because the light will not forgive me

because
the light will not
forgive me

ESSAYS FROM A POET

SHAUN T. GRIFFIN

ILLUSTRATIONS BY ISMAEL GARCÍA SANTILLANES

UNIVERSITY OF NEVADA PRESS *Reno & Las Vegas*

University of Nevada Press | Reno, Nevada 89557 USA
www.unpress.nevada.edu
Copyright © 2019 by University of Nevada Press
All rights reserved
Cover art by Meinzahn and STILLFX
Cover design by Diane McIntosh
Illustrations by Ismael García Santillanes.

LIBRARY OF CONGRESS CATALOGING-IN-PUBLICATION DATA

Names: Griffin, Shaun T. (Shaun Timothy), 1953– author. | García
    Santillanes, Ismael, illustrator.
Title: Because the light will not forgive me : essays from a poet / Shaun T.
    Griffin ; Illustrations by Ismael García Santillanes.
Description: Reno ; Las Vegas : University of Nevada Press, [2019] |
    Identifiers: LCCN 2018051314 (print) | LCCN 2018055896 (ebook) |
    ISBN 9781948908139 (ebook) | ISBN 9781948908122 (pbk. : alk. paper)
Subjects: LCSH: Poetry of places. | Griffin, Shaun T. (Shaun Timothy),
    1953– —Friends and associates. | Poets—Biography. | Poetry in prisons.
Classification: LCC PN6110.P6 (ebook) | LCC PN6110.P6 G75 2019 (print) |
    DDC 808.81/9—dc23
LC record available at https://lccn.loc.gov/2018051314

The paper used in this book meets the requirements of American National
Standard for Information Sciences — Permanence of Paper for Printed Library
Materials, ANSI/NISO Z39.48-1992 (R2002).

FIRST PRINTING

Manufactured in the United States of America

For

Dave Lee
Paulann Petersen
Sam Green

and Sam Hamill in memoriam

I was returning from the drylands. Down below a river valley trembled,
a vega wrapped in blue. Out of the summer night, the sprawling air,
some cricket ribbons, trembling, floated.
    The desert music has a truly yellow taste.

—Federico García Lorca,
Collected Poems, "Border"

In the high mountains, mother,
Where my heart rises over its echoes
in the memory book of a star,
I sometimes ran into the wind.

—Federico García Lorca,
Selected Verse, "Song of the Seven-Hearted Boy"

Contents

Preface

SINCE MOVING TO MASON VALLEY, about eighty miles southeast of Reno, in the late 1970s, I have learned to live with the constructs of place, weather, and aridity, these outward bonds of being in one locale for long periods. And I have learned to recall the names of trees and shrubs I did not know, the occasional flower on the bitterbrush. I have learned the language of clouds, the winter they speak in, the formidable union of wind and ice. I have burned wood in all weather, smelled smoke on my hands when there should have been love or some other reminder of touch. I have worn the blades of my chainsaw clean with dirt from the roots of sage, and I have hung dry in the saddle of my bike on empty highways over mountains. These things taught me to live where I'm rooted, to reach beneath the flourish for what I know, and still they were not enough.

I have written poems and stories since I was a boy, have known the pleasure that it instills. You can never finish a poem, to paraphrase Archibald MacLeish, only stop when you can go no further. This is a kind of effort that mirrors living in the Great Basin, this vast openness for hundreds of miles where nothing tills the imagination and everything tills the imagination. When I closed this book, I returned to the shelves and opened *Walden*. Tucked in the middle of it was a note written in longhand from Gary Snyder. What a fitting end to this journey—the poet who has been most influential in the contemporary American West—was there, wedged in an old copy of the book. I had invited him to a reading from a book of bird poems. It took me seven years to write that book, but it was Snyder, above all others in the Sierra Nevada, who would understand it, and now, twelve years later, I imagined his erstwhile presence in this collection. Early on in this gathering, I wished for something like Walden Pond to reflect upon the nuance of the high desert. Having none and therefore having less in the popular imagination, the desert became its own reward and Snyder, a backbone from which I drew upon to write it.

When I started on these essays, their cohesive thread was the Great Basin. They would emanate out from this place, but my perspective was anchored here. It was what I took to my experience in North Dakota, Wyoming, Zimbabwe, and South Africa. All these separate twinings were shrouded by living, working, and watching what I loved in this landscape be savored and threatened. This is what Snyder knew; this is why I invited him to the reading and why he wrote the card: kinship. Poets who live in this place cannot live outside of its influence. I imagine the same is true for New York City poets and poets in Jerusalem: they infer the lessons that reckon with their existence in a specific location. That influence is also what forced me to look beyond these borders to discover what it was like outside of this locale.

The threads that run through these essays—the American West, poetry and poets, and the people about whom we read and with whom I work—are not apart from this discussion. I never wanted this book to be empty of feeling for what I do to ameliorate some of the suffering of not just the people with whom I share this locale, but of this place itself. This world has bivouacked on a precipice, and as a poet I cannot look the other way. I cannot absolve myself of an obligation to reason beyond our current circumstances, to address some formidable way of living in spite of them. These people and places are extensions of what I hope for every day when I get out of bed: that somewhere, somehow, this same person or place that has been denied can find his, her, or its way forward.

Teaching poetry in a prison has given me an acute realization that very little is free or can be taken for granted. When the men want to learn about poetry they study it like it is food. That's the kind of attention I tried to harness here: a resolute focus on what it was that brought these issues to the fore. Whether it was the magnanimous resolve of an Iraqi poet who escaped his homeland to keep writing or the equally strong resolve of Vassar Miller's spiritual poetry, I wanted to share what they saw. I wanted to crawl inside the lens that opened to Ocean View, the township outside of Cape Town where a poet was forcibly relocated. I wanted to look inside the eyes of a friend who lost her house to a flood, and then fought to save her spouse from a rare disease. I knew each of these people had stories that may not have been shared. Being a poet, I could only see them through that lens, the venerable passage to what dwells inside.

These essays evolved over time and at each juncture I believed in their efficacy, but of course, that was folly. Now, in the many revisions through that venerable passage, I listen again to what these people taught me to do: trust their stories that I may arrive at a vision for what words can do. Without such effort their voices will not be recorded. Or worse, silenced. That is really the final argument: we writers push against silence. We leave the world and ruminate, but upon return, we agitate, if only in the imagination where all great writing lives. I have been given the supreme choice: do something with your life, which I translated to mean— without sharing these narratives, my life would be diminished. I think of the man walking through the desert literally dying to meet Ray Carver. A man who recited William Shakespeare, a hitchhiker in my car, lost and confused. What could he possibly share? I listened and hurt at his every word. This is the silence we abrogate with our work. I am grateful for that work. The poet Hayden Carruth said work sustains us and *this* work—the narrowing of vision to capture someone outside our own comfortable way of life—is old work. It's the work of Herman Melville, Mark Twain, and Muriel Rukeyser. We cannot choose to be outside the human family; it is ours, like it or not. In this simple equation comes the daunting question: What will we do about it?

My two adult boys and their spouses, my own dear, dear friend and spouse, have let me know that I have no choice but to be present, always, to live without chagrin so that my words reflect some habit of desire for fairness. The interior of these essays is equally old—there is willful unfairness on this globe—and each of us finds our way to that realization in time. That is why I believe in the examples of the people and perspectives in these pages. Even those that affront warrant my attention. In the end, if we are lucky, we listen for some fallow truth to set free and yet I cannot be sure that mine is any freer at this book's conclusion. All I can do is describe the journey, the going down to plant. In this stubborn persistence, I am like my predecessors: I start again on the page that belongs to no one.

Virginia City, May 2018

I

Coming into the American West

1

Dressing for Fire

IN THE SUMMER when we lie down to sleep, all of the windows are open. There is stillness in the house. Sometimes we hear a whippoorwill, an owl, or the crazed howl of the coyote. It is only when they stop that sleep comes. Occasionally, if a new bird strays from its migratory path, it startles us from sleep. We sleep soundly, deeply, most nights, but when my wife, Debby, pushes on my arm I know why: smoke has come into the room like an unwanted bird that has strayed from its path. I turn and look north from the bed—is the red shadow on the mountains facing Reno? I walk to the bathroom—is it coming from the west, from Tahoe, or is it further south in the Pine Nuts or Carson Valley? This smoke is a terrible smell. No one who lives here has escaped its reach. It is so dry in summer that fire becomes an element of dread: it can swallow a block of homes in minutes. In 2012, two different windswept fires in south Reno consumed thirty homes each in a matter of hours. We lie back down and hope it is not close, but hope also, it is not near the houses of friends because too many have lost everything.

An earlier memory: I was driving home from the prison when flames consumed Carson City. All of the hills on its west side had burned or were burning. The city was filled with smoke. I couldn't see the Capital dome less than a mile from my car, and I knew it would scar the most vulnerable: pets, children, and grandparents. That fire burned for days before they could put it out. Often it is caused by lightning but sometimes it is a stupid mistake—ash from a barbeque, a spark from a chainsaw, even a controlled burn by the Forest Service.

When I drove up Paradise View on the hills above Carson, our good friends were standing in the rubble—their home had vanished. They had done all the right things—concrete tile roof, cleared the sage and brush to the property edge, and still flame arced from pine tree to pine tree. A spark started their siding on fire, and it was over. The hardest part was that homes fifty yards away were still standing. The flame hopscotched from one home to another but in no particular order. It was so hot the fireman could not get their trucks close enough to fight it. There was nothing any of us could say. Our friends had saved their photos, computer, and dog, but the rest was gone—instantly. Some dervish of heat had torn their lives in half.

Caprice blew down that canyon. Caprice opened a house to fire and left. Left our friends and their neighbors searching for what to do: rebuild, relocate, or leave? The insurance adjusters look good on TV; in person it's not quite so pretty. We were lying on the beach at Camp Richardson on Tahoe's south shore in 2007 with our friends from Southern California. Debby worked with the woman when she was a counseling intern at Cal State, Fullerton. The lake was calm—we were talking, enjoying the summer heat. I turned over to look up and thought it was a cloud but it kept getting darker, bigger, and there was no wind. It grew to the size of a football field in twenty minutes. There was something wrong—it was not a thundercloud. It was fire. "We need to leave now," I said. One hour later they closed Highway 89, the primary north/south artery on the west shore of the lake. By the time we got to the hotel at Stateline—less than seven miles from where we were—one-inch flakes of ash were falling on my car. To the west, where the fire was burning, it looked like an oil field had exploded—it was completely out of control. The hardest part about a forest fire is that it makes its own weather. It creates firestorms so it must be fought from the air and the ground, if it can be fought. The Angora Fire burned more than two hundred-fifty homes. A smoldering campfire started it, and one of those homes belonged to friends. Again, the house across the street was fine; theirs was leveled to the ground. He was a teacher; she worked with people with disabilities. They and their girls lived in an apartment for a year. Their home is rebuilt, but it took two years to settle with the insurance company.

Fire does not ask why. Smoke floats in the room and touches everything. I have lived with that smell through thirty winters. I try to be cautious—I never let the woodstove get too hot or leave it unattended. And yet, it provides: we heated our old house exclusively with wood and since moving across the street, I light the stove almost every winter morning. I installed this stove because a fire calms me. A close friend's son sold me this stove—it is old now; the firebricks are breaking inside. Last year, the chimney sweep bent the flue plate so it is harder to balance in the open position. Cutting and stacking wood gives me more pleasure than I can say. The last thing I do before leaving is cut kindling for Debby. I smoke salmon over a wood fire year-round, and in the summer, fashion a makeshift barbeque of bricks in the driveway. Leandro, our student from Buenos Aires, taught me to cook ribs slowly over hardwood coals. It took hours—if you could touch the grill, the heat was just right. Sometimes, this meant lighting a fire when the cheat grass and the cornflowers had died, when the yard was brown. I had to hose the ground for thirty feet and kept a bucket of water close by.

On the Fourth of July, Debby and I walk to the end of our block and set up chairs. For years it has been the one time when we see all of our neighbors. The wind is usually howling, and the last moisture has disappeared from the Comstock. By the time the show starts we are under blankets—cold, nervous, and excited. Each year we take bets: what locust tree will start on fire, what scraggly sage will burst into flame, what spark will ignite the grass? It is an anomaly of living in this high desert town. Even though fire is what consumes the landscape, they stage one of the best firework displays in northern Nevada. The entire fire department lies in wait: trucks, buffalo water tanks, jeeps, fire engines, command posts, and more to keep the town from burning down. To their credit they do. They have done so repeatedly. When real fire comes to the Comstock, their response is quick and professional.

Twice since we have lived here, fire has threatened Virginia City. The first time I watched from my front yard as the tankers dropped the red borax retardant on the hills, maybe a mile from town. A single-engine aircraft led the DC-3 tankers through the smoke and into the ravines too steep to fight on foot. This aerial support is called in for fires such as these. When those planes come to this little town, we all worry. Another time, at work, the fire came within a half mile of our office. We started to load the most important files in the car and hoped that the tankers and the ground crew could hold the perimeter. Our building was one of three to withstand the 1870s fire. It is restored now, but we could never replace it. Fire destroys. I just wanted it to stop, to move away from the buildings on the south end of town. The wind was erratic, and all it took was one small ember. Our roof was shingles that were over forty years old. They would have ignited in minutes. I watched until the dark came and the fire blew farther south. I went home, ate dinner, and hoped the phone did not ring. Smoke was everywhere and it had come into the room with noise, sirens, and fear.

Strangely, crisis draws a community together—no one is exempt. The morning after I rolled my truck on Geiger Grade, a fireman took me from my home on a backboard. I pulled a snowplow driver from his cab when he rolled his truck. You depend on one another; you do what is necessary to save, to protect, to serve. This is the best part of a small community—in a crisis people pitch in. I imagine the same could be said of a city block—but here we have no choice. If my neighbor's home burns, the consequences are felt throughout the community. This has happened more than once—and it is never good. The woman who stands before you has a child, a suitcase, and dress—the nylon dripping from the hanger. The teacher who lives in a trailer for four months while they gut his house is not any teacher—he sold us our house. The grandfather who hunts must wait out the season with his adult children while the contractor rushes to beat the snow. When the fire burns so close to your house you can see the flame, you immediately feel nauseous—it has shredded someone's life. You know them, talk to them in the post office. You know the men and women standing on the ladder trying to put it out. You know the people who live on either side of the flames. You know what this place has been: many artists lived in this home—painters, poets, novelists, and musicians. It was from the 1870s, almost historic in the Intermountain West and now it is an idea. A friend is battling the banks, the insurance company, and more because he was the caretaker. It is never easy to reconstruct a life, to move on after such devastation. It is an act of will that is further complicated by caprice—why me and not them? Why this home and not that home? Why did it visit my room?

AND YET: I ask my friend with a backhoe to come to my yard. I want him to dig a pit to roast a pig. I have no idea how to do it but I want to, and so I read and ask and practice: surely this can be learned. My friend asks how deep. I imagine six feet. In Jarbidge, in northeastern Nevada, they have dug a hole in the ground and lined it with steel for an annual barbeque. That mountain town of forty year-round residents, the site of the last stagecoach robbery in America, lights a bonfire of softwood and then hard, and it smolders to coals. They throw in rocks, and when they are heated, they move them to the coals at the edge of the pit. They wrap the meat in burlap, put a piece of sheet metal over the coals, another on top of the meat, and return the hot rocks and coals—what amounts to a Dutch oven beneath the ground. They cap it with a final plate of steel and let it cook for twenty-four hours. There is nothing to compare with slow-cooked meat. The whole town gathers to celebrate the passage of Independence Day. A tradition that has been going on for decades despite the fact that Jarbidge almost burned down more than once. The most recent forest fire in 2008 spread for miles and burned out of control in the Humboldt National Forest for over two weeks. The geography was overwhelming and the cost to fight it prohibitive. They let it burn out, but kept watch on the town.

Twice we have dug a pit barbeque in our backyard. The first time was beginner's luck: I spent the day gathering sage to start the fire, and juniper and mountain mahogany to sustain it, and then borrowed oak and almond from friends. I did not know how deep to make the coals and so guessed: at least six inches below and four above. I asked four friends to help, hoping that our two garden hoses and buckets of water would keep the sparks at a minimum. It was September, dry and dusty. Thankfully, there was no wind. Had there been wind, we could not have done it. The flames were over ten feet, almost to the top of the roof. I knew they would subside, but I did not want them to spread. We squirted every spark, every sudden jump of flame, and slowly, the heat began to rise in waves. It took more than an hour to build enough coals to last through the night. I went in the house and brought the pig from the bathtub. It had been sitting on ice overnight. When I carried it up the stairs the day before, my mother-in-law, Gladys, asked if I had a body in the clear plastic bag. No, it's just a pig, I told her, but she had her doubts. My mother-in-law was game for just about anything, but this tested her religion: she thought her son-in-law had gone off the rails. I assured her it would be wonderful, and she rolled her eyes as if I had no idea what wonderful was.

I loved that woman, think of her every day, and miss her like Debby does but probably not as much. When we were in Sacramento to visit Debby's sister, Winni ran into the bedroom

where we were staying: "Mom's in cardiac arrest. Get in the car."
I ran into the hospital barefoot, still not sure what had happened
or why. She had had a heart attack but was supposed to recover.
She would be home in a week and I could pilfer cookies from her
jar. When I got to her bed she grabbed my face and kissed my lips
hard. I held her and then walked to the waiting area. Her heart
literally tore in half. I think she had too much pain, too much
sorrow, trying to take care of her husband. This was a woman who
was in the underground at sixteen, ferrying messages to and from
the allied pilots shot down in her Belgian village of Heers. This
was a woman who lied to German soldiers so that the pilots could
live. One of them flew multiple missions behind enemy lines. One
of them kept the B-17 in the air, burning, until the last man para-
chuted out. One of them kept it flying twice, on fire, to save his
buddies. "One of them" would become her husband. He was in
the waiting room with us hoping this was not the end.

When I used to cut wood for Gladys, she stood outside in
sweltering heat and held the ladder. The chainsaw was over my
head; my goggles were fogged with sweat. "Be careful, don't get
hurt," and then her words faded when I set the blade into the
wood. Tall scraggly junipers, they kept dancing when I touched
them with the chainsaw. They fell all over the driveway and I tried
to push them from the roof. Her husband, Bob, came outside, lit a
cigarette, and thanked me. I watched them for over two decades,
braiding the fine language of marriage.

I knew Gladys was joking when she laughed at me from the
couch. I knew she would love the pig. No one liked to eat more
than she did. Those years of living on root vegetables, in darkness,
with a Jewish orphan in the house, when the Germans stalked her
village, those infinite years when the Allies were farther away than
the moon, gave her patience and perspective. She was frugal—I
teased her unmercifully about the coupons. At the store the ca-
shiers would run when she came in. She was the only woman
who left the grocery store with more money than she brought in.

I didn't know about hunger when I met Gladys, but she would teach me. Her diary of the pilots, elaborate drawings of their faces and flight jackets, read like a telegram from an underground museum. Gladys loved that pig. Winni cut it up in minutes. She was a physician. My good friend threw the pieces on the Weber for a final searing and even the vegetarians went off the wagon for the afternoon. This is what fire brought us. This is how we gathered to share food. This is one thing I could give to Gladys.

DO YOU STOP LIVING because the air is filled with fear? This is what I asked Fadhil Al-Azzawi, the Iraqi poet, when he came to Nevada in 2007. For three weeks we drove up and down the state as he read his poems in universities, libraries, and bookstores. At one point we were driving around the west shore of Lake Tahoe on the same road that had been closed to fire that summer's day. It was March and the road was snowy. We listened to the radio in the silence. It was at the height of the Iraq War. A pediatrician was being interviewed live from Baghdad. The journalist asked, "How can you go on delivering babies when the war will take them from your hands?" Fadhil laughed because he knew the answer. The doctor spoke immediately: "We have endured warfare for centuries. We must go on. There is nothing permanent. We cannot stop living until the war is over."

She continued: "Do you have children?"

"Yes, four, and we may have another one."

"*Now*," she asked incredulously, "when Baghdad is so unstable?"

"Yes. Is it any worse for the refugees of a dozen countries? They have not stopped living; they have not waited for the dictator to leave."

Fadhil leaned forward: "We are not fatalists but we keep on. We have for centuries. If we waited for peace we would have died out long before the British came." Fadhil was tortured for four years, a political prisoner before he fled his homeland. He has not seen one family member since. They communicate through messengers. His house is a home for squatters. He has lived in Berlin since leaving Iraq. He and his wife are writers. His poems and novels poke fun at the idea of permanence, the notion that you could live just as you wanted. In the face of extremes, he laughs to keep perspective, just like my late mother-in-law. It's not death they are afraid of; it's living without the chance to go on that they fear.

SOMEWHERE THEN, the smoke takes its place. We will live each day until the next Fourth of July. We will gather our chairs, walk to the end of the street, and see our neighbors again. We will tell lies about the fireworks and secretly hope that a locust catches on fire. In the cold, unnerving wind, we will walk back to our homes. An ember will smolder, but just as surely, dawn will come and something will appear—a blue flower in the myrtle, a bird at the window. There will be a mark of renewal. We will make our way forward, just as the first miners in this clapboard town. The fire and the wind will exact something from us, but we will wake after the smoke comes in the room.

My wife turns in bed. I look into the night sky. This is how we dress for fire.

—2014—

2

Snowalking

I RETURN FROM THE CITY of shadow to walk the silence of my beloved Virginia Range in northwestern Nevada. Caged in a Seattle hotel room for days, I walk the mine trail, the looping track that connects the Combination Shaft and other lesser-known holes in the earth. Three piñon trees and a desert peach have been cut since I walked its perimeter a week ago. Their scrap limbs lie above and below the trail. Winter has sent my neighbors to find wood. For how many years has it sent us to these hills to cut trees, harvest pine nuts, and dig metal from the soil?

I live within sight of tailings from two dozen mines and have almost come to peace with their brown residue. Still, this is the first time I have walked the three-mile circle to find living trees cut, and the desert peach, one of the few flowering shrubs that bloom at first thaw, is not large enough to warrant dying for heat.

I take where I live for granted unless place becomes an altered landscape, unless it becomes where I *lived*. My community is small, fewer than a thousand people; I am sure the person who is burning the green piñon lives nearby, in fact will say "Hi" to me in a matter of days. What can I offer him but a rhetorical answer to warmth when my own house is heated by wood? The splayed limbs become a testimony to our increasing need to lay down what is living in order for us to live.

After circling the mine trail, my lungs filled with the juniper air, I look east to the successive peaks—Dead Camel, Stillwater, Clan

Alpine, Fairview, Desatoya, Shoshone—place-names that intimate some kinship with the land. Not silent names, but peaks that have endured through centuries of our human presence. I have walked some of them and imagined many footprints preceding mine, as in Mark Twain's account of crossing the Forty-Mile Desert, and found the occasional waterline etched in rock when this place was once filled with inland seas, not shadow. I fall prey to its impenetrable silence, knowing I will spend the rest of my life walking this small, dry ridge.

So many have documented the restraint of the desert that it is foolish to rim their conversations with mine. And yet, out of reverence, I must record the simple wishes of one who lives here, how I intersect with the startling place it has become since the seas receded, since those who were here succumbed to the howl of progress.

Last winter I walked the mine trail in snow and came across blood and rabbit hair. A coyote must have found him sleeping. I could almost accept the red stains, knowing death had left its footprints on the white path. Not because it was the natural give-and-take of predator and prey, but rather because it was emblematic of our own struggle to survive our unrelenting curiosity, our reckoning with the limits of place and species, like the yellow-bellied sapsucker that checkered a lodgepole pine with a grid of tiny circles.

For three days this woodworker drilled for sap and insects from the holes. I stood entranced with binoculars at the window, telling my family to watch this devoted bird. Even when I stepped outside to empty the trash or get the newspaper, it did not move, unlike other birds. It went on working as if it had to complete the grid before leaving. The pine bled sap for days, and I wondered if it would succumb to the broken bark, if it might die at the beak of a bird before spring returned, and how this became a riddle for my journey, a reminder of the choking silence before death.

It is the last Sunday of Lent, forty degrees Fahrenheit, and the lodgepole pine is still alive. Even though the woodpecker left handfuls of bark at the base of the tree and has been gone for over a month, the tree lives on.

Our survival may not be as easy, and the burden of that understanding can overwhelm us to retreat or worse. Still, the lodgepole that hides the mountain shadows beyond is green and living at the edge of the Sierra Nevada and the Great Basin. It is a symbol of reconciliation with this waterless soil. I have written scores of poems about the folly of gardening where the sun eats moisture from every living thing, and yet I persist in trading water for a lone green shoot among the rocks. At least the pine is a buttress against the wind and sun.

In Seattle the barks of trees were green from the rain. It even snowed on the tulips and pansies while we were there. Mold removal *from the lawn* was advertised on the radio. My son and I laughed. Our tiny patch of green grows like a scab, if it grows at all. But I give thanks for every petal of flax, dervish of snapdragon and foxglove, the occasional lily, and the one quick nod of monkshood, even if it fades by day's end. Were it not for the Chinese poppy and the peony that mistook this burnt soil for a garden plot, were it not for the partial rainbow of their annual presence, I would have nailed my name to the long list of those who left the area in desperation.

But they do come up every spring on this infertile mountain, this place that holds more people than water, and they remind me—like the fallen desert peach and the piñon—that our delicate interaction, our weathering of mutual storm and sun, our perennial dance to the next spring is no less a dance because we have history with which to contend. For most of the year, the Virginia Range is the silent home to many, and some revere that silence. Last winter my son's baseball coach saw two bucks at dawn and did not shoot them. In that same winter, our foreign exchange student hiked the trail with me and came upon a herd of deer. Incredulous, he wondered how such wild persists.

Having no answer, I shrugged to the unknown. I have no answers now, only the brevity of hope that our mutual desires as species—whether hunger or heat—will become a covenant for coexistence. The alternative is the foreboding silence, and I am loath to build its tabernacle out my door.

The rocks resume their work. We name them field stones. Before the snow returns, a sapling will divide soil. We will measure its shadow with indifference or reverence as I imagine we were once measured. Now our footprints lap the culture of history and coexistence we have yet to create.

Still another month has passed since I walked the trail in snow. Today the treads of tires mark the dust and hardened soil. Branches lie on most of the mountain path. There was a time when I rode a motorcycle into the mountains, but no more. I am foolish to judge; the trail was given over to us. I cannot choose my fellow devotees; in fact, I must abide our mutual scoring and saving. The rocks resume their work when we go home.

Today, many weeks later, my dog sniffed the carcass of a deer on the trail. Its head hung from the barbed mouth of a mineshaft. The skin was carved from the eyes, leaving two bony white patches beneath the antlers. My dog and I walked on, witness to its unbearable stare. Where will I walk now when I seek retreat?

Whether summer or winter, I will not walk far from the tangle of our lives. The going-away has ended. The perennial species, *we*—the multiplicity of life forms and habitats on this planet— remain together. This is our collective wisdom, this is our primitive tool, with which we return to the dust and snow.

I step off the bicycle at the top of Geiger Grade, elevation 6,789 feet. It is a bright morning, sun after heavy snow, and cold: twenty-two degrees Fahrenheit when I woke. I think of the poet Hayden Carruth writing in his Vermont cowshed:

> Twenty-two degrees below zero
> and only the blade of meadow
> like a snowpetal or foil of platinum
> to defend the house against the glistening
> mountain and the near unwinking
> moon.

I have left town to ride this narrow road to the ridge above

Reno. It is lined with piñon, juniper, and sage. There are token Jeffrey pines, at which I snicker: if only we had a forest of more than ten trees. The locusts and the mountain mahogany substitute for hardwood. Carruth said I have none—"Your sappy pine all but drowns a wood stove."

It is a pretty good year for moisture. As I write this, snowdrops come from the aspen overhead. The last two years have given us snowmelt for most of the summer, and so our taps run to lawns and flowers, also an anomaly in this arid landscape. Last spring, following the wettest winter in ninety years, flowers of every variety sprouted on the mine trail. I sat and painted the monkshood, bluebells, and larkspur. Wild onions and garlic sprouted. Flowers I'd never seen came up. In the lower desert, there were whole families of color that had lain dormant for a score of summers.

This is the paradox of this place—there is comfort in extremes: my sons were flying from the roof last winter, so deep was the snow. Months later, I could not keep the daisies from dying on the slope below.

Out of obstinacy, my wife and I think spring has come and, on a day of no wind and false sun, run to imitate the gardens of Southern California. But we cannot, as our earth is not earth, but ground dug from earth. We live on the mountain of disgorged mine tailings and, below that, bedrock. The man who built my house, a teacher by trade, trucked in yards of dirt to fill his terraces—terraces he made from rock that could not be sold: rhyolite, jasper, copper, and the occasional tufa from Pyramid Lake to the north. This is the land of those who wish for water and, having none, come early to the realization that spring is a deception—a moment in which to flourish and then disappear.

The birds also refuse the obvious signs: the robin, the quail that comfort in all seasons, the goldfinch, and the Cooper's hawk that for days has threaded the trees front and back and then sits atop the dead pine, watching me. Last month we came home to a hole in the double-pane glass: a quail was dead on the floor. Other times, the quail have hit the window so hard my wife called me at work, crying. She picked up the bird and took it to the south side of the yard to be buried. Its body lay perfectly still in the cold until the earth thawed on the ridge above the house.

The hawk reminds me of the balance that we in this mountain town must keep—or not. I will never kill to eat, I think, but I have not been hungry enough to abrogate my beliefs.

I live two streets below the former house of Walter Van Tilburg Clark, a man who wrote, taught, and drank in this town, a writer whom Wallace Stegner regarded as among our finest. His house was a black-and-white clapboard Victorian with a pane of glass large enough to walk through. The window is on the east side of the house and faces the Great Basin. I wonder, did a hawk barrel through his study and inspire his story simply named "Hook"? Perhaps not, but the words gave us the fear in the bird and its prey.

Last week, I saw the first bald eagle in my twenty-five years of living here. It was a cone of feathers shot across the sky, as aerodynamic a bird as I have seen. Weeks before, a golden eagle flew over as I crested Geiger Grade on my bike. I think of them as symbols, not literal manifestations of our sometimes-addled beliefs, but symbols of a certainty: that these species will not go away. This is the order of us and them, predator and prey, whatever dichotomous solution that persists without our knowledge. Emerson wanted man to live up to his means, and these birds, these few flowers, these winded trees and rocks mark persistence, mark our coming and going. They redeem, as he might also say, what we cannot—the unspeakable nature of this planet.

This is why I return to the mine trail; snowalking is an ideal footprint, a place where I leave no permanent tracks, and yet it is an image of wandering from emptiness and fullness, a winter landscape not yet open to spring. In the last big storm, I hiked the mine trail with my dog, a dog for whom the snow is an aphrodisiac—he ran fifty yards, gulped the powder, ran back, gulped more, and ran again. Almost every step of our three-mile journey we were weightless, out of sight of man and footprint. We broke new snow the entire distance. Ice was under foot. There was quiet in the piñon, and I could forgive the cutting that had gone before me—not just the trees, but the Virginia Range stripped of its minerals one hundred fifty years ago, the greed and avarice that drew thousands to this town. Had Mark Twain not made light of it in *Roughing It*, we would still be crying but for its beauty this one day in winter.

The following weekend I hike the trail again, and there is murky water—brown, like the Colorado, like all rivers that run dry in the West. And the snow disappears. "Will this be the last?" I think. "My last snowwalk through these mountains this winter?" Privately, secretly, I hope not. I hope the contrary—that it is May before I speak these words and our annual precipitation will have risen from two to four inches. But that, too, will be wrong; I will have no lens with which to see the light that doubles as a kind of snow in summer. The light that sends to autumn these mountains, and then falls to brown, and the sky, the face of the dying Indian on the ridge, all become the burnt landscape of winter's reckoning. I have wept at this light, and sometimes when the sun breaks through clouds to focus a circle on the flank of Sugar Loaf, I think these woods, however sparse and broken, are woods enough for me.

I have walked in Carruth's New England woods, and they were plentiful, so dense the hardwood lay in leaves and water on the ground. The woods on Sugar Loaf are not his woods. These woods leave us vulnerable to fire in summer—fire always, the smoke a death-bell atop the steeples of our three churches—and to ourselves. We have no woods in which to lose our shadow, and that is haunting to some. To drive for eight hours east or south and name the aboriginal species of drought is to lie before one's god and admit defeat. There is no redemption at first sight. All this emptiness is, and only after years, its own redemption. To walk in snow with the piñon jay or a deer is to return to truth and beauty, the kind poets write of to survive the steady declamation of what they believe—living and working to what end, when to do so peacefully, in a place one loves, would be what? Too easy? I walk to my ends in this burnished landscape, and that is reason enough.

Sixteen degrees Fahrenheit and there is no cowshed, no Vermont to protect me. Snow flurries come to the window. The quail are still on the aspen branches. This is the landscape of memory. It is early March, too cold for baseball, and another Lenten Sunday passed. In some way, this annual recurrence comforts, tells me there will be rhythm to the last weeks of winter, much as the land confides its secrets; in the winter, snow hides the dozing and the road building. The lichens on the north-facing cliffs are covered. But come spring, this place of memory will be altered—a fresh mound of earth will appear on the ridge out of town, some pockmark of our turning to earth for minerals will have left its bruise. So too will come the three-week runoff and in the silence, beneath rock and willow, ice water, close to the blue jags of a spring creek. Sometimes this is a gift, to be stampeded by water, if only in a creek bed, to watch my dog lap freely in the snowmelt. It's incongruous that willows grow on this mountain, but they do and, for a few short weeks, thrive on the apparition of water at their roots.

These same brief creeks gave way to flumes one hundred fifty years ago, when the Jeffrey and ponderosa pines slid down the eastern ridge of the Sierra Nevada into Washoe Valley and then were drawn up here by horse and wagon to become the mine shafts and bulkheads that lean to this day.

In May my younger son and I were on that ridge cutting dead and downed pine for firewood. Sweat fogged my goggles, and my son pinched carpenter ants from the limbs. The sun peeked into the Tahoe Basin, filtered through pine needles, through dust, to his silhouette by the car. I had never seen so much wood; my arms would give out before I could cut and stack a cord of rounds. I heard saws in the distance—more people gathering wood, more hands riding the axe. The sun rose to ten a.m., and it felt like all of us would cook in the heat. To our right, an older man and a woman loaded their pickup with eight-foot logs. He backed down the slope, away from the Forest Service road, and stacked the bed higher. Then came the cussing, the gunning, and the drive wheel spinning until he buried his tires in the silt. The ranger came over, pissed that greed had reared its head again. He felled the tree between the truck and the lower access road, and the man and woman unloaded every log in that bed to back out.

My son and I were in a 1986 Dodge van and we were worried that it would tip over on the way out. We crossed a creek, and I goosed it for both of us; I didn't want to get stuck and couldn't resist the big splash that made the whole morning worth it for him. At the forest gate, the ranger said it was the second time that guy had stuffed his truck in the duff. My son couldn't understand why he would do such a thing, except of course, there was wood everywhere for the taking.

I remember Mark Twain writing of this mountain: penny stocks became elevated to sudden wealth, and the spectators followed overnight. Had we come any further in the intervening years? The history here also confides its secrets: Nevada Territory was rushed into statehood for political reasons. Lincoln needed a two-thirds majority in both houses for the passage of the Thirteenth Amendment (abolishing slavery), not to mention the three electoral votes in his 1864 presidential election. Could the confluence of any greater ideal or president have pushed such a place into a state? That forest we were in was clear-cut to mine this town that only now is recovering, if tourism is recovery.

I have never thought that land equates to memory, but here we cannot escape the obvious burrowing into earth. It is a memory of land before we touched it—of course, this is Paiute, Western Shoshone, and Washoe land. This county is named after Captain James Storey, who marched his men to Pyramid Lake and was ambushed in the Truckee River valley at the lake's southern shore. Blood is the memory of our history here, and yet it is a history of scant record: Sarah Winnemucca's late nineteenth-century *Life Among the Paiutes: Their Wrongs and Claims* is thought to be the first book from a tribal leader in this region. I track this place with books, compass, and stone. But without wood, water, and gold, what is this stone I live on? What is it we have become on its brown shores? What do I claim as my legacy in this place of dubious honor?

Our first house was over the old Chinese dump. A dozen cultures dug the mine shafts, but the Chinese had a visible history, and we lived on their layered earth. Oyster shells and ceramic beer bottles were like stones in the ground. I dug up an opium bottle, and later a man found a twenty-dollar gold piece in the dirt driveway—magnetic poles, I imagined, that we did not intend. The tailings are hard to dig by hand; fence posts will never leave their anchor once erected. Sage is no less formidable—these unwanted soils and plants, these unwanted roots that become our home.

The beauty is transitory, and we see it in patterns that have become ritual: work, family, and rest in the cold, thin air that gives way to belief that, with time, we can heal this land. Then summer returns us to labor and love, however short it may be.

We make a history with which we can live. This land requires us to remember the balance of little things because we have so few of them. There will be no wise man to rescue us. We ask forgiveness, but not in the name of water, air, or sky. We ask for the tranquil, for the subtle. We ask for the genuine. Who has not? Out of subterfuge or desperation, who has not asked?

The miner feeds his daughter, the lumberjack his father, the teacher his spouse. A geologist lives in every town in this state—and the rocks persist—but this next era, the era of fusion, will not tolerate indifference. Some in this country are waiting to rush their waste into yet another hole in Southern Nevada—Yucca

Mountain—and I am loath to support it because the cacophony of voices repeats its claim: we must live with our differences. The plutonium silence will not suffice.

Beneath this desert lives a vowel, an intransigent persistence, a lowercase *i* that wants to live with the land and not eradicate the other vowels that vie for its presence. Eros before Thanatos, the twin landscapes, the double helix I retain to believe that I have sense enough to survive. And we will if these rocks, these empty caverns, these sudden streams persist in their offering: do not forsake me, do not go away with your eyes down, do not forget this hour of our reckoning, which, unlike the past century, may be the century that saves.

Our daily effort to start up this slope toward the peak of Mount Davidson, to gain a perch for viewing the Lahontan Valley to the east, is only a beginning. We have no real presence here without each other. This land will not save us, but we might imitate the secular and surrender long enough to depend on it and perhaps remain in its shadow.

Like the starlings bunched on the power line, we still need each other in this place. Walking beneath them, I imagine they have waited for me to return from the mine trail. And I have. As we shall also do.

—2009—

3

Walking into the Desert

DRIVING NORTH FROM Tonopah, a place as edgy and infinite as wind, I crest the ridge out of Mina, slow to thirty-five past the marooned houseboat in Luning, and find my way back to seventy. When I get the radio signal out of Mammoth, the Dead perform an almost static-free session. It will get better when dark falls.

I have driven this road through four winters for work in the wilderness, seen dozens of images on Highway 95, some lost, some intentional. There have been signs, melancholy ephemera left on the desert floor, but winter remakes the desert. It can change into a landscape of white for miles. At night it becomes a wild light of stars. I try to watch its slow evolution. I see what looks like a person, walking, at least twenty-five miles from Hawthorne. It is cold—maybe thirty-five degrees—and I don't know what he is doing in the sage except that he will not disappear. I drive closer, hope I've mistaken him for a tree stump or fence post, but he is moving, walking on the road north. I come up to him, roll down my window, and ask, "Are you okay?" There is a guttural answer but I can't hear it in the wind. I pull over and ask if he needs some water. He tries to mouth the word "Yes." He puts a plastic tarp of books and clothes and food on the back seat. He swallows the water in one long swish and says, "Thank you, thank you. Didn't know if I would get any water."

"Any water? There's no water in this desert for a hundred miles."

"It's all right, I don't need water. I've been walking for three days. You find it when you can."

"Where'd you start?"

"Some guy dropped me off in Tonopah—said he had to get a room."

"Oh, and you walked from there?"

"I guess—it's all the same place to me."

He reaches for the radio—"I like 'Ohio.' Can I turn it up?"

"Sure. That's how I make the long drive home, with Crosby, Stills, Nash, and—"

He's a big guy, has an army-surplus jacket on and a pad of paper in the pocket. He downs another bottle of water, starts to look more animated. "God, that was good. Water, you know, it's, uh, damn pretty."

"Out here you better have some—"

"So whatta you doing in Tonopah?"

"I work with people, try to help them build—"

"I worked with people too—and then I got fired. Stayed at home as long as Mom would let me, and then she looked at me and said—you gotta get outta here. So I left, been walking ever since. Three years. Left that little town in Texas. I make do. People take care of me. I have my books. I've been reading the classics, you know, Sinclair Lewis and John Steinbeck and Norman Mailer and Shakespeare. You know the play I'm talking about, right? The scene with the three ghosts."

"I write a little—"

"Do you like to read? I think readin's better than food. That's why I carry my books. I trade 'em wherever I go—more classics. Gotta read the classics. You must know Ray Carver—he's my favorite goddamn writer. No one writes like him—or Shakespeare. I used to act and I'd recite him like he was with me—"

Then right into *Hamlet,* and I looked at him in the dash lights— this savant who knew more about literature than most English profs. I wanted to keep up but I couldn't—he was in front of my every breath. "And that Carver story, you know the one—"

"Well, I do know someone who was married to his sister-in-law—a very good friend. A tough writer, and a tough life—"

"My fav' of all time—that one, oh shit, what's the name of it, that one that has the—you must have read that one. God, he's good. How far to Hawthorne?"

"Maybe twenty minutes."

"I can make it from here—"

"You could if you had a car—"

"Well, damn, so you're a writer. How the hell did that happen? You make books, and Jesus, I read them. What a damn coincidence? If I ever move away again, I'm going to do something like that. Just push that old gawddamned pen down the page, make it real in the heart, you know, where the bad shit goes and all you can do is hope it don't break open."

"Yeah, yeah, that's what I do—I write poems and hope they don't break open—"

"You got any books—you know, ones I can read?"

"A few—but I don't think—"

"It's not for me, man. It's for my mind. I have to get them, have to get them all the time. It's the only thing I can do to live alone and stay out here for weeks until somebody stops and asks me if I'm—"

"It's winter. You could freeze out here—"

"Nah. Never happen. That's why I got this rucksack. Everything I own. I got clothes. They're warm enough. Besides, sun comes up and I start to warm. Tell me about your friend who knows Carver. I want to meet him—"

"My friend can't bring him back. Carver's dead—finally stopped drinking and had ten good years, but it wasn't enough."

"No, he's not dead. I read him—he's alive. I can see him, he's just waiting for me. Waiting out there. Take me to him, man. I know he's alive. He's everywhere. I read with him all night, and then I know nothing's gonna go wrong. He's just what I need. That's why I left. Couldn't take it anymore. Those damn lies.

Working in the laundry. You think I liked it there, where the steam and dark angels push those buttons? I liked it all right, liked it so much I told my boss to get fucked and went home. Sat on the couch for six months till my mother said I can't afford you anymore. You gotta leave. And I took my books and left. Knew I couldn't go back. She wouldn't let me. She'd just tell me to fuck off—that's how it is out here. There's no real reason for people doing what they do. They just go on and burn in their little silence. It's almost here, ain't it? The reckoning—"

Thankfully, I see the lights of Hawthorne. Think some food will help. A little edgy—we dodge the looks and ferry the double cheeseburger to the table. He's careful to take the rucksack with him. It protrudes from the orange chair. String and folded paper fall to the floor. He bends to gather them—hides his face from the others. His eyes drive into mine—a galaxy of fatigue, barely visible in the layers of discomfort. I sip my chocolate—I'll eat at home. He says, "Thanks, I can make it from here," but I know he can't. He'll be lucky if he doesn't get arrested. We put the rucksack in the back seat—he was certain it would be stolen. "It's happened. They take your shit. They just leave ya. I don't have any money—they just do it to fuck with ya. Mind if I turn up the radio—I really dig this song. This is Van Morrison, right? God, he was the damn sure thing. Just blew those tracks down. Don't ya wanna be like him? All that ragin' L.A. music. You know when I meet Ray, we're gonna talk about writing. We're gonna work on words. It's gonna be just like in the story where he gets that girl and they go off to some party, kinda wild, you know the story, it's that one where—"

"I know some of the stories—"

"Yeah, he's gonna take me to him. He's gonna make me happy when I meet Ray Carver. Ray's just the goddamnedest. You know, I believe him. I really believe. He's a freaking motor house. There's no way you can take him down. I mean, you gotta find Carver. You gotta read this guy, he just flat blows your balls to the ground. And if you're lucky, I mean lucky, you get to fuckin' get up and read him again. That's why I trade my novels, I keep trying to find new Carver stories, they have to be out there. He's gotta be writing them—yeah, that was one helluva burger. Did I ever tell you why them people keep me down? Why they just can't stand my fucking ass? It's the people, the goddamned working assholes, they're trying to kill me. They love the black people but they hate me 'cuz I'm white. I'm just another goddamned piece a crap in their eyes. They took my job you know. Took it and let me go. Let me run the street. They didn't ask me a fuckin' thing—it's true those people just burn right through me—"

"What people? You're a smart dude. You've read more than I'll ever read—But hey, what's a book, right? People don't read much anymore. Especially poetry. Poetry doesn't have Ray Carver any more. Doesn't have people like you who'll fight for every god-damned line—"

I turn and try to laugh, but he can't hear my words. They're just dust in the dark miles, nothing to stake against his claim. He's alone, as alone as you can be in this desert. I've driven through almost every weather, driven to the sides and the depths, and there's nothing in this place for my passenger. My passenger who needs Ray Carver and needs the solace of medicine, but I am no doctor. I cannot prescribe. All I can do is listen and drive. I worry that the man people run from is coming out soon. "There's a shelter in Carson. I'll get you there. If I leave you here, you'll freeze."

"No man, it's good. I want to get out here."

"Stay in the car. You've got to tell me what's going on. They can help you. I won't leave you if they can't."

"You think I'm some kind of dumb shit—you don't think I know what the fuck those places are? They ruin ya, make you into something you don't want. Why in the fuck would I want to go in a shelter? You gotta be goddamn kidding me. Some asshole tells me where to sleep, when to crawl out in the morning, are you just fucking nuts?" He reaches for the radio, checks the back seat.

Nothing will still him. The darkness between us grows smaller. His fingers on the door handle, ready to run.

"Listen, I'm okay with you being in this car. I like literature and I like you, but you can't cuss at me, and not at the people I love. You got that? Don't push me—I'll drive you to Carson but don't make it worse on yourself. I'm not fucking around. You'll be outta this car in a minute."

"Let me out—let me out here."

"It's only Mound House—you're not gonna make it. What are you doing, man? You're gonna get hurt—"

"Don't lecture me you white-ass sonofabitch. I've been around people like you all my life. You think you know so gawddamned much about me. You don't know a fucking thing about—Stop the car! Lemme out now!"

I brake and wonder what just happened. He walks into the gas station, no money, no words, just walks, and I think he's finally got what he wants—permission. He's almost where he wants to be—in the black unknown. I can't fix him, can't undo what happened in the years before the desert. This is how I leave him in the darkness. There is no willingness to go on.

Tomorrow I will tell my friend who was married to Ray Carver's sister-in-law what a nightmare ride this was. I will tell him all he knew about Shakespeare, about plays and lines I never heard and about his beloved Carver, his only truth in this emptiness in which I drive home. Someone knows him. It is not enough to belong to the desert. Someone needs him or did until the axles came off and he began to spin, endlessly—"yeah it's been three years since I left." Those words like police tape around a house that has been robbed.

I wish he could speak in my class, tell them about *Hamlet*, about *Macbeth*, tell why *Twelfth Night* was so damned brilliant, and then just begin to talk about the novelists, the men and women he prayed to, whom he longed to smoke and eat with, the good ones, the ones who didn't have enough time, who wanted to be alone but were forced into writing their way out of the sorry and the single gun. I wanted him to blur the line between writing and dying to write. I wished he had come to share some part of what he knew, because then I could proclaim his mind for what it was—this corner of raging literature that he stood in, that he bargained from, that he made his bloody truth in. I wanted to be in that room with him, wanted my students to see what that room could be with their eyes, their hands, their smells. It would kill any idea they had of this bold, bold land we believed in, but it will never happen. By the time he reaches Carson it will be dawn, his fingers cold, his eyes closed. He will be roughed up by the cops, by the others in the street. He will know their names. They will eat from his psyche. They will hurt him and he will run to the next outpost where there is something to swallow, or water, or what it was before he came. He will lie down with Ray, asleep in the wind and pray that some night on this desert floor, the book will come back to life, and Ray will be standing over him, all bleary-eyed from the last bad episode, and Maryann will be with him, dragging him to the car, cranking it and cussing the bikes out of the driveway. "Ray," she says, "Ray, we have to get outta here. We can go to my mom's, she'll let us sleep there tonight. We gotta leave Ray—" and in the morning my hitchhiker will steam from the alley into the willingness of one or two who stop to make what they can of what he needs. It's this dire road that's killing him, but nothing I do will change this great friend of Ray Carver.

And so I let him swerve off the edge again, as if it were me he were taking for the next half mile. Let him swerve into the many who turn their heads and wonder if he will do something mad. This is the doorman who lives outside our lives. This is the license to begin the way down. This is the morning where one person is no longer peopled and he must misery through the bones of the day. This is what I try to say to my students but they don't believe me because people don't do this, don't sleep in the cold, unforgiving desert. They rent rooms and go upstairs. They use TVs and toilets. They make mistakes and fall in love. They worship things. And they eat like scavengers, except he cannot imagine what it is like to eat and so I tell them to forget my story. It did not happen. He was not with me in the desert. I was alone. I simply made it up, and it was something I tried to believe. He was something I tried to hold out hope for. He was the solution to my grave, inconsequential highway. He was what I was looking for. There's no getting this right. These strangers on the side of the road who want you.

—2016—

4

Letter from the Blackstone River: Under Fog with the Porcupine Caribou

for Pete Nagano

NINE MONTHS PASSED before I returned to the porcupine caribou. The spring migration of last June seemed a country away—and it was, yet some part of their journey stayed with me through the fall and winter. Like the mammals I watched from a distance, I had come from many places to reach the Yukon.

In the brief time since my friend Bob and I had been on the Alaska Coastal Plain, he had not stopped reading about the caribou. At 8:30 Thursday evening, he dropped his duffle bag in my kitchen and kissed his wife goodbye. I woke him at 4:30 the next morning, then we were off to Vancouver, and two more hours north to Whitehorse, where we rented a car and drove to a small café across from the airport. We were anxious—Bob, his old teaching friend, Dave, and me. The waitress pointed us to the one highway out of town. She was the welcome party, the purveyor of a fine bean soup and homemade bread. She shook the cold air from my hands and understood intuitively that we were lost.

In the Super A Market, we bought lightweight food—not knowing whether we would be snowshoeing, snowmobiling, or sitting in a lean-to waiting to see caribou. Again, kindness swooped down—the shopkeeper directed us to Coleman fuel at Canadian Tire, a combination hardware and outdoor store. After securing the obligatory bottle of Canadian Mist, we left for Carmacks late in the day.

It was nine degrees when we arrived at 5:00 p.m., the first cold, but not cold to those who called this small community home. All the way up the Klondike Highway, I wrote to an old friend, a poet, the one man I knew who would understand this landscape without instruction. Dave was driving when a wolf crossed the road. The wolf stopped and peered into his eyes. Bob saw his tail; I saw nothing but two grown men howling at their good fortune.

In the room we packed for the drive to meet our guide, Pete Nagano, on the Blackstone River. Our gear seemed paltry—army-surplus fleece and outerwear. Even the weighty bags felt inadequate. We did not know what to expect, only that we would report from the snow and ice in the morning.

Frozen Bones, a Whitehorse country-rock band, was setting up for the Saturday night gig. They had driven in from Dawson, four hours to the northwest. The road could not be that bad. We had a beer and then left for the one café across the ice. There were two young women who served what seemed a hotel full of men. How they survived the endless ogling I will never know. One of them wore a sweatshirt that happily pronounced Canadian Women Rock. I believed her. So did Dave; he wanted to take it to his daughter.

In the morning, it was near zero, and we tried to eat breakfast before the drive to the Dempster Highway. At the highway junction was an outpost of dry goods, gas, and the last place you could call for help. "It'll be two hundred gallons if I have to come get ya." Sure, I thought, we might get lucky and see him twice in the same day. I bought a fake Yukon plate to put in my garage collection, doubting that any car I own could make the journey here and back. The Dempster has a reputation: it's almost five hundred miles of crushed stone and in March, sanded ice and snow for the occasional rig connecting the few stops between here and Inuvik.

The road up was opaque; there was no measuring the distance. We had come to the land of cloud and wind and snow. This was the hundred-year forest of "drunken" black spruce, all of them smaller than pine saplings. Poplars lined the riverbeds and, farther north, birch colonies stood by the roadside. We surrendered to the indifferent rolling ridges. On a bluff a car was stranded. Dave peeked in the window—not knowing who might lie below the fogged glass. It could have been any of us in that car, waiting for the next vehicle, waiting for the one sign of flesh.

At kilometer one hundred twenty-one, in the middle of a valley east of the Ogilvie Range, we saw a Canadian flag blowing at the edge of the frozen Blackstone. We turned on the ice and found Pete's Toyota, heavy with a gas drum wedged in the back. And then he appeared, dressed for "forty below," as we would find him the next four days. He had a sled hitched to the back of his snowmobile. We threw our overstuffed bags and groceries on the icy carpet and walked to the cabin, still incredulous there was shelter in the vast openness of this land. I heard echoes of Jack London and a Robert Service poem Bob had sent before leaving. I heard the spittle of the bemused miner in "To Build a Fire" crack in midair. I wondered how long the cold gave you before it stopped hurting.

I remembered flying onto the Coastal Plain the previous June. We let go of the familiar to wake on a riverbank, and like that day, this land, where man and mammal have coexisted for several millennia, flooded in. It was not a foreign land to Pete. His eyes were small orbits of acute observation. This was his birthplace, a long and singular existence with rivers and mountains that sculpted his people, the Ta'an Kwäch'än Nation. He drew on a napkin to describe the seven tribes in this valley trying to coexist, to hunt and survive the onset of outsiders. He said it was stressful, and I wished that word had not found its way north. I wished he did not have a definition for what we had left behind.

In the cabin we warmed to a pine fire and sipped tea. Pete tried to imagine us in the Ogilvie Mountains on snowmobiles. In a few hours, he found out: we were pretty much worthless. I likened riding them to goosing a Harley in the sand. They were responsive if you knew motors and balance. Richard, Pete's brother, showed up a day later and told me, "Ride it like a horse or a woman." Having insulted half of the readers, he meant ride like you mean it. Low visibility made day one a veritable picnic on the six-hundred-cubic-centimeter sled.

Pete sipped black tea, as taciturn as a man must be in the North. Then he opened smoked salmon and we thought the moon had risen in our cabin. He started dinner and asked what we brought. We remembered the few thin chops in the bag. Pete snickered, "That's barely enough for me," then cooked all of the chops—his and ours—when he was visibly tired. Our bellies were full. We offered cookies and thimbles of whiskey. We sat by gaslight with Blackstone water in drums and a barrel stove, six feet from the table.

Pete arose in the gray light, put water on for tea, and percolated a large pot of coffee, although it was not his drink. He fried bacon and eggs, apologizing for not having enough to share, and we sipped river coffee and oatmeal from tin cups. Before we left the table, he went outside, filled the tanks with gas and oil, and started the Ski-Doos. We took our snowshoes, thinking there might be an opportunity to use them. Dave packed cheese and apples, still crisp from the Whitehorse market. To our eyes, the terrain was empty, without features because the clouds were low and unforgiving. But to Pete and Richard, it was more like a house they had lived in for forty years—it had context in low light, white light, and darkness. It was home to dozens of species, not just the caribou, but most large mammals that have dwindled or died out in the lower forty-eight. And it was their home. More than once Richard said, "I don't have any ambition to leave here." We respected their desire and understood the failure of our notion of travel. To be of a place is to be more than what it promises—and they were.

At one point, I went ahead with the two of them to break trail and when they circled back for the others the landscape was completely devoid of earth and sky and tone. The cloud had come to my feet. I couldn't see twenty yards and realized as they rode away that this was my moment alone. I had no compass and could not have told a mountain from a bone in that light. I could not hear the least living thing. My heart was a strobe of heat. I took my jacket and hat off, hot from riding the few miles. I imagined that it would be an hour before they arrived. I put my camera on the pile of clothes and took an automatic shot, not believing the solitude. I tried to find their tracks but saw what looked like prints from two long poles—my front skis. This is how you come to lie in the snow, I thought, but quickly put the thought to waste. If I had to get out, I would do more than lie before a sunless sky. Cold is a weather of few mistakes. I waited.

They came. We rode farther on and had lunch. Emboldened by our progress, we rode to the next ridge where the caribou were. This was the surreal moment Bob had hoped for: to see them in their natural habitat fifteen hundred miles from the Coastal Plain. We edged up the backside of a slope, shut the Ski-Doos down, and walked to the ledge. Below were forty caribou, attentive and prominent in the treeless landscape. Richard sat, told us to do the same, and made the sign for quiet. The herd split and one group began to come up the ridge where we sat. They walked closer and stopped. They heard my boot on the snow, then loped down the ravine. Richard said they had come to him many times—we needed to be still. I fumbled with the camera. The caribou were bountiful, and I could not capture them.

Riding back, we were filled with the unexpected: we had begun to witness their migration. On the ridgetop were fresh scat and hoof prints. Beneath them, the tiny lichen grew against the rock. This was the caribous' diet for the winter; lichen sustained them. I think of lichen as painted rocks. These mammals are larger than deer, weigh up to four hundred pounds, live for about seven years, and subsist on lichen and tundra once they reach the Plain. They move across the most forbidding territory in North America, survive wolf, fox, coyote, and hunters. They have done so for more than ten thousand years on a diet of plant matter that is barely a plant.

Coming back, the clutch in my Ski-Doo gave out and we doubled up for the last miles. Richard rode as if he were alone. There was no wasted effort. I began to understand how close he was to the snow and ice beneath us. For him, this was a day off, a way to let down and relax. He wanted nothing more than to be in this wilderness.

At the cabin, we were tired but happy. Pete was in the kitchen, the gaslight soft above the stove. "Do you like moose?" turning his knife on the fat. He sliced the flank into chunks that simmered for more than an hour. It was sweet, tender meat mixed with pasta. On the table was a bowl of salad. We ate slow and quiet. By the end, we could hardly move to our beds.

The next day, there was sunlight and very little wind. I saw Pilot Mountain to the south, the Ogilvies to the east, and the runway where hunters flew in to the north. A perspective on the land returned to us; we could ride in this weather. We wanted to go as far as we could. We rode over snowfields for miles, Pete and Richard stopping with field glasses on the ridges. A helicopter tracked the caribou. Pete wasn't happy; helicopters traumatized the herd. We spread out, and for the first time I had no desire to follow closely. I floated behind until we reached Seela Creek and angled through the poplars. Pete stopped to make sure we saw the water. He did not want us to puncture the ice and dry by fire. We went up a ridge that looked to Mount Skukum. The creek bed flowed south; the lines of poplars were like sumi strokes on the white field. Pete shut down his engine. In a pocket diary, given to me by Richard, I wrote, "Sun and blue spots, today we can see. All of us are learning to ride. Everyone's doing well. There's wolf scat here—a caribou was killed." A hoof was on the snow. "They killed him here," Pete said. I tried to imagine that wolf on this crag of rock satiated with fresh caribou. Bob put the hoof in his jacket, and foolishly I kept two scat pebbles, believing they would tell me of that day.

Pete turned and said, "I don't bring many people here." The hunters would leave him without the few annual kills that sustain his father and mother. We were in the private of his homeland, and he opened the one door that few visitors went through. He uncovered what we came to observe, trusted the strange new faces in his backyard.

Bob and Dave ate and shot picture after picture, and I hoped my black-and-white roll would render a small part of this beauty. I flicked away the apple core and we set off for the next valley. My limbs tingled with joy. I had no thought for miles, the snow a cushion below me. On the ridge above us Richard rode in sunlight, arcing the herd toward our sleds. We stopped and watched: hundreds of caribou in all directions. It was like going to a kingdom of hooves and horns and brown and white fur. At the base of a chute, there were forty caribou right above our heads, incredulous that we were in this place with *them*. This was the last time I doubted their magnificence—they lived without the twentieth century. They fell prey to one instinctual need: to procreate and give birth on the Coastal Plain. What more could a species hold out for the skeptical?

Our journey had taken us fifty miles, and unbelievably, we had come full circle to my broken Ski-Doo. No topo map, no compass but the weather of snow worn on a man in the Yukon. Richard towed the Ski-Doo back, breaking trail all the while. I might have said fearless, but he would defer—"This ain't nothing." Then sleep came on our bunks—we were too tired to eat.

In the morning I fumbled my thermometer—ten degrees in the thin green bunkhouse. I lit the *Yukon News* and the pine stacked from the night before. I was fully dressed and tried to warm my Sorels on the stove. My fingers and toes felt the burn. Outside, it was minus thirty-five degrees—a gray sky and light snow. I closed the door and stoked the fire. No one moved. A shaman had come to the Blackstone. His name was Cold. He had been in the book of many peoples. There was a silence in the room. The steam rose from my hands and socks. A crack in the window glass defeated my glowing fire. Dave had the heavy bag.

He swore by it that morning. Bob and I had drifted in and out of sleep, our limbs like swallows in the wrong spring.

The door opened to a smoke-filled bunkhouse with three old men. It was Pete with coffee and hot water for oatmeal. This is what comes from river water: the end of isolation. Pete said, "It's a little cool today; we may have to wait for Ski-Dooing." Waiting seemed fine. We tested the air. My mustache froze as I made my way to the woodpile. In a few hours, if the car started, Pete thought we'd drive to see Elephant Peak, and beyond if the weather and gas held out.

We passed a desolate road crew outpost and two itinerant campers. Nothing more than a canvas shell and a stovepipe between them and minus twenty-five. At the hot springs I took my first shot of running water but I could not be idle outside. We pulled the car off on a bluff above a valley, and I tried to remember all its feeling for the watercolors in my bag. On the Coastal Plain I had painted, but here my fingers were crude instruments.

That night we ate tacos with the hunters. A dozen of us were at the table, and the food was almost as good as Pete's. There was an uneasy quiet; our groups were separated by the *idea* of wilderness, and despite the cold there was little to say. The lodge was home to those who paid for the privilege of coming to this landscape, and neither group could lay claim to living with the caribou. We wanted the wild on our mutual terms, observations, and skills. I am not the angel who will dispel belief in guns—I would shoot a bear if my life were endangered. I found a natural affinity in the rank way we decided not to converse. Each came for time in their temple and each would leave without hesitation for the world left behind—work, wives, and every postage stamp accorded to the eyes of children. Are we different? I think not. We are animal and prey, but we want different silences.

Dave woke at 2:00 a.m. and lit the fire. For an hour I listened to it sputter and release its combustion to stars. As we stayed wrapped in fleece in the army-surplus bag, rest came with the hoofprints of caribou, their "split-heart" tracks and scat in the snow.

For the first time I painted in the sunlight of our bunkhouse. I wanted to heave the door open and paint on the step, but the cold forced me to the stove where I found the color green, the first primary color beyond the dinner table. Mostly the paint was smoke, the disappearing gray to white that confounded our eyes for four days. Then, the primordial effort to hike the duffle bags to the Toyota, which Dave started at twenty-eight below. A good thing, I thought. The generator would have taken hours to warm the block. I was not inclined to diagnose the mechanics of dead motors. The day before, I barely held the gas nozzle for Pete to pump enough fuel into our tank to get to Stewart Crossing. Silly me, a tool in this cold was a piece of wood that did not burn, except when it touched flesh.

We settled up, an awkward punctuation to the days of living by other cycles, and started down the Dempster. The sun was out; we saw the landmarks that had been hidden from view—the Tombstones, the lakes and rivers twisted to land. The car Dave spotted on our journey up was gone. Perhaps the owners had come to retrieve it before spring cast its snowmelt on the highway, or they were lost still and it was in a Whitehorse junkyard.

We snapped photos as if the view would escape us and drove into Dawson for a burger and a beer at the Eldo'. Dressed in fatigues and a snow hat, I looked in the mirror behind the bar: my gray-and-black-speckled face, my eyes wrinkled with happiness. Bob and Dave phoned their loved ones in the country below and I bought a few cards for the disbelievers. We crisscrossed the icy streets of Dawson, tried to imagine how Pete and Richard lived, but could do little more than imagine a shower and a bed. In our stupor, we came upon the cabins where London and Service had stayed for a brief time. Their log homes barely stood, and yet their words remained. Is this what a writer does? Relinquish his spirit to the river that he may lie in peace?

Not high-minded modernists, these two let us into the Yukon, let us live beyond the four walls of routine. *The Call of the Wild* is the dream song of a dog and an explorer, the affirmation of greed in the wilderness, what we face today with different prose and different guises. That night in the bar in Carmacks, the drunk Indian was a daguerreotype for the hunger these and other men left behind. We left the bar, left the young women pouring coffee the next morning, and my friends posted me safely in the hangar in Whitehorse.

In Vancouver, I sat at the window watching rain. We flew in by the river of logs, and the city was overcast but beautiful in the way all gray things are beautiful: it held no pretense, it was part of a tradition of clouds. I remember walking the dock days before, that same river home to boats and shipbuilders and the first daisies of March. I remember meeting Dave, half-asleep in our room and the cold Guinness that marked our gathering for travel north. I have lived in the sanctuary of poetry and wished for one simple truth to affect me: without declamation, we go to river and mountain and sky. And this day, this rain-gorged day, I boarded the last plane for home and knew it had. Miles below, the city of thousands ran to their destinations. For a moment I was free of mine, knew only the cardinal time of caribou hunched in the White Mountains. I was part of the other landscape, a sapling left in their midst.

— 2005 —

5

Minot, North Dakota:
When the Sky Begins to Unravel

IN THE LATE FALL I left for Denver, then on to Minot—fifty miles from the Canadian border. The airport was small. ShaunAnne came around the carousel to grab my bag. Real winter had yet to come, but there was worry in the air. The streets looked abandoned—piles of mud and debris had floated over the crest of the Mouse River. Heavy rains in Saskatchewan pushed the levees to the limit, and soon water was running in the streets. Minot is bisected by elevation, and those close to the river could not run. We pulled up to Russ and ShaunAnne's house—a formerly beautiful brick home that abutted the river. Mud and water had reached seven feet up the exterior walls. Nothing was the same and they feared for what it meant: where to rebuild, how to reclaim what was lost?

Still, she managed to bring me into the folds of NOTSTOCK, an annual printing, art, and music extravaganza at Minot State University where she taught. I turned to her and asked, "Do you think we should be doing this? Seems like you have more to attend to." She laughed her stoic laugh and told me to be in the bar at five.

Downstairs, the rodeo pros were in the hotel lobby. We sipped a beer and she began to tell me how things had unraveled. They were home and knew the water was rising. They spent three days emptying the house. Then the sirens and the horrible sinking that followed. Russ is a musician and has more records, guitars, and amps than a good retro rock station. ShaunAnne is a bibliophile.

The two things that kept them alive—books and music—were about to live in storage for eighteen months. She has written many poems about this—staggeringly sad and strong, trying to feel her way back to that beautiful idea: normal.

She didn't want me to know it cut deep, but the sixteen months since the flood had bent their lives like rails beneath a train. They lived in a FEMA trailer, which is shelter, but little more than four hundred square feet of it. They knew what the other did every moment in the aluminum cubicle. Their drain was hooked to the drain for the house. Heat tape circled water and waste pipes. They could wash enough dishes to eat but had to slither through the kitchen when their meal was finished, so tight was the space. I think of places where people live, of uniforms to wear in the darkness. They could neither live nor wear a uniform in this space. It was claustrophobic and still.

She took me to the college and said, "They're yours," and they were. For five days I met them: high school kids bused in, rez kids bused in, college kids trying to fit them into their classrooms and all of them buzzing like flies over the possible hiatus from learning. Poetry doesn't have an argument in this dialogue; it must find its way into a life. If you are lucky enough to be smitten by a line, give thanks, but I found myself wondering at the blackboard—what had I just gotten into? There were over five hundred visitors from every wheatfield in a hundred-mile radius, and I was the lone foreigner. Well, not really—there were several outstanding printmakers, musicians, and painters from Chicago, Minneapolis, and beyond. I could feel the excitement that comes when people gather to celebrate art. Her students were like disciples; ShaunAnne was revered. They wanted to know what this thing called poetry was. They had written poems, studied them with her, and made every attempt to rollick in the stanzas. ShaunAnne thinks we met at a Robinson Jeffers conference—she is a scholar of the poet's work—but I think we met when his poetry came into our lives.

I tried to find a word to begin, a word that would let me explore its nuances for five days, a word I could hang exercises on and yet not be able to fully define, a word that had already been thrown like cordwood against the wrongs of the world: *power*. I asked them to pair adjectives and verbs with ten synonyms for *power*. Soon the words were like popcorn flying out of the pan. They became aggravated because *power* has so many connotations; from peace to war, they ranged like crows looking for the precise meaning of this word. We left some of their found poems on the board like this one from Joe: "It is hard to stand against the unrelenting hypocrisy." Some we let go to chalk dust but none were exempt. Every student wanted to be a part of the words emanating from the board. Something more came from their constant poking at its intent, its seemingly benign presence on the green wall. I erased and erased, making new columns. They could not generate words fast enough and slowly began to be facile at this game, this game that pretended to undress power. There were so many intelligences in the room and ShaunAnne, Sarah, and the other teachers watched, helped, and mentored. The subtle differences were everywhere—the high school thieves that take us away for that brief time to become unseen. Not just the bullies and jocks but the innocents with their leitmotif: I cannot possibly belong. Everyone knows the rules but me. The college kids didn't care a damn—they jumped in with both feet and soon were helping the younger ones try to articulate this notion of what power meant, when to any outsider, it was all over the room: what the haves and have-nots take for granted—this is how it is.

Because it's not enough to write and leave words on the board, even for the long weekend with a note to the janitor, we had to find a way to preserve them, to make them real. Someone suggested the hallway to the English Department, a fitting place to adorn with the paper cranes of power. I asked ShaunAnne for colored paper and had the young people write their words like they were stakes in the ground. She wrangled permission from the on-highs, and on Saturday morning a young mother showed up with home-made bread and coffee; Kristina took off work, found a sitter for her daughter, baked for us; fiery Joe hauled words to the wall. Molly and Lisa helped too. There was a tall, lanky woman in her thirties whose name trailed into the wheat, but she was so taken by the process, she declared her love of poetry at the top of the third flight. I thought of Dickinson lying beside a perfect couplet.

We found some spray glue and plastered the walls with orange, yellow, and red. Every pastel had bold black letters to define the scraps of paper. Soon it was a collage and the random juxtapositions made the phrases even stronger. I didn't think it was possible when we came—didn't think we could find our way into the stairwell of the brick building. I imagined much less than they did—which is the joy of letting the genie out of the bottle.

That night we made the first of many forays into the Blue Rider, a bar Walter Piehl started to survive the long winter and to carve out a place for painters and painting. Walter is known throughout the Midwest and beyond as one of its native sons who is an excellent abstract painter. Before the trailer came, Russ and ShaunAnne kept Walter's paintings—some made for them—in the basement of friends with whom they stayed. His paintings were in almost every venue in this community. He was gone during my time there, but I heard legions about his influence, his presence, and once again learned art's life-saving genesis—he chose to stay, to make his street the haven for art. His late, good friend, the Native American painter Fritz Scholder, was so taken by the bar that is really not a bar but a perfectly made gallery that poses as a bar, that he painted an original on the wall where it remains to this day. Walter covered it with Plexiglas so that in the case of some imminent demise—too much fun in the name of art—it would survive.

Inside, the patrons were schooled; they knew what painters had come, what visions were on the wall. I felt honored and ignorant—somewhere an artist had risen from this soil to claim his home. But for the address, it could have been a SoHo exhibition, and this is when art brooks no patience—what you do with your ability is the lone marker. The rest is for the critics. This is the satisfaction that comes from being still—Walter did not make a case for his art; he made art. Many former Minot State students created 62 Doors, an underground artist's collective in the basement of a building owned by Walter. Its hallways are lined with sixty-two doors, something whimsical and magnetic with an art store to keep everyone honest. I have seen this kind of bravery in other small towns—think Russell Chatham in Livingston—and I have seen it in my own town. There must be five painters in northern Nevada who wrest from the jury an acclamation but choose to remain where they are and do so without attention. Maybe the power slid from the stairwell to the long shadow of *Der Blaue Reiter*, whose name derives from a school of painters in Germany.

I sat in the FEMA trailer waiting for the meal to light on the table. I ate in the adjoining chair. It was quiet—like the water was still rising. We sipped cabernet, and I searched the walls for what to say. The week had been inverted—what words could convey such loss? Russ never wavered. He worked tirelessly on the house, sawing, painting, restoring, and salvaging the hardwood from its interior. There was an itinerant carpenter living in his camper with a dog. He was sawing too. They thought it would take another three months before they could move in. I did not have a mind to forecast. I did not come to interfere, but I wanted to stay because I could have helped cut down the dead trees, move the mud, replace the windows.

On Sunday, the day after we put power to rest in the stairwell, Russ drove us to the Upper Souris National Wildlife Refuge. It was clear and we walked its rim—swans, coots, and cinnamon teals in the cattails. It was more than a refuge, it was something unshaken by the water. How such beauty and torment can abut one another is without explanation. We stood in the October light, and I could feel the wind rise from the west—some dormant cousin of the peace in this place. It would bring the cold. They would have to live through its tendrils in the trailer for three more months. They understood what little heat there was.

ShaunAnne graciously coaxed twenty people to the reading. I must have sounded like a merganser that had gone off course—a Nevada poet whose desert was not far behind. They were kind, and I took most of the books home. But what does a book mean in an auditorium that was lucky to be standing after the flood? Not much, I imagined.

In the morning dark, I got on the small jet with the Air Force reservists whose rifles were carefully locked in the cargo hold. They were half my age, trying to prepare for the day they may be called to fight. The guy sitting next to me—most of the guys sitting next to me—were coming back from Williston. The fracking boom was on. They were flying home to families in Oregon, Idaho, Montana, states without an address in Minot. The Walmart couldn't stack the shelves fast enough. They put bottled water on crates out front, and it was gone by the end of the day. The man closest to me worked fifteen-hour shifts, slept in the truck, washed on Sunday. He got tired of fighting the crowds and stocked up in Minot before he drove out to sweat the rigs. "The money's good"—that refrain followed the wind all the way across the plains. I couldn't blame him—at least that's how I rationalized it from the small window looking out on the black circles below. But there wasn't much to let go of—my friends were in the trailer, their friends trying to teach through the winter that would bring more snow, ice, and long nights. As T. S. Eliot said in the *Four Quartets*, "And the end of all our exploring / Will be to arrive where we started." Russ and ShaunAnne were winding back to what they knew—the misgiving of living in spite of the river's cut bank, and still not living enough to know if it would suffice. It takes a subtle courage to stay here, and that was before the flood, a determination to see the plains, the wheat, and the soy as friend. Their ancestors, the homesteaders who came from Norway and Sweden, did not ask to be here. It was land to begin, land to frame a life. Inside the small trailer, my friends try to frame their life. They have no guidebook, no relief line, no anchor to set down. They could float away again. They could end up miles from here, but they choose to remain. Like all good visitors, some part of me stays with them.

THREE YEARS LATER, ShaunAnne sent an anguished note—Russ had whooping cough and they could not stop it. This went on for one hundred days and something cracked. He lost his venerable touch. She was alone and doing everything. Later that spring they flew to the Mayo Clinic twice. There were no specific answers, but his health grew worse until the doctors isolated the cause: Creutzfeldt-Jakob Disease. In the fall, thirteen months after contracting whooping cough, came the disquieting news that he could no longer stay at home, the place he had rebuilt from scratch. She could no longer take care of him. She hoped his care would be sufficient in the downtown nursing home. She hoped her money would not run out and leave Russ alone. She hoped her letters to friends, now written in the stupor of a caregiver, would suffice. And then came the last: he had gone.

I live a long way from Minot and all I wanted to do was hold her, comfort the lost person who was left without her lover. But I could not, and so I wrote feeble notes to her, trying to assuage grief's empty chair. This was little more than a rebuttal, a subterfuge for what could not be said. Her mailbox filled with frayed and unspoken words.

In May, she organized a block party outside the Blue Rider—something Russ would have played at until the sun came up. She knew that his spirit, wherever it had gone, would come back for the Memorial Weekend gig. Her family and friends were in the house, the house I saw for the first time: every window, wall, and door refinished and lived in like a home. The yard was green, not brown. The geraniums were potted, not stems in the silt. Her books were on the shelves. Her mother talked to me about art—she knew more than most art historians. ShaunAnne led me into the basement. Five bookshelves were filled with Russ's records. Amps, turntables, and recording equipment were stacked on the concrete floor. In the wild, last moments they had rescued what they loved. She pointed to a painting Walter Piehl had done for her—Russ in a collage and another of Russ by Jon Olson, his face as full as the moon. I left early and slept deeply in Tom and Barbara's house where Russ and ShaunAnne had stayed before the FEMA trailer. Tom and Barbara were like olive branches amid the grief. He had taught English with her at the college; they did not need a reason to say yes.

In the morning we swept the garage across the street from the Blue Rider. Eli, the son of another former bandmate of Russ, found a bobcat trailer and parked it perpendicular to the entrance of the bar. Eli carried Jeffers with him in his pocket and had lived off the land to play music. It seemed the most natural place for a stage: in the middle of the street, the street that would bear up under the gathering weight. We finished sweeping and drove to the city auditorium to get chairs and tables. Walter secured them with rope in his hay trailer. He felt safer in a saddle than a car. It was out of filial duty to Russ that he worked and gathered so many to make this event right. Just as we finished lining up the chairs, Eli noticed a cloud in the west and then it began: the dust and rain and darkness of a Midwest storm. Russ was here all right, and the storm grew until the glass shattered in the garage, a pane blew from the ridge on the roofline.

Slowly, we brought the amps and guitars back out again. The wind was loathsome, but over two hundred people were coming to eat from the taco stands and play the music Russ loved. I went and showered, but the dust would not relent. It was a dust I knew from Nevada. Maybe it was the same dust that circles high above to land once again at our feet. ShaunAnne bent over the makeshift stage; her back was inflamed with pain, but it was more than pain—she had carried all that Russ was for five months to make this day hallowed. It was the pain that belongs to phantoms. A pain she could braille.

Outside the Blue Rider I finally stood with Walter. He was as affable and ready a man as I have ever met. He wanted to know how I knew ShaunAnne, where I had come from, what I had done. All I wanted to know was how he made his abstract art. It was the way the weekend went—me looking in, so many looking out. Walter's son, Shadd, was on the stage, and John, one of Russ's former jam-session mates, was on lead. Andy was on the bass. They were singing a song that survived opening night years earlier in the Blue Rider. A bar that I now understood was in Kandinsky and Klee's shadow. The artists broke from tradition to remake the canvas in pre–World War I Germany. Now it was post–Iraq War Minot, and the tradition of rebellion was everywhere in the street. ShaunAnne rose to the stage and tried to shout what Russ had meant to all of them. The crowd quieted. Her parents and friends were standing in the wind and sun, friends who had driven or flown from all over America to remember Russ.

An outsider has no place at such endings. I watched from the entrance to the Blue Rider, slumped in the certainty that the beauty here could not be replicated. It was the best of a small town: intelligent, magnanimous people gathered by one man who understood this and who were drawn into his orbit yet again. It grew dark, and Eli asked if I would go on the stage. An order of words and notes prevailed. I looked down to ShaunAnne, the bar was crowded, and the lights dangled at the taco trucks. No one heard me, and I started to recite William Carlos Williams's poem, "The Locust Tree in Flower," a poem I recite to myself every May because I know we will be all right. We made it through another winter and the locust, a stubborn bone of a tree, bloomed once again. ShaunAnne wept in my arms; she wept in everyone's arms. I left for bed, but Eli and the others played long into the night. In the morning I looked at those same black circles. Fracking had come and gone. The airport was new, but the people were missing.

The Midwest started to flower. I wondered where the men had migrated to—what nexus of commerce had drawn them in? At 35,000 feet, I was no less itinerant.

ShaunAnne sent me a picture of us on the street in front of the bar. She was smiling in the tears. The windstorm had passed. Maybe she knew what lay ahead for her and her friends, the ones you cannot make in a single visit, the ones you make over blood and headwaters and nights in the Minot dark. These friends who are like hardwood and live in the perimeter of things held close. These mighty farmers and teachers who will not cross the single boundary of No. These men and women whose land and art are synonyms for staying alive. These young lives that emanate from stairwells. Their journey goes on. They need what it represents: a way to hold out against the bulwark of misdeeds by smaller men and women. Most would have run by now.

—2017—

6

Walden Pond in the Desert

It would be simpler if there were a place with a small cabin, a retreat to which I returned, a meadow in the mountains with a creek nearby that defined what this landscape might mean for a poet. Then I would know what instructs me, how to behave in this open land. I would have a template for moving into the expanse of language, because this is the example that has been held up for so many years—once you are settled in the routine of place, you may begin. But there is no such place here; *this* ideal locale for creation is imaginary. I must look elsewhere to discern what is missing, what is given.

When Henry David Thoreau set out for his twenty-six-month stint on Walden Pond in 1845, it provided an intrinsically valuable structure from which to explore his many themes of self-reliance. The image of Thoreau at the desk in the simplicity of his wooded cabin is, by now, a cliché, but the Great Basin—while also beautiful—is more than its obvious referents: hot, desolate, and dry. These small tenets for living without an exact beauty—what is missing, what is given—require a longer gestation, a willingness to be without formidable knowledge of a path to such a place. I have wanted this answer, this recollection to be filled with recognition, but it is not. In thirty years of trying to find such a place, I have learned, instead, to depend on qualities of character, not place, to order what is missing, what is given.

Didn't I know this when I moved here? My cabin could have been in another place, close to a Sierra Nevada stream, or maybe a lake at elevation? Didn't I know that coming here with such expectations would fool me? And yet—what I could not define drew me in. I wanted to write poems in a place that was hollowed by sand, wind, and extremes of weather, by a history of struggle against those things. I wanted a retreat that was earned. Not to diminish what Thoreau did, but rather to claim this undefined place of mountain, high desert, and alkali flats for definition and, after years, for retreat. The simpler choice would have been obvious, but the choice to locate in a land without clear definition put me closer to clouds, stars, and worries that I might not ever truly settle. I envy those artists who don't need these things, who can sit down in a café and write as if nothing were going on around them. I am not that person. This blue-to-purple-to-brown horizon may as well be my desk and the sun, my immediate shelter and source of discomfort. I too have a cabin. It continues to grow outside every day. It grows farther from me to include all that I may or may not see, and my small pool extends to everything that flourishes. If there is water beyond May, a handful of wildflowers pronounce its presence. That recognition may take a decade, and nothing comes to this pool easily.

After so long here, there is little delineation between the internal and external geography of this place. When I am away, I am struck by its absence, by how empty, vulnerable, and hopeful it is. Clearly, this is no image of beauty, no pond by which to sit, only qualities of existence. A quality of mind. People ask if it is possible to know such things about a place; I have come to *need* them. It is no longer an ideal that I imagine.

Until you step into a place as large as the high desert of my home, empty sounds like an abstraction. At first glance, it has no geographic center, no unifying altitude, depth, or circumference. To the outsider, there appears to be little *here* save a desire for all that it isn't. Empty connotes being alone, and in much of the Great Basin, I am alone. When I travel from west to east on Highway 50, I may drive for hours and see more antelope than cars. Being alone does not intimate being lonely; rather, it is a place in which to discover what is unsaid—a poet's place.

Paradoxically, people are drawn to the high desert because of this perception of it being an empty place. This perceived lack of definition, this empty landscape, is what stirs many to move and root here. The vocabulary to describe it is expansive: endless, open, vast; and it is also described in foreboding terms: dry, brown, barren. These are not opposites; they are qualities of living here, what I explore in my poetry and painting. I link myself closest to this intersection, this emptiness and its foreboding unknowns. The horizon is mountain and sky; the flora, piñon and sage; the fauna, coyote and bobcat—at once unnerving and comforting. In a word, the emptiness is a vacuum of our rich and variegated lives in this place, and the poem is a reference to this soliloquy. It is the supposed emptiness here that produces tension in my art. Whether isolation or contemplation, I never travel far from this physical experience of geography. I personally cannot, and so I have chosen to embrace its consequence—the poem as testimony to the riddle of this environment. A riddle I leave unsolved.

A visitor from a tree-laden landscape might remark, "You cannot hide here," or, if a person does manage to hide, it is temporary, but the visitor and this place remain unchanged. This can be disquieting; what so many seek in the high desert is open to friend and foe, feral and final demands, and, of course, serenity of no limit. This is a contradiction and why, in part, the American West is so elusive; its descriptors are transient, its coordinates restless, and its attraction endless.

My threshold for peace is out my door. I am minutes from being vulnerable in it, but I must relinquish myself to the openness, the untamed motion of being in a place with few borders. Out here, the horizon passes from one corner of vision to the other. This wide space is enthralling; it can also be terrifying. There is no perceived entry or exit; it is an inland expanse of soil and light, mountain and occasional creek, silence and distance.

The name, Desatoya—the mountain range in central Nevada—is loosely translated as "to lose one's bearings," as the early Basque sheepherders no doubt did.

Consequently, I find myself in this emptiness without a compass, without a reference point—where is that familiar footing to steer my course? It is *here*, directly in front of me, which is difficult to remember, and yet I keep looking for some other reference to home. To live with this beauty, I must first assent to it. The poet Joe-Anne McLaughlin Carruth has said laughingly of it, "I could never live in the West—I couldn't take the competition." As a poet, this rightly means letting go, giving in to what will come from not knowing, not being in control of my destiny. This is an unpopular notion in the "every-man-for-himself" West. The rugged individuality that once characterized its many residents is now almost a myth. But does that require the poem to conform to this myth? I don't think so. Within the context of my daily life here, a far more vulnerable reality is the norm. This is the grist that informs my poems—the struggles with weather, work, political views, and the trusted reticence of thirty-year neighbors. Even when I am misunderstood, our differences are not grounds for divorce. To take art out of this context would be disingenuous, and that is different from other locales. What I call my home is first and foremost a place. One reckons with a place. If it were easier, it would be another place—a city, a bus station, an office—where the environment is more controlled. I surrendered that control when I came here but embraced something altogether different: a willingness to live without it.

The opportunity to partake in this conversation is constant, and art is the supreme offering in such a conversation. A poem distills; it is a magnifying glass through which to examine my experience of vulnerability in this landscape. What better way to render surrender than through art—to salt flats, sage, or ridicule? Yes, ridicule of the human kind but of the feathered as well—think magpie or piñon jay.

For in surrender comes solitude, and the mind quiets, redolent with possibility. This is hard for me, after decades of being here, but it is in that moment when poetry speaks loudest. It is most clear, a concise expression of emotion and perception. The literal translation of belonging to a place is without pretext and therefore germane. In this, the poet in the West is not unlike Thoreau—he also belonged to a place that allowed such concentration. It is just harder to belong to the physicality of this place— not something easily chosen.

Some will disagree and say that poetry has little function in this landscape. The poem is a tool of the mind, not to be rendered in service to another descriptive power, whether greed or praise. Perhaps, but this landscape, like all landscapes—think of Pablo Neruda in Chile, Federico García Lorca in Andalucía, Matsuo Bashō in Japan—is such a rich, primordial place to start a poem that I cannot resist. The poetry that infuses my search for definition in this land is rooted in engagement with the outside world, the one beyond my window that I must abide in order to survive. A bird might be a talisman or a bird, but within the context of this landscape it takes its rightful place as messenger of tree, wind, and water. Likewise, I cannot escape the portents of these soundings in the immediacy of my life any more than I can escape the thrall of sleep, hunger, or love. I try to find resolution in these discrepant elements, take refuge in the silences of this high desert where the poem is shrouded by nothing—a temporal reality that I acknowledge. My poem is therefore also vulnerable, my art as elusive and inscrutable as the wind. Wind is a defining characteristic of this dry land, but what is a poem conceived with this recognition? It is "an avowal," as the poet Hayden Carruth has said. My choice is to avow this experience of being vulnerable.

And then, finally, on to hope, which of course, is the point of this reflection without Walden Pond, the one I make with art, yes, but also experience with my hands and labor. Hope, because I cannot argue with the sky—which is everywhere and glorious. Hope, because in the ruins of rock fall, alkali flats, and occasional water, there remains a history of more than us, of being in this place for millennia—whether antelope or Paiute, mountain goat or settler. There is also a record of survival against interminable odds. The diaries of those crossing the Forty-Mile Desert in the mid-1800s are rife with suffering—drought, dysentery, and insects—all to find the panacea that was the West. Even Mark Twain's description of living here in the mining boom was filled with passages of tears, humor, and foolishness, but also of optimism that, despite it all, the town's intrepid miners would prevail.

I turn to Gary Snyder, Richard Hugo, and other poets who are known for their variations on hope in this waterless place. As they did, I make my home where hunters and gatherers once made theirs. I can no longer afford to be nomadic. There is no more West in which to escape. The West, as has been said, is *here*, so I must learn to live in it and pay attention to the obvious for illumination: seed, leaf, and stone. The elements are harbingers of what I will soon experience. As an artist I thread them into my stories. I speak on behalf of the dying birch as much as I sing the praises of the prospering child. Why?

This is the substance of my day. I cannot shed the particulars of existence for the sake of art—not if I choose to be defined by them. These particulars inform the range and topics I descend into with poetry and paint. I have tried to paint in other colors but the burnished hues of the Great Basin return to almost every watercolor: sienna, auburn, saffron—the dry hues as I like to call them—just as my poems are infused with the value of these hues. How can they not be? Unless I was an entirely cerebral poet, description without them would confound me at every turn.

William Carolos Williams said this long before: "No ideas but in things." These physical things provide a lasting measure of reflection—comfort in the knowledge that the dirt below my feet has both questions and resolution, that in my absence, *this* tale will nevertheless unfold.

I choose to be a part of this narrative, to direct my attention to the arid land and the daily bath of wind. I choose to drum the collective storm of seasons and the promise the place might hold, with or without my signature. There are others for whom this place is simply a desert. That's fine. This dialogue with the expanse out my door enchants me. In coming to know a place, I come to know my place in it, which enables me to care for it and to plan for its continued use. In other words, it is a place of competing expectations, and in order to reconcile these, I write about them. Thankfully, I have metaphor and image on my side, which lets others into this example of unparalleled beauty and greed, and the corresponding knowledge that these two ideas portend.

I have grown stubborn in my belief that beauty can transcend greed—even as our very refusal to listen chokes off yet another river. Listen to whom, you ask? Certainly not the profligate offerings of the land barons—they have already come and gone—but those other signals that portend the greater promise of species survival. That is a valuable continuum to work on—everything is up for grabs and there is tension in the choice to listen or turn away—as the taps run dry and the flood of migration continues. I believe this is the responsibility of living here—to share in this dialogue, to help push it further, listen, and take sides. What artist has not, and what artist can afford the luxury of supreme disaffection? I cannot. That is why hope remains for me.

The job of the poet is to refract, much like the razor light that startles my eyes because of the lack of water molecules. This then is my task: to refract what comes to bear on this place that endures our presence. As I've said, it is in the silences that the poet works. This place is perfectly suited to my labor. The challenge is to listen, hard for all of us, especially the artist who must record these unspoken realities: emptiness, vulnerability, and hopefulness— what is felt but perhaps not shared. Thoreau did not start here; he shared the practice of retreat with others before him, but it is difficult to know if such practice is possible here. I believe it is.

That is why I depend on the intrinsic qualities of this place for guidance: emptiness, vulnerability, and hopefulness. There is no counterfeit currency, no surfeit of knowledge that will suffice without them. At least for now—what remains unseen is its primary attribute and why so few choose it. I should be thrilled to write where I live, but I too retreat to something not quite seen, not quite known, for a fuller, more precise understanding of what is here. These three things became habitual cornerstones that exerted their presence on my poetry. Time was the one thing I could not account for: only after its passage did I tire of the simpler explanations and welcome this unconventional notion of being a poet in the West. I'm grateful for Thoreau's example but equally grateful for what is largely unknown—a place in which to begin with little distraction. How else could I know its name?

—2017—

7

Because the Land Is So Bare: The Poetry of Joanne de Longchamps

THERE ARE A HANDFUL OF POETS from the Great Basin to whom I look for a reckoning with this place—an understanding of its light, its bearing on the mind, its presence in the cultural landscape—how, in a word, a poet adheres to its rigor? Joanne de Longchamps struggled to address these questions and to form an identity beyond a regional poet—a pejorative description of any artist. Yet, in her long-written rebuttal to anonymity she found an extreme exposure to light, collage, mythology, and love. Her body was a crucible through which these things manifested themselves, and in her art, they found expression. Most women during the 1950s and '60s were fighting to share any of these ideas. Her well-known peers fought off similar shackles. I'm thinking of Adrienne Rich, Denise Levertov, Anne Sexton, and Maxine Kumin to name a few. A woman was not supposed to intersect with more than the feminine. How unlikely a curse for de Longchamps. She worked at one remove from the flesh and was never certain of its name: sorrow came quick to claim her. She lost her son to suicide, her marriage broke up, and she had repeated health issues throughout her life.

The author of eight collections of poetry and collage including a posthumous edition, she moved to Reno, Nevada, from Los Angeles, as a young bride. In the pre-feminist 1950s she wrote poems that railed against its leaden antecedents. Witness these lines from the sonnet "Portrait: Housewife" in 1957:

She makes a fetish of her faithfulness,
whose private loathing is the double-bed;
a public symbol of the willingness
that, absent, breeds a halo for her head.
She spends bleak passion in domestic rites,
forcing a rigid pattern on the days
that corset conversation, appetites,
and leave her victim to a stern self-praise.

De Longchamps was a vital presence in the Reno arts community. She supported what would improve and coalesce its nascent existence. She worked with several Nevada writers and artists—Jim McCormick, Walter Van Tilburg Clark, Joan Arrizabalaga, Robert Caples, Harold Witt—to name a few. She trusted these artists to guide her and listened to their feedback, especially Clark's. Her poem to Clark at his passing will not leave me ("Late Letter to Walter Clark"). She remembers friends gathered on "a snowhill / for the opening and closing / of cold earth given you," and finds a way to say goodbye using Clarks' words in her poem: "a hawk sailed up / out of the white mountain." She could not write lines for the writing; she understood them to be patterns of existence, how a poet lives in a world without derivative meaning. This was the scrutiny she brought to her art—how can it elevate thought and belief across time? Is there some way a collage can be viewed as an instrument of science put to elementary understanding in the hands of a child? These are redemptive questions and although de Longchamps was never freed from their unanswerable quality, she nevertheless returned to express what color could be drawn in its service, what line exposed in its fealty. In this, she is like every poet in this volume—searching for what cannot be expressed—but to live without such purpose was unthinkable for her.

With *Eden Under Glass* (1957), de Longchamps took the first steps toward fully imaging her artistic vision. Whether it was through pre-feminist or anti-atomic sentiment, her observations were acute. Two in particular document life in the 1950s: "Tea-Time: Atomic Age," a sober portrait of the housewife "ringed with . . . dry mist of cigarettes"; and "Exitus," a revealing look at Oppenheimer—"World there was / that spun in darkness down." Both poems were written long before objection to nuclear war became fashionable. Her early fascination with mythology became a strong personal mythology and compelled her to write through the spell of Greek myth. Rooted in the etymology of Greek words, student of its culture, architecture, and geography, she formed a threshold from which to interpret much of what she viewed and experienced in the Great Basin. She repeatedly contrasted the light and space in these two, distinct landscapes.

The Hungry Lions (1963) was the twenty-fifth book in the Indiana University Press Series. Among her predecessors were Carolyn Kizer, David Wagoner, Conrad Aiken, Josephine Miles, Theodore Roethke, and Federico García Lorca. She was forty years old and it saddens me to think she would not end her life as a well-known poet like the others in that series. She was a Nevadan, and that circumscribed her existence as being separate and apart from mainstream literary America. This is another theme that reoccurs throughout this volume—to be a poet in the American West is to find the solace of wind, aridity, and light. Not, to most minds, the literary laurel of a different locale. She knew this; she talked often about it—how living in the Great Basin was like a surrender to its beauty and a recognition of its literary isolation.

The Wishing Animal (1970), published by Vanderbilt University Press, was her most authoritative and challenging to date. The voice in these poems was dramatic and precise: "Our blood / enters the earth, / black wine / for the thirsty stones." These are poems that writhe on the page. They move with ease and manage to mystify, torment, and restore. Many of these poems informed her collages—later collected in two limited-edition, small press volumes—and she began to think of herself as much a collage artist as a poet.

Then came her strongest volume, *The Schoolhouse Poems* (1975), from a Nevada publisher, William L. Fox. He remained de Longchamps's publisher for the rest of her life. This volume marks her days spent on a family acre near Galena Creek at the base of Mount Rose, the site of a one-room schoolhouse. The title page is Robert Caples's eerie portrait of de Longchamps, painted in 1975. Though de Longchamps spent a lifetime observing and re-creating Nevada's stark light, air, and soil, it wasn't until *The Schoolhouse Poems* that she began to write about Nevada, the *place*. Perhaps her early belief in Greece sustained her until the landscape of the Great Basin became part of that myth. Certainly her interest in the physical environment was heightened by living at the tree line, under the watchful eye of hawk, squirrel, and owl.

The majority of the poems in *One Creature* (1977) were taken from earlier collections, but seen here with the collages they become three-dimensional. The collages focus on mythology, animals, death, and the nexus between science and poetry. Paradoxically, although many of the collages were of the idealized human body, none depicted her personal struggle with failing health. She was unrelenting in her search for the exact words: "tracery, hymenopteron, sievings." *One Creature* is scientifically precise—the poetry captures the essence of life forms:

> Yet bees dance.
> Their pre-prescribed circling,
> set to sun's position,
> reveals (to bees)
> the direction of sustainable pollen.

She captured the specific motion of species and linked it to our own inexplicable journey. In her poem "Cygnus," she likened marriage to the swan's monogamous mating: "We choose as swan or skylark. It is said / the swan sings only as it dies." De Longchamps drew connections between the animal and the human and in these parallels she saw larger ones—the ghost of the sea bear—and smaller ones, too, in the geometry of the beehive. But precision, a desire to know and represent the thing in its fullest, was the strength of these poems and collages.

She expanded the depth of her vision with *Warm-Bloods, Cold-Bloods* (1981). Her eel, jellyfish, and bat poem-collages are seamless re-creations of species in words and images. She tore these striking images from scrap paper *after* she wrote a poem about that creature. Her elegiac poem to her son, Dare, needs no commentary. If you were looking, as she must have been, for a way to record a mother's loss of a son, it is here and it is hard. Friends say she never got over his suicide. It is remarkable that she could go on given the medical complications in her own life (one of her later poems laments the thirty-one surgeries she endured).

In the posthumous unpublished manuscript *The Glass Hammer*, de Longchamps chronicled the rituals of a failed body, drink, and killing pain. The poem, "Philosopher" begins, "Survival is learning what to keep / and then not letting go—." This was the only time I spoke to her. I asked if she would read with Carolyn Kizer, Mark Strand, William Matthews, Richard Shelton, and Pamela Stewart. She declined in a raspy voice, but was "honored" that I asked her. She did not feel she could do justice to the reading, her health getting worse by the day. I pleaded with her to reconsider but knew her decision was final. This is when I began to edit her posthumous selected poems, *Torn by Light*, which closes with eight poems from *The Glass Hammer*. Each of the selections from the eight books begins with a black-and-white reproduction of her collages. Carolyn Kizer wrote of her selected poems,

> Joanne de Longchamps was a . . . beautiful poet. Her last years were all agony, but she had the courage of a tigress and she prevailed. I am so grateful to have this gathering of her poems.

Throughout de Longchamps's life there was an absence of religious belief; her belief was in Greece, animals, and ultimately in the struggle between love and death: "We're afraid of being without love. And we're afraid of death." Nowhere was this struggle more accurately expressed than in her poems on love—"My love, I know no more of love to say." She could be merciless too—"Not in a firm-fleshed beginning / are love's disguises known." This opening line is from "Grimdeath and the Bones": "Lovers die but caution kills / the living while they move." From her earliest work—"I love—in loving I was never wise"—to her last—"It is love, the artisan, the glassblower / . . . who takes our fragments into flame"—she wed emotion to words until finally it became a "vessel / holding light once more."

Although she found ". . . a quality of air and light and movement of light and shadow that I saw in the Aegean that is [at] Pyramid Lake" in Nevada, there is a "feeling of unity simply because the land is so bare. . . . We're fed by our being hungry. And you do hunger in this state [Nevada]. You want some kind of reaction and it's damn slow coming." As if to reconcile her presence here, "You learn to live with the absolute elements." Toward the end of her life, de Longchamps was asked if living in Nevada had in some way limited her career as an artist. To this she responded, "If I had wanted to be great I suppose I'd have gone to New York or I'd have gone back to Hollywood and picked up my contacts. What I want is the feeling of being around people who sense and try to create or recreate this marvel of just being alive. . . . I don't believe in all of this, the rewards of position and power. . . . No, I don't think Nevada is a cop-out at all."

How many mornings have I awoken to the light that would not forgive her? How many mornings have I found myself staring endlessly east across the Great Basin? I turn to de Longchamps because she could not resolve its presence in her poetry; she needed what it intimated: carry on. Do not look elsewhere; do not ask why. An artist only gets a few minutes on the grand continuum and then, it is over. In the desert, time can feel obsolete, as if it has melted from your hands. For de Longchamps, this brief yardstick of light and time forced her to choose what she must do with her art. There was nothing else to propel her decision. No ego, no dance with the luster of the city. This is an obdurate decision: you struggle; you may find your way. You may also fall into nothing. It is a choice that embeds authenticity in your art because it cannot be replicated. She took the risk to do this. No one else. It is something to emulate when much literary aspiration runs contrary to notions of craft, born of durance in a place.

— 2017 —

8

Adrian C. Louis and the Fire Water World

*Eerie how my impotent mind ghosts through redneck
counties glued together by Christian radio.*
—ADRIAN C. LOUIS

ALMOST SINCE MY first reading of Adrian Louis, I have asked myself what it means to be a writer from the Fire Water World, the white one I cannot escape any more than Louis can forsake his Paiute origins? This reflective lens comes at some cost: this is not New England. I am not wrestling with Frost, with the demands that were made on those in his shadow. This is its own geography within the West, rife with the half-life of our paired histories. I do not own them but I cannot disown them. This is not something to outrun. It is the buttress against being in this place. I am confronted by its history throughout Nevada and I am loath to give it a name save sorrow. Even that is not cost enough. To not acknowledge the storm that Louis writes from is to live in abeyance. I cannot do that. He reminds me to shut up and listen. He reminds me that no belief is worth losing a culture. He reminds me that poetry cannot put a shine on what was lived and felt as death. Maybe the Sufi poets were right: pay attention. The mystic is all around but on the edge of this mountain, Louis can intimidate if I look too closely.

An enrolled member of the Lovelock Paiute Indian Tribe, Louis was raised in Wabuska, the valley where I started teaching in Nevada. If I think of the poets from the Great Basin, they simply do not share his perspective. He has stood outside its parameters since his first book. When I want a refresher course in how to remove the skin of complacency, toss off the barbaric synonyms for so many lives on the rez, I turn to Louis. Among his contemporaries, he is writing from an edge that few are willing to negotiate. It is an edge filled with the drubbing of common decency.

When I moved to Nevada to teach in the late 1970s, there were stories of the Washoe and Paiute locals being drug down the street on Saturday nights. This is the place that Louis was born. This is the root of his story and why it cannot be assimilated like the beautiful stories of others. It is fraught with an isolating thrum. He has long since abdicated responsibility for what is right and wrong here; his poetry is the slow drip of antidote to what he sees and hears. It does not distill why this is so. Consequently, he has free reign to move across the reservation and tie his words to the belief that things are okay now, that the reservation has evolved. I drive by the reservation and sometimes I stop. I look for the Cooper's hawk that is Adrian Louis circling over. I wait for the constant shadow overhead, the one that will telegraph just how far I am from this bird. This bird that defies what I want from a poem, this bird that comes for me in my sleeping and waking: "Our cleanliness and savagery, our love and hunger / were white lies / that we told in the night." These last lines from "Dead Cows at *AGAI PAH*" are from *Fire Water World*, his fourth book. The Fire Water World is the white man's world. Joseph Bruchac said of the book,

> Although his realism may be hard for some to swallow in comparison to the romantic lyricism of certain contemporary "Indian books," this work should establish him as a major presence in Native writing.

Published in 1989, I could not find words to describe the artery he had just opened. Thirty years, almost twenty books, and multiple awards later, my artery remains unchanged. The poems move within and without me; I have little chance of escaping them.

People tell me their opinions of poetry every day. I listen because I want to believe them and when the conversation is about to end, I ask if they have read Louis. Some answer in the affirmative. Some claim him as first responder to the desolation that has become commonplace in our lives, people living without dignity or well-being. Some say he is like others who write from this tradition. Some say nothing at all. I choose to affirm the tradition of Adrian Louis. It's not that his poetry and novels have changed what is still very real on the reservation; it's that without him, there is much less definition of this place and its people. Surely you could learn this from his contemporaries—Sherman Alexie, Sherwin Bitsui, Joy Harjo and many others—but you could also find that their chorus is not complete without him. His refusal to write within the lines of contemporary literary tradition is a preamble for staying present, for tolerance, if that can be said, of the duality of his situation: living beyond the distrust of his feelings and experience. That's not a lot to go on. I could not make sense of such disparity. What saves him is that his poems are audacious. If some are not fully realized, it is because they must carry this other world in every line, the white one he cannot outrun.

In 1996 Louis published "Earth Bone Connected to the Spirit Bone." It could have been a long prose poem in *Ploughshares* but it was an essay of poetic rage because his partner, Colleen, was dying:

> I listen to the ghost talk of tumbleweeds, nightcrawling, rasping across the dry desert heart of my distant homelands. I listen and listen, but there is no real amen. A word comes, an English word with harsh Germanic overtones. A solitary word comes and erases the connection between earth bone and spirit bone. That word is Teutonic and Nazi-sounding. That word is Alzheimer's.

He offered prayers to the Grandfathers, the Spirits of the North, and the West Wind that she might be healed. He asked again and again why this torment should come in the middle of her life? He received no answers and turned his words on himself: "And now, fuck all the words I've ever uttered, it becomes the only word in our world." In 1998 he sent me a copy of the chapbook, *Skull Dance*, which included a long homage to grief that I reread to know her, "This Is the Time of Grasshoppers and All That I See Is Dying":

> Today, like most days, I have you
> home for your two-hour reprieve
> from the nursing home prison.
>
> And let's not call
> these bloodwords
> 'poetry' or a winter count
> of desperate dreams
> when reality is so much simpler.

In this life that will not account for our shared, unwanted history, he refused to diagram his days without her, refused the outline of living alone. Again, I learned the solitary preface of kinship: what love we have may disappear any day.

I return to "Wabuska" in *Savage Sunsets* (2012), in which the magpie rises to take him back to the farm valley where he grew up:

> I became a citizen of my heart
> & turned as gray as the lie
> that at any day I could scrape
> all the asinine clichés & excuses
> from my old tongue, cook them
> down in a silver spoon, resurrect
> my wings & magically flap back
> to the ghost clouds of childhood.

This is the messenger from my early home in Nevada. This is the man who wanted to be a poet and left to study at Brown. This is the man who was a journalist before teaching at Oglala Lakota College on the Pine Ridge reservation and later at Minnesota State University in Marshall. This is the messenger who shredded any idea of "recollected in tranquility" from his childhood in this place. This is the messenger to whom I return for a bearing on what lies below the landscape of the Great Basin. Without this messenger, there is little to recommend the reconciliation of the Fire Water World in which he finds himself. So much has been made of the discrepancies all around us; he and his peers are writing about the white man's world that few acknowledge or address. What has not changed on the reservation is the contempt for this dialogue.

When I started reading Louis, I imagined he would be well known in three decades. In my naïveté I believed the trespass on their land might be acknowledged. Paradoxically, he chose to live in the heart of its poverty and solace. The poems emanate from the backyards of friends and family. Some may think this is not the aim of poetry. It is inconsequential when you live in the subjunctive tense that is the reservation. By some random accident, I was on a panel with Sherman Alexie when he started to write his poems, and he has become that well-known writer. More than two hundred and fifty kids from the nearby reservations were chanting his name when he read to them in Reno. But Louis's work is not parallel to the universe of literature that others convey.

> While I slept, God groped
> his frozen wand & spewed
> snow upon the enervated
> reservation of my mind.

This poem, "Toxicity," is from the award-winning volume *Random Exorcisms* (2016), about which Sherman Alexie wrote:

"Adrian C. Louis is profane, angry, and deep in love with this sad-ass world. He is the primary reason why I started to write poems. And he is one of the poets that I constantly re-read. He is one of my personal prophets." I can think of no higher praise from a peer. It is futile to compare poets; both of them starve in their lines. I have tried to bring Louis to Nevada to read but there are too many hardened memories here. The only place he wanted to read was the prison where I teach. Maybe it is because they do not need a scorecard: these memories are the stones that lie on the desert of living without recourse. In the other history of this land, there are stories like his that occasionally seep from the ground to become the lateral achievement of sorrow. They make their way. They need very little to survive because they perfected the art of living alone. In his poems Louis finds redemption, I think, but it may only be a synonym for loss of belief. It may only be what looks like redemption in the far morning of what he sees as in, "My Fine, Feathered Corpse":

In this dry dying
of American night,
an old eagle fell when
it flew past her house.
If you venture her street,
please don't tread upon
my fine, feathered corpse.

Random Exorcisms is a book with which I measure the man who opened my artery so many years before. When you live long enough to write many books, you have the privilege of outliving your first words. But those words were telegraphed to what could not be imagined—redress for the four-hundred-year-old divide between his people and their home. In the end, that is why I read Adrian Louis. I cannot say how or why he finds the courage to return to this place of undoing. He lives in faith that out of the words will come resolve, but he offers no solutions.

He has learned to manage the drift of age, doctoring, and loss as in "RE: Infection":

> A tumbleweed of fear,
> my spinning brain
> looks for escape
> from the creeping dread
> & my tightening scrotum reminds
> me I *am* in a white doctor's office
> where I seem to dwell these days.
> I scan memory for distraction.

I think of Thomas McGrath's coordinates, his elemental reach into the Midwest, into the unfinished resin of what stood for the American character. Louis is charting that same territory, that yet to be uncovered residue of the place beneath. It's a fair question to ask why we do not read the likes of McGrath today, as it is with Louis. It is more than fear; it is a winnowing we cannot countenance. Something inside is revealed when this skin is pulled back, this skin of our nation. Now retired from teaching, I try to keep track of the man who writes "Plan 9 from Inner Space":

> To fit in better
> with the god-fearing
> zombies who populate
> southwestern Minnesota,
> I decided to get one
> of those chrome fish,
> the kind true believers
> stick on the asses
> of their cars
> like some futile,
> End Times frat pin.

A frat pin for the End Times on the coast of American muscle cars. This is the reflection of an unwanted mirror. Whether in

Louis's caricature of Verdell Ten Bears, part boozer, part trickster, or the wrangle of Facebook in the neon dashboard, his verisimilitude refuses easy explanation. He rides into our lives with a diction of broken tongues, upends perceptions, and dangles tendrils from the reservation. It is easy to look away in disgust—just as Louis asked his grandfather to forgive him for being ashamed of his Indian blood.

There is salvation, too, in the persistent declaration of survival, an urgency that circles in and out of his poems. This is the strength of his poetry: he continues, he finds another exit. He is not alone in this pursuit. There are dozens who have tilled the spoils of consciousness but he manages to couple anger and delight at its telling, or the appearance of it. His is a legacy of unforgiveness, of willing to be broken by the words that defy and devolve. He listens to the outside walls, the ruminations of a past as he turns to its frontier on the page. From the Midwestern prairie, the ghost of a people rises to haunt and there are no answers to the questions. There is little to abide in this outpost of writing. Adrian Louis is standing nearby, trying to negotiate the clouded history of what remains.

Author note: Since writing this essay, Adrian C. Louis left the Fire Water World on September 9, 2018.

—2018—

9

The Desert Outside:
Thinking about Richard Shelton

RICHARD SHELTON LISTENED as I drove him to the reading and finally said, "Be patient. Don't rush things. The books will come." I could not understand what he meant. He had published widely, and I was barely out of grad school. It was in the early 1980s. I had bent the corners of Shelton's *Selected Poems, 1969–1981* until they frayed. There was something in that volume I had not read elsewhere—a kind of bone truth, a vision of the desert Southwest and its people that was mesmerizing and unmistakably his. In a word, the poems were rooted, not just in place, but also in anguish. I cannot unlearn the lines from "Letter to a Dead Father":

Sometimes I touched the membrane
between violence and desire
and watched it vibrate.

. . . I needed
your love but I recovered without it.
Now I no longer need anything.

In the mid-1970s the *Los Angeles Times* did a major feature essay on Richard Shelton. I read it with interest—it was my first exposure to him. Of course, not knowing any better, I wrote to him. I was particularly interested in his work in the prisons. Out of some two hundred letters he received, he wrote back to me. I was stunned in that grateful, self-conscious way: how could he know how much it meant? Some time later he read at Cal State L.A., and I realized that this was a person from whom I would pattern my own study. I was a loner in college—at least in the creative-writing world—and his letters became the solace for that time spent writing and revising because so much of my work was unfinished, just not ready. I didn't know it but he did, and he encouraged me to look farther, go deeper, and strain to see what lay below.

I was attracted to his poetry because of its refraction of his Tucson home—an homage to the flora and fauna, but also a willingness to reveal the desert outside—the dozers, the roads, the endless growth that was eating the very place in which he lived. In "Survival," he writes:

> Watched closely by the birds,
> I gather the things a man needs
> to build his strange nest:
> stones for a wall, sand
> for mortar, the ribs of dead
> saguaros for a roof. A dry
> country is for those who choose it,
> for those who are fragile
> and beat down by such gentle rain.

This is the story of so many places in the American West, and for Shelton, it was the way in which he could articulate its peril and his coexistence in it. How does a poet name what comes to silence beauty? It seems to me he has spent his time trying to answer this question that may not have an answer. He chose to live on the outskirts of the city, and like his home, his poetry resides in the outline of the desert, what can only be imagined by the absence of its essential elements: rain, cactus wren, bullsnake, and the carefully woven history of people in that place, as can be seen in "Desert":

> If I stay here long enough
> I will learn the art of silence.

When I have given up words
I will become what I have to say.

Shelton is fond of telling the story of a journalist who called to interview him because "he was Idaho's most famous poet." Shelton paused to ask about Ezra Pound. There was a long breath before the line went dead. Shelton has tried to name the ubiquity of his history in southern Arizona; *Going Back to Bisbee* may be one of the truer narratives of living in the West. Prescient and vulnerable, it is a chronicle of his coming of age as a young writer who grows to need that arid place. I have felt from the beginning that Shelton was its spokesperson, its referee in the time of cutting parcels from its boundaries:

> On warm autumn afternoons when the cotton from the
> cottonwood and the tiny parachutes of desert broom
> seeds drift through the air and the sun slants through
> the foliage, everything turns gold and magical, and time
> seems to be a remote and unimportant abstraction.

In my mid-thirties I wrote to Shelton to ask, "How do you teach poetry in prison?" He wrote back: "Just start. Go in and begin talking about poetry. The ones that want to learn will do so; the others will go their way." It sounded simple enough, but it wasn't. I had no idea of the poets I would meet and what they would teach me. It is well known that Shelton taught Jimmy Santiago Baca, Michael Hogan, and Ken Lamberton, to name just a very few. Equally important, he changed the culture of incarceration in Arizona. He and his graduate students worked in almost every facility, and that gave the men a way to express themselves within the confines of prison. I couldn't express it then, but I would learn that his workshop was lifesaving—it gave the men an identity beyond prison. A way back to feeling. This is not something the warden aspires to do. This is not what is expected when you are sentenced. It is an anomaly in the long chain of events that leads to loss. Again he turned to a question with few answers: how does poetry speak inside?

For years he and his grad students have edited the *Walking Rain Review* (later *Rain Shadow Review*), a journal of the men's poetry, and in every issue they answer this question. His students gave my students the courage and conviction to write their journal, *Razor Wire*. They gave them impetus to articulate what it is they experience. I have heard endless adjectives to describe the men with whom we work, but they are rarely dignified. Shelton moved beyond what others expected. He started the workshop because he knew it needed to be done. There were voices inside that needed to be heard. I believe he had an intuitive sense that it would keep them from further harm. Poetry does not ask if you are good, only that you spend time with it, that you release some part of yourself to its vision. In this way the men began to carve what was theirs from the fog of isolation. These lines are from Rashid Sultan in the 2013 issue of *Rain Shadow Review*:

> Like a leaf
> in a windstorm
> the dope-sick thief
> contemplates one final tug
> on his straight shooter
> ignoring
> The Harvester.

Because of Shelton's gift—encouraging me to go inside—the men changed what I believe about poetry and prison. Inside, poetry is closer to butter or black bread. It is the thread of strenuous grief in all quarters—even in so small a thing as a stanza. Inside, there are no arguments about why prison matters or doesn't matter. It exists; people live in it, and without poetry it remains a fixture of vengeance. I will never be able to repay my good friend for this thirty-year odyssey of teaching inside. It has made me a better person, one whom I would not have been before, and as he writes in *Going Back to Bisbee,* "Somehow, you don't expect to run into part of the American dream in a state prison."

But it would be a misnomer to limit Shelton's influence to the yard. While he is clearly one of its few heroes, his poetic labor is without peer in the Southwest. He and his late wife Lois have hosted poets from all regions at the University of Arizona's Poetry Center, a steel-and-glass refuge for poetry like Poet's House in New York. It began in a small cottage on the campus and when the poets visited they frequently stayed with the Sheltons in their guesthouse. That room is lined with poetry books and the memories are legion. I can't think of an American poet who has not visited. Shelton wouldn't tell you this; a man who works in prison doesn't need the boasting of others. Before long, you understand that he knows the inside of a poem because he studied alongside many, many poets. He has read voluminously, by his own admission, more nonfiction of late than poetry. He read in Nevada with Ann Zwinger, and read again, numerous times alone. Each time I listened, tried to ferret out the muscular identity of his poems and prose. His stories of the stones, their movement under moonlight, are luminous. Again, he brings our attention to what we rush by—the ocotillo, "flagellant of the wind"; the idea of water—"we wait for the promised rain / for the second coming / of water"; or the fresh tracks of progress:

> Tonight at the end of a long
> scar in the desert a bulldozer
> sleeps with its mouth open
> like a great yellow beast.

This is the illumined cathedral of his homestead, the story outside, but it is a further story, an uncovering of what is so often seen as unnecessary, the desert. I'm sure he would say the same of the men whom he teaches: they are not seen, not known. Perhaps that is why he is drawn to their solitude. Nothing can prevent their outlines from being exposed. They are like Keats's negative capability—defined by what is missing. His life is central to this belief; he moves within their twin spires—the unwanted desert and the unwanted men—to redress the unseen.

Another blessing that I will not repay: the poets whose stories he recalled—James Wright, W. S. Merwin, and several others I had read about who then became real. He always deferred; he was not of their stature. And yet, what is stature in the desert?

When I last visited him he was thinning his books—thousands of volumes. He picked *The Last of the Menu Girls* from the shelf, told me how much it would mean to me, a new issue of the *Rain Shadow Review*, and signed his autobiography, *Nobody Rich or Famous*, a fitting declaration of his start in long-ago Idaho. Ken Lamberton had sent the excerpt of it from the Tucson arts weekly with Shelton's picture on the cover. It was vintage Shelton—straight ahead, hard to fathom, and still yearning for an explanation. We went to breakfast at KG's Westside Café in the industrial section of Tucson. You knew he had been there dozens of times. I ordered the homemade *chalupas* and hash with eggs—something like Mexico on the tongue. He continued to regale my wife and me with stories—mostly true and mostly hilarious. Back at the house, he pointed out the birds—new names to me—his names, names he had earned. In the upper reaches of the saguaro, a miniature owl had been his companion for seasons. In Lois's long illness, the owl and their big white dog had kept him company. This is how you learn to live alone—with the things that cannot be seen save by those who insist they are there. For decades he has insisted that the desert, its people, and their history be seen. I wanted to take more than the books with me, wanted to know I would see him in the near future. He promised to call on his next trip to Oregon to see his son, Brad. He promised to divert from Winnemucca when he and Lamberton return to Idaho. Until then, his poems stir in the house, the repeated consequence of caring:

in the heaven of the poor
the past keeps going away but is
never quite gone
I was young I was
so young I thought I would
get over it
and all I've learned
is that we never get over anything

Like all good teachers, he has given me what he knows but has done so with caution—if you must write about the land and if you must teach in the prison, carry your person with you. Do not let go of the humanity that matters so much in those two isolating places. There is a figure on the outline of the Santa Rita Mountains south of his house. I think of a man walking into the desert, looking for the path to its summit, looking for the observatory that may, at last, shed light on what's below.

—2016—

I I

Most of What I Believe Was Found in Poetry's Ancient Hands

10

My Journey to Hayden Carruth:
Falling Down to Understand

I. Values

IT WAS ONLY AFTER TEN YEARS of working on a book about Hayden Carruth and three decades of knowing and caring for him that I realized something crucial: it was his values that so attracted me—service, responsibility, and an insistence that poetry be of this world, not an imaginary one. There was more: his work ethic—tireless in labor and in the pursuit of literature—and his acute awareness of others, particularly those who suffered.

Doubtless this empathy was the product of his travails—but it was also an awareness that the reason for this suffering was the greater political and social order that maintained it. This is an essential element of Carruth's legacy—his literature encompassed the whole of his humanity, not slices of understanding but the entire apparatus of his suffering and logos. His values brought forth a skepticism of the Modernist belief in poetry of the imagined world. His poems, he often said, had a social utility—meaning, they were written in service to his belief in a poetry of use.

It is no secret that Albert Camus was his first major influence—Carruth wrote an autobiographical novel to him, *After the Stranger: Imaginary Dialogues with Camus*—and existentialism was, for Carruth, testimony to the role art would play in his life: how could one ignore the camps, the atom bomb, and the inequities that produced them? He could not, which meant he had to incorporate them into his poetry.

I learned to respect his values, his tenets for writing poetry, because they gave credence to my own tentative attempts at writing: "A poet must first have a vision, an imaginary life"; "poetry is essential to goodness"; and "this goodness should be put to use in service to others."

These are tough commandments and he tried to integrate them in a unified vision of his art—whether in the struggle of his farmer neighbors like Marshall Washer, or fellow Vermonters, or Syracuse city-dwellers, or his deeply felt poems to the physical world, like "The Loon on Forrester's Pond." Of course there were contradictions in his attempt to place his values in the central locus of his poetry and criticism. Carruth was vehement in his lack of religious faith but took pains to examine living without it. *Sonnets*, Number 15 begins:

> O Jesus, thou who sittest up there on the right
> side of the fence, help if you can (which I doubt)

and ends

> Two things exist. They are Cindy and the grave
>   [a former girlfriend].

This does not efface the fact that the majority of his poetic effort was suffused with these values. It simply makes him more human for knowing nothing "but love and death."

II. Reviews, Letters

It is probably futile to try to recall this journey that led me to Carruth, but one year after completing *From Sorrow's Well: The Poetry of Hayden Carruth* in the summer of 2013, I cannot shake the desire to write it down. After reading his anthology, *The Voice That Is Great Within Us* in college, I turned to his reviews in 1978. His quarterly poetry essays for the *Hudson Review* covered dozens of books and were rich with humanitarian ideals: a more peaceful world, a belief in the common good, and a desire for authenticity in the work being reviewed. In other words, an absence of ego. When the late New Mexico poet, Keith Wilson, came to Reno to read, I sought out Carruth's review of Wilson's *While Dancing Feet Shatter the Earth*. He praised its careful rendering of the desert landscape, its inhabitants, and its fragile presence in the late twentieth century. Wilson's poetry left me wanting the desert in my life—the one outside my door that I had yet to fully appreciate.

Carruth was the poetry editor at *Harper's* in 1979, and impetuously, I wrote to ask if he would read some poems. He wrote back and said he preferred "poetry that was direct statement of acutely perceived experience." That was twenty-nine years before he died—twenty-four before I would start on the book—but every word that came from him in the interim, and there were thousands, accumulated like paper cranes in my room. I have so many letters I cannot count them—they are in shoeboxes, envelopes, and mailers. In the late 1970s this note came on a postcard: "I have three books forthcoming and no faith in forthcomingness." I must have read it a dozen times. How could he be disillusioned with the impending birth of *three* books? Thirty-two years later, I asked the same question of myself, when three books that had languished for years were published. I was not left with hopelessness. Despite Carruth's professed loss of faith in forthcomingness, he continued to care, albeit imperfectly, for his family, friends, students, and neighbors. He could not shake his need to be in the milieu of others, even though his agoraphobia was crushing. It was labor that saved him—labor with and for others, and the community of writers that he served.

III. Mentor

After nearly ten years of correspondence, I was in New York in 1988. I found his number in the phone book and called him from the Staten Island Ferry building. Incredulous that he answered the phone, I asked to come visit. He paused and said, "Okay," not knowing if I was for real. By then, the threads of connection had grown—Carolyn Kizer, Denise Levertov, Richard Shelton, and Stanley Kunitz had surfaced in his life and work and, through the caprice of small angels, in mine. A patchwork of images coalesced—this is who he was, what he did, how he worked, drank, smoked, and lived—but it was never the complete person or poet. I wanted to form my own impression and that could only come from being with him to shake his hand or share a cup of coffee.

When I drove up to the little red farmhouse on twenty-three acres (that he purchased with a lifetime achievement award from the NEA) I did not know what to expect. From the moment I arrived, he was affable, inquisitive, and serious. His kitchen library, a small, elongated room, had thousands of poetry volumes in it, more poetry than I had ever seen. This was from the two decades of reviewing for the New York quarterlies in his former Johnson, Vermont cowshed. I tried to surmise how he accumulated this much knowledge about a subject as diffuse and unknowable as poetry. There was no answer to my prodding. Carruth was canny with me, the acolyte. I would not learn anything about him easily. It would take effort, I realized. His jazz albums were equally staggering despite the spines being sliced up by Smudgie, his and his wife's, the poet Joe-Anne McLaughlin, cat. Maxine Sullivan and Ben Webster towered over them in black-and-white stills.

He was still smoking then, pipes, cigarettes, even cigars, and the apparatus was everywhere in the house. I can't begin to think about *his* first impression: silly me, driving six hours to meet a man with whom I had only corresponded. But the pictures from that time tell a different story—genuine regard for one another. My wife, Debby, and I drove away from the little red farmhouse with the hope of a relationship being kindled. Clearly, McLaughlin, his final spouse of two decades, had much to do with this. She was a published, prize-winning poet before she met Carruth. They had known and corresponded with each other for nearly ten years prior to marrying in his later life. She welcomed Debby and me with open arms and soon I began to read her poetry and understand what a vital role she played in the editing, selection, and revision of Carruth's many late volumes. Later, I worked with her at the Frost Place. When she read her poems, she left nothing on stage. Sometimes we talked for hours and I realized that her poetry and her teaching were elemental to their relationship. If you read Carruth's "Testament" to her from *Scrambled Eggs & Whiskey* you will understand the depths of their love.

I will never forget arriving in the mid-1990s with a Christmas wreath and she calmly telling me, "You know, Hayden doesn't believe in Christmas *or* God." I said, "Well, give him the cornbread and I'll hang it on the door anyway" (at least I knew he loved cornbread). We had become good friends by then, and it was a friendship of mutual concern: I to learn from him and he, I imagine, to belong to a younger generation of writers from whom he was feeling steadily disconnected. No matter, we were good together.

IV. Human

From 1983 to 1993, I was working on my first book of poems and Kizer suggested I ask Carruth for a jacket quote. I did not know what he would say or write, but he assented. By then, I had poured over his criticism like it was a lifeline. It was smart, eloquent, and imaginative and I wondered if this meager offering would measure up.

I was also painfully aware that it might not—Levertov had responded negatively to my poems when I was in her workshop, and she and Carruth were close. Carruth recalls in the introduction to *The Voice That Is Great Within Us*, how moved he was by her poems. I was a long-time admirer of her work, but as can sometimes happen, that stood for nothing with her.

His jacket quote was understated and careful to lead the reader inside this first book. Affirmation, yes, but more—the poems would hold up.

Then came the first of many letters from the hospital in 1987—he had tried to take his life, spurned by love, by sorrow again—it must have seemed the only door left him. Stephen Dobyns and Douglas Unger have written of taking care of him through this period, as have many others, and indeed, Carruth had a way of bringing a phalanx of caregivers into his life, most gratefully, because it was usually an equitable exchange. Dobyns:

> The day after Hayden regained consciousness, my wife gathered up our two girls—three and seven—and went to visit him. I was astounded; she hardly knew him, had hardly talked to him. But she's Chilean and believes that even if you hardly know a person, you go to the hospital to encourage them and let them know you care about them. Hayden, too, was astounded.

He could be as vulnerable as a leaf in the wind and then recover to write about it. As I have written, I cannot reread the essay about suicide in *Suicides and Jazzers*; it is too painful for me. In this, he could also hurt—his son, David, and his former spouses, Sara (mother of his late daughter, Martha), Eleanor, and Rose Marie. Rose Marie and David were Carruth's pillars of support in Vermont and witness to the all too real episodes of wreckage, and so visiting the man they loved in the hospital yet again was most difficult.

It was shortly after his suicide attempt that Joe-Anne McLaughlin answered Carruth's call to come "rescue" him from the sorrow of loss. I recall asking her what she had hoped for and she told me, "Nothing, really. Only to be there, to be with him. I loved him and I wanted him to live." I said, "That must have taken a lot of guts." I grew to respect her as I did Hayden. They were cut from the same cloth—poets who could not forsake an understanding of their roles, their values in this time. In other words, poets whose essential worth derived from Edwin Muir's belief in poets as public people with public responsibilities.

Thirteen years later, in St. Elizabeth's Hospital in Utica, The Bo (Hayden's affectionate name for his son, David) and I stood as Carruth was in and out of ER after a massive heart attack, mostly due to his own recalcitrance—he tore the IV from his arm, stormed out of ICU, and lit up with the oxygen tube in his nose. When the New York state surgeon said, "I won't operate," Joe-Anne pleaded with him to reconsider and threatened to expose him to the media if he refused. In the chaos, I opened a letter from Adrienne Rich and read it to him—". . . Hayden, don't go, you can't go, we need you, your son needs you. *I* need you."

The doctor relented, and two weeks later Joe-Anne and I drove Hayden home and he quit smoking for the last time. I got out the ladder and fixed the weathercock on the garage—it was rusted in a southerly direction.

His life was a public account of resolute will, and because of his voracious reading and corresponding, when he fell, which he did, Levertov, Kizer, Adrienne Rich, Donald Hall, Galway Kinnell, Jim Harrison, Geof Hewitt, David Budbill, and a score of others reached out. So what could I say in the waiting room, what could any of us say? This was an American poet, exposed but nonetheless trying to find a way back. Hayden never wanted any of the sorrow—rather, it was a kind of ruthless shadow that he tried and tried to outrun.

On most of my visits to his farmhouse, Carruth and I drove to town, and he, the inveterate namer, pointed out the flowers (chicory, heal-all, white daisy), and the trees (sumac, oak, shadblow, and other hardwoods) all around his land. (Rose Marie met him when he was standing in a ditch looking at wildflowers.) I took a photo of him in those woods with his Whitmanesque beard, cane, and overalls. He tolerated my ignorance of the physical world with thoughtful response: "How could you live in a place for twenty years and not notice the late migration of the lone robin in winter?" he asked. "I finally *saw* them," I said, and then he smiled, as if to confer an understanding—*you will*. And I did. These moments, fragments really, are what stayed with me and they gave an urgency to my attempt to edit a book about him. Ultimately, it was how I came to balance all of the impressions about him and to make my mind adhere to what I saw—this fragmented soul, this regimented mind, this deeply feeling, opinionated, hardscrabble poet whose generation represented some of the best American poets. He was a paradox of impressions and real, consequential effort, effort that he would eschew. When I asked what he was working on, it was nothing—and then the books would trickle out: *A Summer with Tu Fu*, *Beside the Shadblow Tree*, *Letters to Jane*, and so I knew it was in deference to his character: let the work speak. Let the poems and criticism come to the reader.

V. Research

Against this backdrop of friendship, came the letters, packages, books, and references to Carruth from editors, former students, colleagues, and friends. I began to gather them, thinking I might *try* to edit a book about him. In 2003, I wrote to ask for his blessing to begin the project. He agreed; I never knew if he thought I could succeed. I also had this disquieting notion that he would not be recognized in any meaningful way without such a book. His legacy was large but misunderstood. He did not have easy access to the center of literary New York—by choice, by design, and by the uninviting example of some who sought the limelight. Carruth was a loner, or mostly alone outside of his literary life and he needed the correspondence of others (Philip Booth described *Brothers* as "the social art of a solitary man"). He was deluged until the end; his last letters to me were like those of Williams, the words broken to their fragments. He would tell me about the weather, the birds at his feeder, and the wood in his shed—that he by then could not burn because it hurt his lungs. There was never much about poetry and poets. It's not important, he intimated, but you are, we are, and that is something altogether different.

When I told him of the tentative title, *From Sorrow's Well*, he shrugged, "I've always been frustrated by that label." I asked him if I should change it. Again, he shrugged and I can't remember what he said except to imply, leave it as it is; they're going to make up their own minds. I have never read of Carruth's interest in Lorca's *duende*, but I am certain it is the same sorrow, the dark creative force that emanates from within. This was his strength as a poet, the ability to take that sorrow into poems of masterful thought and provocation. I'm thinking of "Essay," "Paragraph 25," "On Being Asked to Write a Poem Against the War in Vietnam," and "Song: So Often, So Long I Have Thought," which ends with these lines:

> Something has made me
> A man of the soil at last . . . Year by year my hands
> Grow to the axe. Is there a comfort now
> In this? Or shall I still, and ultimately, rebel,
> As I had resolved to do . . .

I also sensed what was not written: he longed to be included in poetry's gathering music. This, finally, is what led me to try and right a literary wrong: in his time he had written over thirty volumes of a poetic depth to emulate, and still the great silence enfolded his literary oeuvre. *The Sleeping Beauty*, his book-length masterpiece from Harper & Row, fell out of print until he wrote to Sam Hamill to ask if he would republish it ("Poor little book, *The Sleeping Beauty* died." *Sonnets*, Number 39). With the exception of New Directions, most of his work was published by university or small presses and not widely distributed. This exacerbated the conundrum of his career: he was the editor at *Poetry*, a thirty-year critic for the *Hudson Review*, editor of the seminal twentieth-century poetry anthology, *The Voice That Is Great Within Us*, creator of a poetic form, the paragraph (a highly evolved fifteen-line sonnet with a rhyming couplet in the middle), a jazz critic and essayist—in short, an accomplished literary figure.

His letters led me to continue working on the book. When I was most afraid that I would not get it right, not fully represent him, a small epistle arrived that would, in its nuanced way, assure.

For three years I woke early to read everything by and about him. I wrote to several publishing houses, notably the University of Michigan Press, as he had published two books of essays with them, but the Great Recession had come and their poetry series was on hold. I edited the volume down to six hundred pages of interviews, essays, and reviews and foolishly thought I was close. I shared the contents, introduction, and headnotes with Hayden and Joe-Anne. They approved; I was on the right track, but I still had no publisher. In desperation I wrote to Marilyn Hacker in 2010. She was the editor at Michigan's Under Discussion Series and had suggested I send it to her if it didn't work out at the previous presses—five years after I first wrote Michigan.

Marilyn Hacker was fearless for Carruth's sake *and* for mine, but I could not know it then: it was overwhelming to cut the book by almost half to be considered for the Michigan series. Yet she prodded: you can do this; you can manage this triage. Cut to the concision of the poet and his work. I had no contract but I loved Carruth too much to let him down. There were new essays, previously published reviews, interviews, and poems but were they enough for Carruth's standard of excellence? Somewhere I heard Carruth's voice—doubt is a writer's companion, every writer's. Solace comes from the work of writing, nothing more.

I had the example of other books in the series to emulate; the question was, did the architecture of this volume do Carruth justice? The book was organized chronologically and developmentally around the four major themes of his life: realist, jazzman, survivor, and innovator. I had to show his intellectual and artistic growth across this very divergent stage of thoughtful commentary and impressions, and my own knowledge of his development as a poet.

VI. Dissolution

Carruth's death in 2008 was especially hard. It was the dissolution of something unspoken: the man from whom I most fully came to understand poetry was no longer alive, and I had not yet acknowledged that debt. The book was still unborn. This tempered my resolve: I contacted Rose Marie to ask if I might visit. She led me into Carruth's twenty-year odyssey in the northern Vermont town of Johnson. It was there Carruth rebuilt a cowshed into his writing room, heated by a woodstove and deadlines. It was also there he befriended Marshall Washer and a host of other poor rural farmers. Rose Marie took me to the origins of Carruth's poems from that time: the brook that ran alongside their property, Marshall's farm, and the garden where they grew their produce. She made Debby and me cherry pie and listened as I tried to explain this journey to understand Carruth. She read the introduction on the porch and said it was still a bit stiff, and in the months to come, she was essential in tracking down references—Rich's sons, Kinnell's influence and support, and their early friends, David and Lois Budbill, and Geof and Janet Hewitt.

Rose Marie recounted numerous evenings when Denise Levertov and her husband, Mitchell Goodman, were at the Carruth house for dinner, and how much Carruth and Levertov needed each other as poets and friends. The same was true for Adrienne Rich and her husband, Alfred Conrad. Mitch and Denise lived in a beautiful old Maine farmhouse, and Alfred and Adrienne rented summer cabins in New England.

The Bo, Carruth's son, was no different. Early on he showed me a picture of Marshall Washer so I would know his face and copied a picture of Hayden standing next to his pickup at their house in Johnson. The Bo talked often and fondly of Wendell Berry, and their family visit to his Kentucky farm. Many people kept me alive on this journey—not least was Berry. His letters and reminders that the book needed to be done, in fact would be done, were invaluable. Berry's essay, "My Friend Hayden," written for the book, is a portrait of Carruth, the man and poet, by his peer of forty years. Likewise, Baron Wormser, who wrote an essay on Carruth's jazz poetics, never equivocated on his belief in the project. Carruth suggested I go to the Frost Place because he wanted me to meet Don Sheehan, who was then its director. That's when I met Wormser and Howard Levy, another ardent supporter. Carruth's former colleague at Syracuse, Douglas Unger, went out of his way to see the book through to publication. Both Wormser's and Unger's contributions set the tone for their respective sections.

It was to all of them—family and friends of Carruth—that I felt a responsibility to get it right, which sent me down the rabbit hole again, to reread Virgil, Camus, William Wordsworth, Edwin Muir, and others. Books were piled on my floor like thieves who stole my time, but I had to know what Carruth alluded to in a poem or what a colleague intimated in an essay. I could not presume I knew. This forced me to grow more in my fifth decade than any other pursuit—intellectually, emotionally, and spiritually. I read and reread Kizer, Kinnell, Hall, Rich, Robert Frost, James Wright, and Paul Goodman. What I could not locate, the astute Betty Glass, special collections librarian at the University of Nevada, Reno, doggedly tracked down.

VII. Permission

In 2011, one year after I had started revising the book down to 250 pages, Ellen Bauerle, a senior editor at Michigan, emailed to tell me they had accepted the book. I wept—for Hayden, Rose Marie, the Bo, Joe-Anne, and Marilyn. There had never been any assurances except for my belief in Carruth and his work. That the book would finally appear in Michigan's series on American poets was almost surreal. It could have ended in ignominy. It still would have been worth doing, just not as satisfying, because what Carruth gave me was an education. I had to learn enough to ride out the effort of banding together twenty-four voices that would comprehend Carruth. That must be why he let me pursue it—I needed to understand the consequence of what he knew—something, I confess, of which I am still not certain. But I have a sense of what this consequence is, what he hoped to achieve in his six decades of effort: to change the arc of poetry, and by inference, the reader. In a word, he wanted to impact its vast and contradictory landscape.

Carruth taught me something else—in order to fully appreciate poetry, you must surrender to an ideal, a form that is not completely knowable. That can frustrate and take years. To watch the arc of his mind develop over more than thirty books was something to marvel at, but more than this, it was his example of willingness, his ability to return to the desk when there was no apparent reason to do so. His insistence on being present as a writer in the dialogue of reviewers, editors, and poets, was in pursuit of this ideal. He repeatedly told me how much gratitude he felt toward Frederick Morgan, the founding editor at the *Hudson Review*, because of his steadfast belief in Carruth's critical ability. This gave him a lasting platform from which to examine the ebb and flow of contemporary poetry and simultaneously confirm his core values as a poet. It was his determination to move poetry beyond the status quo that helped me understand *how* to go on such a journey. Clearly Carruth was not alone in his desire; this is the dilemma of loving the art form: risk in service of perfection. In the end, I think he extended a hand to his readers so they might join him. There was no parallel truth to discover—his cowshed winters were conveyed with the ice on the glass of his hut, just as the long poems in *Tell Me Again* . . . were waves of breath and loss and grief. I take them to mean all of this, and more, or as Kizer confided, "I read Carruth when I cannot sleep."

Carruth left few tracks but paradoxically this helped me to see the journey to poetry from his vantage point—that is, not knowing, not being a full participant in the give and take of literature. Only in this way could I fully appreciate what that outpouring of sonnets, paragraphs, haiku, and syllabic and free verse aspired to. Even then I can only imagine what it was to learn the art form as he did.

VIII. Coda

It was October 2013 when I joined Carruth's friends and family to read from the book at the Vermont Studio Center in Johnson. The old, restored opera house was cold. I introduced the book, and each of them sang from his many songs: David Budbill recounted listening to jazz with him for twenty years, Geof Hewitt gave a wonderfully animated reading of "Johnny Spain's White Heifer," Rose Marie Carruth read the early poems to the birds and wildlife of Johnson, and Baron Wormser read three sections from *The Sleeping Beauty*. Over a hundred people were there and we read and laughed and cried. Afterward, Mary Jane Dickerson came up and introduced herself. She had been a pupil of Carruth's for a year when he could not find much work and was still very agoraphobic. She was an English professor at the University of Vermont who was able to spend one afternoon a week with Carruth because the university had hired him as an adjunct professor. She confirmed what so many had shared: he was a brilliant teacher. Later, she would send me her first book, *The Center of Things*, completed in her seventies.

His erstwhile spouse, Joe-Anne, was unable to attend because of health reasons, but she was there in spirit.

George Drew, whom I had not met until that evening, drove four hours from southern Vermont to hear the reading. He told me Carruth asked him if he, George, had ever read my work. Drew said "No," and Carruth replied, "Read him."

After Hayden's death I learn still more: just today the Italian translator Fiorenza Mormile wrote to share her drafts of poems from *Dr. Jazz*, which were later published in *Poesia*, Italy's foremost poetry journal. Carruth influenced a generation in ways I will never fully articulate. Each of us manage to hook our names to the ladder that he so willingly extended but Carruth knew poetry intimately; he read for four years in the basement of Dartmouth's library to edit his major anthology of American verse. He also knew its cost; his Bloomingdale poems—written in the mental hospital in White Plains—literally hurt to read. Now the ladder returns to Carruth, to his readers, to those left larger by his magnanimous example. He would defer or laugh, as he did when I called him from Thailand on his eightieth birthday. He flippantly asked if I was in a brothel—"No, Hayden, just at the beach with my family." Then I think of the end of his poem "Ecstasy": *the great pain assuaged.* Last week, just before what would have been Carruth's ninetieth birthday, I was interviewed by WPFW, Washington, D.C.'s public radio station for "jazz and justice." How fitting, I thought. When the interviewer, Giovanni Russonello, asked me why I edited *From Sorrow's Well*, I hesitated, then said, "Solace, a measure of resolution for Carruth and what he set out to achieve." Russonello found a recording of Carruth reading "Emergency Haying," about the day he and Marshall Washer put up five hundred bales of hay, his most personal elegy to the labor of man. "I read him for my survival," I said.

—2016—

11

From Sorrow's Well:
On Hayden Carruth's Resolute Poetics

IN THE SEVENTH DECADE of his life, Hayden Carruth published seven books: four volumes of essays and poetry; two collected poems, shorter and longer; and a collected essays and reviews. Most poets would be daunted by such an undertaking—at any age. As for Carruth, a man who disavowed spiritual faith, it was symbolic of a belief in the edification of poetry, its abundant ability to reclaim a moral and intellectual footing. Early in life he wrote, "Love of poetry is the habit and need of wise men wherever they are." He would later write (my paraphrase) that this love is subjective; the act of writing poetry must be in service to this love.

As a whole, these books represent a rare document of survival, a catalog of a life spent in literature that has not been widely read. I suppose this is the fate of poets at work in our society—they are relegated to a marginal existence, save those few very public literary individuals—something that Carruth was simply not able to be. He lived on a small rural homestead in upstate New York, looked out to corn silos and cow pastures. He had little use for the machinations of modern poetry except insofar as they came to his door—the manuscripts that arrived from all geographical points, the bewildering correspondence, and the editing he continued to do in the red house on Bear Path Road.

Among serious readers of contemporary poetry, few disagree with his status as a major poet, and most regard him as a candid and humane critic—qualities that served both to alienate him from and ingratiate him to readers for over fifty years. It is virtually impossible to catalog his oeuvre; he wrote prodigiously for so long and in so many genres (from novel to translation to a highly evolved Carruthian sonnet—the paragraph) that each book must be read slowly, as they successively bear witness to his life as poet, Yankee activist, and town crier of the disaffected literary public. I do not presuppose the distance of years required to examine all of his literary endeavors; these few words focus on the later books in the context of a lifetime of principled effort. There are gaps here—his love of jazz, his arduous editing, and his relentless efforts to open the house of poetry: ". . . The man or woman on the other end of the park bench, is the bozo I'm interested in."

I remember finding a yellowed copy of the 1963 essay "Poets without Prophecy," in which he lamented that in a year (1961) of reading *Poetry*, not more than two poems were published on the bomb. Doubtless there were many poems of dissent at that time, but it was Carruth who voiced their absence in the *Nation*. I suspect because he demanded that art be above artifice—whether as critic or poet, and those roles were frequently confused and contributed to his exile from mainstream literary America; his readership was of a like mind and therefore small. To oppose the status quo through the McCarthy, Vietnam, and post-Reagan eras, to question one's role in those politics, was to remain of a mind apart, and he did, but it did not stop him from expecting the same of his contemporaries: "I don't believe that one can love language without loving the otherness for which it stands. This for me is axiomatic. In other words poetry and compassion are inextricably intermixed."

Poetry, to almost any mind, is a sort of tonic for being-in-the-world, at once not understood and understood by the vast majority of readers to belong to a select group of practitioners. Within this narrow band, Carruth carved an unfailingly honest and uniformly demanding niche. He had no will to lie except when, of course, it was understood to further the truth. And his truth was frequently seen from the cage of failed expectations—his and ours. This self-imposed restraint, this steady return to the orthodox domain of language-as-revelation made Carruth a reluctant participant-observer. Hence, the perspective in some of the poems is not always kind or inviting, for they regard their subject with unerring detail. I am thinking of the long poems to his mother, his daughter, the Bloomingdale poems, and the delirious alter-ego poems of Tanck. A good deal of his prose is likewise drawn from sorrow's well and tempered with a refusal to narrate beauty. He must in the end refrain, remain at a distance to harvest the full effect of literature: ". . . for how / in that great darkness could I explain / anything, anything at all."

Much of his nascent development as a poet had to do with his early publisher—James Laughlin, or Jas as he refers to him in *Beside the Shadblow Tree*. Theirs is a story of symbiotic evolution. When Carruth had little money or prestige, it was Laughlin who found him work and kept him in the fold, whether at the offices of New Directions or at his estate in northwestern Connecticut. In a word, he provisioned Carruth, kept him able to write when few others were aware that he was hard at work cultivating his peculiar combination of New England pragmatism and highly stylized literary drama. Of course, Laughlin did this for dozens of writers who were initially shunned from the mainstream by subject or style, and who for the most part went on to create our lasting literature—Williams, Ezra Pound, Vladimir Nabokov, and others.

New Directions was precisely the kind of place for Carruth, an outcast by definition. Laughlin, while diffident, gave him an outlet, a way to be in the world that only required he write, use his growing literary acumen to full advantage. So it is not unexpected that Carruth would pay him tribute in a book of reflection on their life together. As a testament to literary friendship, it parallels Henry Miller's tribute to his time with Lawrence Durrell in Greece, *The Colossus of Maroussi*, a book some feel was Miller's finest. To write at any distance from the person who may have saved him (Carruth) from a protracted period of drought, is to harrow from the past what might have been. Clearly, for Carruth, the teakettle would have simmered and his works steadily evolve with or without Laughlin. But to the extent that it would have been disseminated to those in the know, time would exert the greater pressure of silence. I return to the *Shadblow Tree* out of reverence, to know what it was like to grow and develop as a literary figure in the shadows of Delmore Schwartz, Lawrence Ferlinghetti, William Everson, Kenneth Patchen, and Kenneth Rexroth, and how without them, our lives—we few in that narrow band in this country—would be diminished.

There are five shadblow trees in Carruth's backyard. They are saplings, planted in the last decade, after he won a lifetime achievement award from the NEA (which permitted him to buy the homestead). I suspect, although I never asked him, that they stand for a kind of literary permanence, a passing on to the next generation of his resolute poetic intention. I watched them age with the years, not unlike him, moving to distill shadow from sun.

Reluctantly, the sad, ephemeral title of his late essays, has a section in which he comes upon a frozen bobcat while woodcutting. It is thawing in the spring snowmelt, and even then, almost forty years ago, it was for Carruth, an image of passing from this world with dignity. It is also a passage of manual labor, the kind he struggled to emulate in "Emergency Haying." I am in thrall to the sheer joy of cutting and splitting cordwood for the coming winter, as if the task itself were reason enough for living. So much of what Carruth aspires to in his art is embodied in his life: the cantankerous wit, the "buller and a jammer" yanking on the chainsaw, the red-eyed critic walking out of the "ninefootsquare hut" at dawn for a last cigarette, then sleep before the day's chores woke him. A kind of serene existence except, of course, if you had to live it. I once read in his diary the words, "Poetry and poverty are very close." And further on, his meager income ledger derived from the words he wrote to eat. This is not news to the uninitiated. All artistic creation has its due, but there is something that doesn't want such human toil, to paraphrase Frost, to lie between the creator and his art. It is hard not to wish that his affinity with the working class did not come at such personal cost, that his life was closer to Seamus Heaney's than John Clare's.

Out of respect for Carruth, I could not reread the essay on suicide, collected earlier in *Suicides and Jazzers*. That he would live to write again is reason enough to turn away from the darkness that led him to such devastation. And here I make no apologies for him, only that he suffered lifelong personal loss and it led him to believe it was the cost of making art. In this, he identified with the jazz musicians of his time, those charismatic and troubled horn and reed players, people who drank before breakfast, and drank again when it was over: "And I hated especially to see them [jazz musicians] falling into oblivion, working in funeral parlors and pool halls, dying in poverty and neglect." Carruth put down some booze in his time, and anyone who knew him, knew of his love for tobacco. An entire essay is dedicated to the thrill of smoke, which for all its edification still can't justify dying. He finally quit at eighty, and found solace in small things, letters from friends, the proximity of his son, the abiding love of his wife, poet Joe-Anne McLaughlin. They endured much together—but what couple has not?—and it is this theme, durance, that speaks most clearly in this late volume. At one point, the prose was interrupted for a year, so painful was the writing. Yet he returns to it, summons the courage to finish the essay, and whimsically asks, how was it that I stopped?

A truer portrait of the artist may have been given to us but I am beseeched by the truth in this volume. It harkens back to reluctance of a man who, after seventy-four years, reconciles the rhythm of poetry to the rhythm of letting go, even as those he most admires were leaving him to the task of saying what must have been their coda: write that you may uncover your art, that you may release its subtle, unrehearsed supplications.

The work ethic that enabled him to gather so many volumes late in life was similarly directed at helping a constant stream of poets and novelists, yet he was conspicuously absent in the footnotes of contemporary literature. Charles Simic wrote an essay in the *New Republic* on "The madness of my homeland," meaning the former Yugoslavia. A colleague sent it to Carruth and yes, he had read it, in draft form. I suspect his willingness to help so many comes from being acutely aware of literary indifference, how with very little effort one could disappear from the creative landscape altogether, and thus became a champion of those who, like himself, sought to make of their literature a separate place to be in this world: "It happens that my own personality, this particular combination of defects and fervors, has made me generally more willing to speak for others than for myself." A careful, Carruthian reading of one's work was something of a gift; even the discarded elements were returned with import. This is why he remained an active editor: his intellect was daunting, reading wide, and coupled together, they formed a magnetic tension that created undue balance, an attention specific to the task.

Much as Laughlin found a niche for Carruth at New Directions, Sam Hamill, the late, indefatigable publisher of Copper Canyon Press, brought new readers to the poet's work in the early 1980s. At that time Carruth wrote to ask if Hamill was interested in republishing *The Sleeping Beauty* and Hamill wisely answered yes. They could not have been more alike in their literary tastes and temperaments; they stood alone on opposite shores buttressed by a belief in uncompromising literature. Hamill was keenly aware of the Eastern tradition; he translated numerous volumes of classical Japanese and Chinese poets. It was out of his enthusiasm for their work that he shared the poetry of Tu Fu with Carruth. Five years later, Carruth wrote "A Summer with Tu Fu," first published by Brooding Heron Press as a chapbook, then later as a section in *Scrambled Eggs & Whiskey*. This long meditative response to Tu Fu, written during a summer in the Stockbridge Valley, is that precise intersection of introspection and lyrical acumen that approximates Tu Fu's own meditative time spent in creation. Carruth perfected the tonal characteristics of the poet to marshal a classical affirmation. "I've always been a perfectionist; I don't know what else to be." The poem "Old Song" is a series of breath notes.

> An old song on a hot
> midnight patio of summer.
> "The House of the Rising Sun."

> Look at the hazy stars
> so soft in the coal-dark blue.
> Cicadas. A woman singing.

The other poems in the book are vintage Carruth, snappy, surly, carefully constructed poems apropos of their subject. They register the freedom of one who has lived long and are occasioned by the timeless concerns of the working poet: love, death, beauty, birds, his embrace of the natural world and disdain of the political one. Sung from a distance of years, these poems escape the valor of contemporary poetry.

In the fall of 2001, several of Carruth's close friends gathered in the Great Hall of Cooper Union College to celebrate his eightieth birthday and the publication of *Doctor Jazz*, his recent collection of poems. The night was filled with reminiscences and readings from Galway Kinnell, David Budbill, Adrienne Rich, Marilyn Hacker, Sam Hamill, Joe-Anne McLaughlin, Jean Valentine, and others. In the audience were hundreds of friends and admirers, poets who had watched his evolution from University of Chicago grad student to editor of what is arguably our finest contemporary American anthology, *The Voice That Is Great Within Us*. The New York poet Howard Levy commented that Carruth's poems sounded as if they had been written for the readers. Carruth wrote fluidly in so many traditions that Marilyn

Hacker could read a sonnet; Galway Kinnell a long free verse poem; and David Budbill a syllabic blues riff.

When Carruth stood to read from *Doctor Jazz*, he discovered that he did not have the book with him—an unintentional omission few could help but notice. And yet, laughing, he borrowed a copy of *Doctor Jazz*, and read a poem as if he were reading to friends at home. He was visibly happy to be honored, despite his trepidation about such events and the long journey into the city. For a man who had worked to avoid the limelight, this was the veneration of a lifetime of effort, a moment of supreme joy in the poet's life, when those who most loved him celebrated all he had written and stood for.

The *Doctor Jazz* poems epitomize Carruth's lifelong struggle to articulate the poet's central theme: grief and its attendant resolution. In the middle of this collection is a long series of poems entitled "Faxes to William." "William" is a sounding board, a muse to whom he directs his thoughts in the aftermath of his seven decades. Like these faxes, this is a book of recollection, of peacemaking with the shadows that have dogged him all his days, and that his art, no matter how fully realized, may not suffice.

> The fallen hibiscus flower
> that was so exotic, intricate, and splendid
> lay on the floor, a reddish
> pulpy mess. I took it
> to the container of unpleasantness
> for the compost heap. Inevitably,
> William, hopelessly I thought
> of all the poems I've written.

There is a healthy tradition of New England poets, and this is particularly true of Vermont, Carruth's former home and the location of his signature poems and the Vermont hill people who steadily slip from view. These are poems from a period in American history when the farmers made their living with their hands, when Carruth befriended them for who they were: individuals who left their mark with their livelihood. Like him, they lived where it was difficult. His long poem, "North Winter," written from the purview of a converted cowshed, foreshadowed his poem to Tu Fu; it was a meditation on living in the Vermont wilderness, with only ice and wind and cold to befriend him: "Morning ice on the window / opaque as beaten silver / while the poet / in his ninefootsquare hut stamps . . ."

It was these attributes of self-reliance, of stubborn refusal to be overcome by the elements that drew him to the region and its people. They stood their ground and they stood against the prevailing wisdom of American largesse. In them, I imagine, Carruth found a touchstone and believed that, with persistence, he could hew from this land a literary tradition that embodied its values and recreate the musical cadence of its folk wisdom. To do so, he would live and work in virtual isolation for twenty years, writing reviews and essays for most of the literary magazines that emanated from the Hudson. His family suffered; his personal luxuries were limited to pencils, stamps, stationery, and the like. This is not written anywhere per se; it is evinced in the testimony of the poems from that time. They are worn and worked in like old gloves, boots, farm implements that fade with use: "Almost 500 bales we've put up / this afternoon, Marshall and I." It was during this time that he wrote his most enduring criticism, his long essays on Alexander Pope, Paul Goodman, and jazz, prose that defined him, a contrarian that lived outside the literary tradition.

This extended period of reading, devotion to craft, and commercial failure gave birth to the resolute survivor that Carruth emerged to be. Despite the tribute at Cooper Union, I can't help but think he wanted more in his lifetime, wanted to be known for the tremulous undertaking that became his Vermont poems, wanted to be addressed by the inclusive pronoun "We" in modern literature, but it did not occur. And, clearly, he would abjure any effort to change late in life: when he was invited to the Clinton

White House, he turned it down in a huff. They stood for chicanery, for idolatry, for the mendacious fools of the state, against whom he had dedicated his life and art. It is no coincidence that his peer would similarly act out of conscience: Adrienne Rich wrote a stinging reply to a similar presidential invitation. Indeed, it was the letters and support of many of those gathered at Cooper Union, who, like her, kept Carruth turning back to this world after a near-fatal heart attack in his seventy-ninth year.

Literature is rife with personal and political tumult; the thoughtful reader has only to look beyond its border of safe and certain virtues to understand the suffering from which it derives. Carruth understood this early and began to intimate a vision of another kind of literature, one that accounted for a reading and thinking public. That he succeeded in defining a unique body of literature, redolent of possibility, rent with human turmoil, as aesthetically demanding as the formalists of his day, was his laurel. What he surrendered to attain it may never be known; he gave us the argument of its loss.

— 2004–2018 —

12

Before I Knew Her Mind:
A Dream of Carolyn Kizer

THE MOST DIFFICULT PART of this story is its conclusion, which gets altered with every telling, and as much as I try, it looks very different from in those heady years when I opened the door to find her brimming with the subtle rewards of the "po-biz," as she called them. Anyone who knew Carolyn Kizer will tell you that until the last decade there were dozens of people in her orbit: poets, professors, students, and wannabes. It is hard to name her collage but, like her poetry, humanity and intellect are at its core. There is something to behold in a woman who can manage the lightning strikes of jealous writers, literary curmudgeons, and D.C. bureaucrats. It is also hard to imagine someone with a better pedigree, coming from whip-smart parents and going on to study with Theodore Roethke and Stanley Kunitz at the University of Washington. Richard Hugo was also there, having graduated two years earlier.

The first book of poetry I gave to my wife was Roethke's *Collected Poems*. I told her that if she liked these poems there was no turning back. I read that book until it broke. Roethke pushed Kizer—especially when few women poets were taken seriously. His poetry was anchored in the landscape, hewn from labor, themes she would draw on as she developed her voice. "I started to write poetry seriously when I studied with Theodore Roethke. . . . He taught me to understand the difference between relying on the unconscious and writing when you have control." Kizer was a single mother then, whose struggle to raise three young children defined her as a woman and poet: there is no excuse for banal effort.

I was in my late twenties when I phoned Kizer to ask if she would give a reading in Reno, Nevada—which must have sounded like coming to the ends of the earth. She did not know me but assented and months later I stood in the airport waiting for her to emerge from the plane. By then I had learned of her friendship with Richard Shelton, Hayden Carruth, and Denise Levertov—poets who would impact me deeply as I started up the long staircase to poetry.

At the reading, I introduced her with trepidation: I was beginning to understand how much more there was to learn. Despite the small venue, she left those in the room in awe. She ranged from Virgil to Vietnam but somehow pulled it off in "A Muse":

You can see that I am rife with possibility; a dancer, yes,
and it may be a choreographer, and a poet, a poet who
dances to her own music, her own words. In the tradition
of the revered Isadora.

This was in the early 1980s—a particularly vulnerable point in her life: she was without a publisher. But I did not know that. After three wonderful days, I took her back to the airport. While we were sitting there, she asked me to read the poems from the manuscript that would become *Yin*. They were typed and pasted on the pages of a black notebook. I looked down at them and wondered—why me, what could *I* possibly say about them that would mean anything to *her*? In retrospect, time peels away slowly and, whatever small pleasure I took from that moment, I will not be able to convey how it changed our conversation about poetry. More important, it brought us together as friends—two people working at something far more difficult than I could articulate at the time. These spontaneous gestures of trust became a signature of our relationship and without them my own poetry would be diminished. Later, that same trust would dissipate, and still later return, as it must in all real relationships.

Carolyn Kizer could be intimidating—I can feel her eyes on mine now—and my only recourse is to try and capture what I can of the relationship throughout the many days and nights of that time, knowing it is closer to parable than truth. There is no definitive picture; Kizer moved fluidly among poets and poetry and this only added to her mystique. The woman I knew was down-to-earth and cared for my wife and our children. I valued that quality in her because I did not have any overt cachet. I could recite none of the verse that enchanted her—but she could and it was like water to me, listening to her redress our existence in "For Jan as the End Draws Near": "The ones with everything to lose / will mind it most."

When my wife returned to graduate school at Stanford, I sat in on Kizer's class. She went over every word of my first book, a gift of her concentration. I remember a poignant moment: at the end of a poem to my wife, I could not find the right word. After reading the poem aloud several times, Kizer said, "Reticulate." I asked her why? "It is precisely the feeling you are trying to convey, the sense of your lives fanning out together." My wife looked at her from across the room and then at me: "That's it, that's the exact word." It was not an easy time for my wife—she was studying, always, and our son was born weeks after we arrived. The birth was rough; I nearly lost them both. But somehow when Kizer came to our apartment it assuaged that difficult transition. That may have been the thread that kept our relationship alive. When Kizer read those early poems in that book, it was an acknowledgment of practice, of belief, much like she had asked of me in the airport. She managed to see them as they might have been, and in some cases as more. It would take another ten years for the book to be born, but it was her attention to the details of every sound that I recall.

She remained ever the paradox: in late spring of 1985, she and Sandra Gilbert showed up at our married student housing apartment to give a reading later that evening. I had just gotten off work in Stanford's personnel department. I worked with refugees, single moms, and people with disabilities. It was a breezy San Francisco Bay Area evening. She came in and asked if she could use the phone to call her children; she had just won the Pulitzer Prize for *Yin*. I was stunned, could not imagine why she came for the reading and knew that this would forever change things. She countered with, "What better way to spend the evening," and then laughingly added, "This is the last night I'll be reading for a hundred dollars." Sandra Gilbert and Susan Gubar had just published *The Norton Anthology of Literature by Women* and predictably, the reviewer was unkind because she was not included in the breakthrough anthology. Yet Gilbert was thrilled for Kizer and for that brief moment, the world outside disappeared. We sipped chardonnay before Kizer would share the news at the reading. The next day there was a full-page feature on her in the *San Francisco Chronicle*.

When we returned home to Nevada, I continued to send her letters and poems. She was the first to suggest that I do more with my work, so I took a hiatus and went to Nepal with Jiwon Bhurtyal, one of the refugees I had hired at the Bay Area campus. He was from the small village of Pokhara. When we arrived, much of the village turned out to greet him. A goat was slaughtered for the feast. I wrote poems and read from the base of Annapurna. It was the rainy season and so for days, I listened to the thunder and rain howl against the tin roof of Hotel Snowland. When I returned, Kizer suggested that I write a book of poems and illustrations and, although I wanted to, I did not know how. It would be years before I painted and knew what such an idea meant. But she could envision the book and that bold thought was what I took from her—that the possibility of the unwritten word is reason enough to set down a poem and a drawing in its service.

I visited her large home in Berkeley on my work trips but the city became too much for her, particularly the people who were forced to the street. This is because she was a political poet. "I remember after a reading somebody came up to me," she relayed to the *Paris Review*, "and said, I love that political poem of yours, and my husband, who was standing next to me, said, Which one? They're all political, and I was pleased by that." She knew this was wrong; people should not have to live on the street, yet to fight the incoherence of local politics was a maelstrom that kept her from art. It took Kizer months to write a poem and her output was slow, which may explain the move to quieter Sonoma. There was serenity there—not unlike the serenity I returned to Nevada for, which was something she understood immediately. When so many questioned our decision to return to Nevada after my wife finished grad school, Kizer simply said, "You must go where there is less distraction." I did not have to explain why silence was its own reward. Wendell Berry has said that Hayden Carruth gave him the courage to make a similar choice when he moved from Greenwich Village to rural Kentucky in the 1960s. Carruth had moved to northern Vermont to begin writing his major poems and because of this, Berry could trust Carruth's decision—rural isolation did not mean cultural death; it was a way of staking out one's place to begin a life in words.

When I came to visit Kizer in Sonoma, we walked the downtown courthouse square. There were many small shops and in one, there were handmade plates and dinnerware. My family had very few matching dishes, and Kizer and I picked out a set for my wife. They were hand-painted, so each one was slightly different. We still have them, although many have broken, but I can hear Kizer ask, "You don't have any money—how can you pay for these?" Foolishly, I replied, "I'll find a way." It was her attention that let the day pass as if it were stretched from time, and conversation slowed to the most elemental, necessary coordinates. At her house she began to read from my second manuscript, her eyes focused on the poem at hand. John Woodbridge, her husband, walked into the room. She looked up. "I am reading Shaun's poems. This will take a while," and it did—while I read from the spines of her floor-to-ceiling poetry library.

By then I was a long-distance consultant to four universities in the San Francisco Bay Area and for the first time in my adult life, had time to write in our small, Nevada home. I began to edit a book of Nevada poetry, followed by a book of Joanne de Longchamps's *Selected Poems*. Kizer knew de Longchamps because they were both published in the Indiana Poetry Series. To finish the Nevada anthology, I started translating the poems of Emma Sepúlveda, something I had no preparation for except my rudimentary Spanish. Kizer's example of "Keep Hidden from Me" by Rachel Korn encouraged me: "Translation is what I do when I cannot write poetry":

Keep from me all that I might comprehend!
O God, I ripen toward you in my unknowing.

Although some translators quibbled with their quality, the translations sustained Kizer through long periods of drought and, equally important, framed her perspective, her worldview on writing: it is not a private undertaking; rather, it is something much larger than one cultural myth or belief. Kizer was of the mind—not unlike Carruth, Levertov, and Rich—that poetry's place was in the grist of our lives. More than once she said, "Get a job," when young poets asked where to start.

This belief in poetry's intrinsic value to change lives, its social utility—to use Carruth's phrase—helped me translate Emma Sepúlveda's political poems. Sepúlveda is a Chilean exile that fled Pinochet's soldiers at the height of the coup. She and I worked for three years on her book, *Death to Silence (Muerte al silencio)*. When we submitted some of those poems to *Calapooya Collage*, we were excited to learn they had received the Carolyn Kizer Foreign Language and Translation Award. Sometimes you back into things and they become their own reward. Translation has remained something I cherish. It is as difficult as writing poetry but with an added twist—the poem must sing in two languages— and in multiple layers of context, sound, meaning. It is the most challenging—and rewarding—writing I have undertaken.

Tom Ferté, the late editor of *Calapooya Collage*, was an old friend of Kizer's. No surprise—as the doyen of Pacific Northwest poetry, she was friends with most poets and writers from the region. At each year's publication celebration, Kizer read from the new journal to a packed room at Powell's Bookstore in Portland and then announced the awards in her honor. This was Kizer at her most flamboyant, the celebrated poet on stage with her retinue. She made us feel as if we were part of the poetic tradition. For years, my wife and I went to Powell's every August. Those gatherings of so many Northwest poets—William Stafford, Ursula K. Le Guin, Vern Rutsala, Madeline DeFrees, Ingrid Wendt, Ralph Salisbury, Paulann Petersen, and dozens more who were associated with the journal—became a ritual, a coda to the eclectic voices inside the journal. Ferté's tastes ran wide, as did Kizer's, and they jousted long and mightily at the podium at Powell's. They were a singular force of mind, and their performance was something to behold.

In the summer of 1989, I asked Kizer if she would come to a writing conference in nearby Carson City, Nevada, where ironically Stafford was also presenting. Their personal styles could not be more different—Stafford's was subdued but carefully articulated and Kizer's, direct and trenchant. One of the poets who attended her workshop left after a stinging rebuke. This was not the first time, nor the last, that I would see this side of Kizer. I tried to assuage my friend's concern. He was a good, if eccentric poet, but certainly not a beginner, someone for whom her criticism might have been valid. Kizer was tough and you did not want to cross her: he disagreed and the sparks flew. He still has not gotten over it but the stories of poets and their behavior—good or bad—are legion. I have witnessed the best and the least come back to their rooms with glass in hand, leaving a trail of misspent words behind them.

What finally matters is what gets done on the page. The words remain and if they do not always console, they lament our greater sorrow. I remember Kizer telling me that she read Carruth all hours of the night. I have no doubt he read her, trusted insomniac that he was. What a cacophony of 3:00 a.m. poets, reading, distilling, and praying if they could pray, for some rest before dawn. Kizer's essay on Carruth disputes his supposed atheist beliefs, preferring instead to find in his vision a spiritual domain—not unlike the one I saw in her, although she, too, would not ascribe to any belief. This is the belief of the poet, a fundamental regard for the value of human life, insofar as it can be expressed in poetry, as written in "To My Friend Who Rhymes with Peace":

Now I am able to be still and know
God *is* us, because so clearly, God is in you.

Neither Kizer nor Carruth was religious, not even close; but they wanted to believe and felt responsible for that belief—to women, the poor, those suffering, those for whom poetry was not idea but a necessity. In this way they circled the idea of belief. It was belief of meaning—existential and corroborative.

In 1992 I was in Southern California and read Kizer's review of Gary Snyder's *No Nature*, in which she described her young daughter's chance meeting with Snyder on the steps of a Tokyo train station—crying, disconsolate at having seen the memorial at Hiroshima. She was a foreign exchange student and Snyder's poems were in the Kizer house and her daughter knew of him when he, Snyder, stopped to lend her comfort. Only in the whirl of Kizer's energy could this have happened. How many people have cried on those steps and left with only tears to show for their discomfort?

Kizer went on to describe hearing the young Snyder and Allen Ginsberg read at the University of Washington, just after the famous Six Gallery reading in San Francisco. Snyder was twenty-five years old and Kizer was thirty—and this time was preparation for the work to come.

Hers was a devouring mind; she read widely and led me to many poets I did not know: Janet Lewis, spouse of Yvor Winters, whose poem on the atom bomb, Kizer said was among the finest on the topic; Robert Peterson, the poet she selected for the National Poetry Series; and the women with whom she had the greatest affinity—Diana O'Hehir at nearby Mills College, Josephine Miles at UC-Berkeley, Sandra Gilbert at UC-Davis, and so many more. I could not return from her house without another ten voices in American poetry. They were penetrating voices, poets I reached for to understand my own work, whether translation or writing. When Emma Sepúlveda and I translated a volume of poems by the children of the Disappeared (those who had been abducted or killed by Pinochet's military), Kizer suggested that I ask a well-known poet to write the introduction. When I called, her graduate students would not let me through. But the poems do not need promotion: "Today is already late. / It's already twelve o'clock, / thinking when I will be able to eat, / verb that can be conjugated / but one cannot taste her" (Lorena, *For All The Lands We Will Pass Through*).

Gently, and sometimes not so gently, Kizer showed me her mind: fierce, unrelenting, and exacting—qualities of stubborn precision. Sometimes she was mistaken. She thought Czeslaw Milosz passé, but rereading lines from "Dedication" I can't waver from their urgency: "What is poetry which does not save / Nations or people?" Occasionally this storm of intellect withdrew to pettiness; I asked her to submit some poems to a friend's journal but she would have nothing of it. And so there was silence for a good long while, until years later when I began work on a collection of essays about Hayden Carruth. I reread an essay by Marilyn Hacker, noting Carolyn's influence on and importance to Carruth. I reread Kizer's essay in the *Seneca Review* and Hacker was right— the essay did need to be in the book. I called Kizer's husband, John Woodbridge, and we spoke for five minutes. Then he asked, "You don't know what has happened, do you?" There was a long pause, and then, "She has Alzheimer's." I swallowed—this towering woman diminished to coping with the basic requirements of staying alive: eating, sleeping, bathing.

Almost thirty years had passed since that night Kizer read in Reno. I had a vague sense of her not being present in the literary milieu—her name was conspicuously absent from the quarterlies and festivals. Her correspondence with friends had fallen off and I did not know why. Her husband's words left me with no doubt: her voice, her vision, had been muted.

Some months later, my wife and I visited Kizer. Her caregiver, Peggy, made a fruit salad, toast, and eggs. Her son Fred kept us company for more than two and a half hours. Slowly, we tried to piece together the past—this was when we were together for that event, that reading, that surprise recognition. Like the nights at Powell's when Kizer captivated her audience with anecdotes— mostly true—and recitations of Catullus or Shakespeare. At one time she was teaching a class at San Jose State. When I stopped in on a business trip, she was reading from a small book to once again familiarize herself with the poet's work. She discouraged me from the weekly travel to the Bay Area and I relented. It was a class on Pope or John Keats, I can't remember. But I wanted to know *her* poetic cartography and then I understood: her poems were telegrams from an earlier time, which made them relevant in this time.

AND SO THE INTIMATE reversal of a mind. Whatever song she was given to sing, she held its note for the crescendo and that might be at a literary conference in Poland, a preeminent gathering of Virginia Woolf scholars, or a faithful admonition to a friend—keep writing. In her sultry swagger, she could overpower, and in her most timid, she could refract what was asked of her time and talent. Our friendship came from the belief that poetry could create a common bond, a place in which to share and discuss the most vital of truths.

Sitting in her kitchen with Fred, she read the *New York Times Book Review*, ate toast and fruit, and tried, I imagine, to understand who these people were at her table. Fred showed her the book I had sent so long ago—with a note of thanks for the careful reading, for the instruction years before. She did not remember the book, but it did not matter. In the light of her home, there was comfort: she read poetry for days on end and perhaps discovered there, some fulsome place that, given her limitations, was a place of beauty or recognition or tolerance. A place in which she could survive.

This is why the shadow of that woman we sat with at the kitchen table was so devastating. Her genius was precision. She could name, recall, finger, or ferry the one right song, poem, or story from the endless reservoir of her reading. She could leave you doubting that you knew anything and then ask you for help. For Kizer, feminism was an opportunity to fully express the province of women *and* men with a fierce and biting humor that frequently relegated the literary influence of the latter to its dustbin. I'm sure she said to me more than once, "There is nothing here we cannot share." A new literary standard? No—a recognition of the obvious. Kizer sculpted a different literary tradition and she made no excuses for it. This was the woman with whom we shared toast and eggs, and it does not mollify what truth remains. Her hardscrabble knowledge served her well but still, I wanted to go home with a vision of Carolyn Kizer somehow restored. I guess we must live with these inglorious thieves, these cells that somehow rise to steal the mind away. But I don't like them and don't want them to cheat her of another day. And so I will reach for her poems to restore a dignity of mind, of each day without the searing presence of its loss.

—2016—

13

If I Had Wheels or Love

Grief requires no credentials.
—Vassar Miller

It was May and I was walking the streets of Houston. Downtown was empty and humid. I wandered back to the apartment in the shadow of the Astrodome and happened to read of Vassar Miller in the Sunday paper. Nearly everything about her intrigued me: her face and eyes, the subtlety of her words, and the sparks in the few poems reprinted in the article. We would not meet until several years later at a poetry reading in Reno, but I made up my mind to learn more about her. I now know that she is widely regarded as the finest poet of her native Texas, and she is the first to have her collected works published. Born in Houston sixty-nine years ago, she is the one Texas writer for whom Larry McMurtry "has unequivocal admiration,"—strong words taken from a 1981 article in the *Texas Observer* in which he lambasted Texas writers, all of them, except Vassar Miller.

"I have been called a religious poet," Miller said in 1970. "I think I still am, in the sense that my poetry deals with basic human questions: life, death, eternity, time, love." Today when she reflects on being labeled—whether religious or disabled (she has had cerebral palsy since birth)—it is with distaste, and she refuses to speak for either camp save through her writing. She questions why these characterizations have taken her out of the realm of modern poetry. Surely her predecessors (John Donne and Gerard Manley Hopkins, for instance) found eloquence in religious themes. Eliot has been criticized for many things but not for being a religious poet.

As I write this, I am painfully aware that to capture her with words is to watch her struggle with the simplest of acts—dressing, eating, and sleeping. In the fall of 1992 I returned to Houston three days before the presidential election. Texas was politically torn but there was calm on Vassar Street. Two years had passed since I last saw Miller read her poetry, too long for any friend to accept. But distance separates and she has little choice in such matters. Her home is her refuge, though were she able, I believe she would return to Europe or the fifty states, as she once did: "If I had wheels or love, I would be gone." This line from the title poem of her collected works, *If I Had Wheels or Love*, gives a glimpse of the joy in her veins. Like the late Kenneth Patchen, she must cope with a body that won't listen.

When I arrived at her house last fall, it was near eight in the evening. Her caretaker had made a dinner of pot roast, fried potatoes, and greens. Ms. Miller was in her room watching television. As I sat down on the bed, she took one look at me and in seconds picked up where we had left off after her Reno reading in the spring of 1990. There was no hesitation, no awkward pause, only the voice of happiness upon seeing a visitor from far away. I asked if she had been doing any writing. "Yes," she stammered, "I am working on the 'Christ' series." We fumbled with the computer and the printer spat pages of text until I turned it off for fear of its never stopping.

Dr. Richard Ashman, a New Orleans physiologist and founder of the New Orleans Poetry Journal Press, selected and published Miller's first book of poems, *Adam's Footprint*, in 1956. Since then, the editor of the press, Maxine Cassin (who co-edited that first volume), has been a lasting influence in the poet's life, publishing book reviews, poems, and a second volume of her poetry. In the nearly forty years following the publication of that bellwether volume, Cassin has been an advocate and a lighthouse for Miller in the Southern literary world, though she too is now in poor health. Among her peers, the late Howard Nemerov was one of the first to take note of *Adam's Footprint*: "Brilliant works of language, with a fine energy flowing through one passage after another, the hard-working vocabulary, rich, strange, accurate, beautifully paced." Later, as a consultant in poetry to the Library of Congress, he arranged for a taped recording of her poetry for the library's holdings.

Donald Hall is not certain where he first encountered Vassar Miller's poetry. He believes it was either while reading for the *Paris Review* or in the anthology he co-edited in 1957, *New Poets of England and America*. He urged her to send her second manuscript, *Wage War on Silence*, to Wesleyan University Press and recalls in a recent letter being delighted "that other editors agreed with me about her work." *Wage War on Silence* was nominated for a Pulitzer Prize in 1961 and reprinted four times. Miller said of the book: "The title . . . reflects my conviction that poetry, indeed all art, is the striving to say the unsayable, to express the inexpressible," as in "Without Ceremony":

> Except ourselves, we have no other prayer;
> Our needs are sores upon our nakedness.
> We do not have to name them; we are here.

In the next eight years Wesleyan published two more of her books, *My Bones Being Wiser* (1963) and *Onions and Roses* (1968); both went to second printings. Some of the finest poets in the country were publishing with Wesleyan during that period, including John Ashbery, Robert Bly, Richard Howard, Marge Piercy, Louis Simpson, and James Wright. To be among this company was an honor, but she returned to the smaller presses. (Miller is not sure why Wesleyan turned down her next book; no doubt editorial tastes changed in the tumult of the late 1960s.) Clearly her poetry started to change with the publication of *If I Could Sleep Deeply Enough* in 1974. The former book editor for the *Houston Chronicle*,

Ann Waldron, wrote: "Miller's new book is . . . different from her four earlier books of poetry. The poems are tougher and less traditionally religious in nature." Miller responded by saying, "It was a gradual change; maybe it was Cynthia's [McDonald] class [at the University of Houston] to some extent, although I had already begun to change."

The founding editors of Wings Press, Joanie Whitebird and Joe Lomax, chose *Small Change* for their first volume. This chapbook contained sixteen new poems that Vassar read at Houston's Contemporary Art Museum in June 1976. This "tribute to . . . the First Lady of Texas Poetry" also marked the first Texas publication of Miller's work and, for her, a steady departure from old poetic roots. In her words, she felt her poetry becoming "more humanistic, dealing more with human relations, more open and more personal." Wings Press published *Approaching Nada* the following year. In an interview with Karla Hammond, Miller describes the chapbook as a spiritual biography and as a single poem in five parts. "I've seen only one review that was entirely favorable." Writing in four intense days, she set down a narrative poem in numbered sections to ". . . seek my roots of shifted waters / shifting toward nada." Shifting toward nothing, toward the ineffable, she began to explore her history in the desert Southwest. This was a long poem made all the richer for having shed early poetic patterns.

Robert Bonazzi, editor of Latitudes Press, published two thousand cloth copies of Miller's *Selected and New Poems, 1950–1980*, in 1981. *Library Journal* selected the volume, which included an introduction by Denise Levertov, as the best small press book of poems for 1982. Every copy was sold. In 1983 the New Orleans Poetry Press released *Struggling to Swim on Concrete*. On the back cover of this volume, Miller's staunch supporter McMurtry is quoted from the 1981 essay in the *Texas Observer*: ". . . Hardwon, high, intelligent, felt, finished, profound. To Vassar Miller, if to anyone we have, belongs the laurel." The Pulitzer Prize

Committee wrote to Maxine Cassin and requested that she nominate the book for the prize, though, again, Miller was not selected.

Like Maxine Kumin, who thought poetry too fragile a vessel for political statement early in her career, only to write some of the strongest poems about nuclear war later in life, Miller turned to editing to synthesize her beliefs on disability and art. The University of Texas Press published *Despite This Flesh* in 1985, an anthology of stories and poems by and about people with disabilities. A controversial book, *Despite This Flesh* met with mixed results among disability advocates. Some felt it was not a strong enough indictment, others dismissed it because of the poet's religious background. Southern Methodist University Press released her collected poems, *If I Had Wheels or Love*, in 1991. This was SMU's first book of poetry, and though it received considerable advance praise from Denise Levertov and Richard Wilbur, few reviews appeared outside of Texas. A notable exception was the *Kenyon Review*, in which Jessica Greenbaum said, "I hope the crust of silence that has insulated Miller from the reading world will be broken by this volume, since these poems address the tyranny of silence, both within and without." The book was passed over for the major awards and for the annual poetry prize given by the Texas Institute of Letters (which, coincidentally, she received for her first three books). In March of 1993 she received the Lon Tinkle Memorial Award ($1,500) for a significant career achievement in Texas literature from the Texas Institute of Letters. Today, when hands and heart permit, she is at work on her autobiography, *Speaking My Piece*. She has rewritten it, starting with the last chapter. A former housekeeper stole the first chapters of the earliest version and never returned.

I am reminded of the line, "If you don't want to give yourself away, don't write."

In a 1983 article, the *Houston Chronicle* said, "Few people in Houston seem to know the internationally acclaimed poet's name or work, and Miller, on bad days, gets so discouraged she doesn't seem absolutely sure she cares whether people know her or not." In this role she has many predecessors; certainly Emily Dickinson comes to mind. She finds some measure of contentment in Hopkins and Dylan Thomas, her two favorite poets, but she returns to her own writing for solace, as in these stanzas from "Meditation after an Interview":

I speak myself, and my name
is only smoke
and less than smoke.

I explain myself, and my name
turned witness against me,
puts questions I cannot answer.

But if You say me, my Lord, my name
I meet in Your darkness and hear it
singing content in your silence.

Back in her bedroom (which doubles as her place of writing) I was reading the notes on her wall and noticed "Freewheeling Poets" meeting on Saturdays from eleven to noon. Still wanting to teach, she offered this program through leisure learning and no one came. In any other major city, a poet of her stature would be paid well to conduct a workshop for the general public. Today Vassar Miller barely makes ends meet. She has lived for years off the interest from stocks and bonds (through a trust set up by her father) but is constantly threatened with being moved to a nursing home as her money runs out. When she gave a reading in Reno in 1989, her first west of the Rockies, she received a $1,000 honorarium—the most she had been paid for a reading. For thirty minutes at that Reno gathering, she read from nine Xeroxed poems, distributed to the audience held captive with her halting voice. Those who were in the theater have not forgotten her. It wasn't a reading she gave; it was a life played out on the stage. Struggling to move from one poem to the next, when she closed with "If I Had Wheels or Love," there was only silence in the dark.

Still later that fall evening, I climbed into bed in her guest room out back. It was raining hard. I couldn't help but feel as if I was about to sleep at the door of a figure in history that, with luck, might be rediscovered by a future generation. Years ago, *Texas Monthly* did a story on a painter, Forrest Bess, who lived in obscurity on the Gulf Coast but painted scenes that leave me awed. Although no two Texas artists could be more different, they are not understood, which translates into a flickering belief in self and for her, belief in God. She knows theology in a way most theologians crave to know it. In this she abides, though readers familiar with her work know her belief in God is haunted by doubts—there is no guarantee of self-worth or righteousness in this world. Paradoxically, it is the thing that comforts her and yet makes her sleepless, for fear of not measuring up. Witness "Defense Rests":

> I want
> a love to hold
> in my hand because love
> is too much for the heart to bear
> alone.
>
> Then stop
> mouthing to me
> 'Faith and Sacraments' when
> the Host feather-heavy weighs down
> my soul.

Although I trust her when she says "I did not need [critical] attention," many a lesser poet readily accepts that she is steeped in belief and that is enough to sustain her. Any person who has a cursory exposure to religion surely knows that to love something is to know first one's own shortcomings. Again quoting from the

Hammond interview, Miller says, "No doubt most critics and other poets consider my religiousness at best an exotic hobby, at worst a disease."

Miller's stepmother taught her to walk (her natural mother died when she was one year old). Her stepmother's stubborn insistence on self-reliance gave the poet freedom from a life of dependence on others (until much later when the cerebral palsy grew worse). She bounced down the stairs on her bottom, a mode of travel she recalls with much pleasure. But it was her father who brought home a typewriter, the tool that would change her life. She was kept out of grade school, and it was her stepmother again who taught her to read, but Vassar demanded to learn in public school. She enrolled in Lanier Junior High at twelve. After high school, she went to the University of Houston, where she received her M.A. in English in 1950. Six years later her first book, *Adam's Footprint*, was published.

Miller is uncompromising in her desire to portray the world in which she lives. Reviewers said *If I Could Sleep Deeply Enough* was more honest than her earlier work. To this she responded, "I was as honest as I know how to be in writing all my poems. Most critics seem to think that any expression of religious faith is dishonest." In "The Tree of Silence" we know her most fully: "For when was language ever food for human yearning!" As a poet, she names without decoration or contrived loss of feeling. She refuses sentimentality or piety when unwanted, and chooses instead carefully constructed lines that fall, one to the next, with no hope of letting go.

Vassar Miller has never married; she loves children though she has none of her own. Hers is a family of old friends. She has a special affinity for animals; her two dogs, Regal and Cricket, give her great company ("They're my best friends"). She lives alone and is under the constant care of a household helper who assists with all of her daily activities. For years she has known the daily indignity of being dependent on others to help her dress, eat, bathe, and leave the house. She had a motorized cart of sorts, but after two hard falls she is afraid of using it. The lone exceptions to her isolation are St. Stephen's Episcopal Church and its priest, Helen Havens. They are her lifeblood, the things that give her reason to live. Outside of this small group of friends from St. Stephen's, a handyman who repairs the house, and a handful of others, she lives in virtual anonymity. She rails against bouts of depression and medical problems, and has a constant fear of choking, which in turn forces her to drink Ensure for nutrition rather than eat solid food. Her time is divided between the Houston Public Library and writing, though as her dexterity decreases, it grows increasingly difficult to operate the keyboard on her computer.

How is it that one so tenacious as she has slipped past us like a cloud?

Nevertheless, Vassar has her champions. *Heart's Invention* was released in 1988, to my knowledge the first major critical study of her work. Edited by Steven Ford Brown, the book is part of the American Poets Profile Series. And there are other individuals who have been helpful to her through the years. Donald Hall wrote a very thoughtful letter and was happy he played some part in her early publishing with Wesleyan. Maxine Cassin said, "We have published many first books since 1956 but there will never be another *Adam's Footprint*." Doubtless there are others who read her for pleasure or affirmation but are not known in the world of literature. But I was most heartened when I received these words from Miller Williams, who, prior to becoming the director of the University of Arkansas Press, taught Miller's poetry in the M.F.A. program at Fayetteville: "So far as my reading has taken me, Vassar Miller is the only poet writing in English who has given us a body of serious religious work, I mean in the fashion of John Donne and Gerard Manley Hopkins." Indeed, Williams goes on to say, "She makes her poems of passion, creed, craft, and wit, so clearly hers in the deftness of the balance that we might know them without her name."

Not long ago I asked her why she writes, and without thinking she said, "Because I love it so." She is an essential part of our literary history, a writer who has known obscurity and yet perseveres. The will to live is strong in this woman. Unlike those who use their strength to build or break down, she takes the world on her tongue and swallows to know its place in her life, in her poetry. She moves away in wonder and fears always it will come to an end. There is no limit to the letting go that one must abide to live. For Vassar Miller, survival is the moment at which you say goodbye. People mean so much to her, and she has so few people any more. Feebly I said, "Keep writing," and she said, "Yes."

> *Pity is a distraction,*
> *I'm too mean to die.*
> —Vassar Miller

Late at night, I was nearly asleep on the couch when the phone rang. It was Jay Leach, the Baptist minister from Houston. Did I remember him? In my grogginess, there was no mistaking his tone: at seventy-four, Vassar Miller's seemingly endless life had been eclipsed by a final silence.

Vassar Miller's life was a confluence of desire, hope, and dire suffering. Few writers have been so unfailingly honest and determined to chink from the bounds of American letters a place for themselves. Paradoxically, except for the admiration of a dozen of our most respected poets, she went to her grave in virtual anonymity. Miller wrote predominantly in traditional forms on religious themes during the height of the Beats and the Confessional poets. For Miller, this was an act of love—she wrote the poems that had to be written. Those who cherish finely crafted poetry about spiritual issues, the struggle to find one's self amidst a mostly godless world, read Vassar Miller, not just for her countenance but for her unflinching attempts to name the experience of an invisible woman, as can be seen in "Posthumous Letter to Thomas Merton":

I ask you, self-styled marginal man,
Does not each sufferer always inhabit
The edges of the world as pioneer
To prove how much humanity can bear
And still be human, experimenter in
The bloody laboratory of our lives.

Out of that contemporary isolation came her strength—she could not aspire to any artificial liking. Her words were the harbinger of religious feeling not imagined in American poetry since the death of Eliot.

When I visited Miller at the Stoneybrook Health Care Center in Houston, most people did not know who she was. She was a woman, like any other, whose flesh was giving out. I asked what she needed. Books, of course, was her immediate answer. Then I read poems to her. She was transfixed, so focused on her craft that nothing could penetrate that concentration. Even in the throes of a nursing home, her mind was more lucid than many in their cars speeding the street outside.

Miller has had her champions, but the brooding silence remains. Perhaps this is because at some intrinsic level her poems both comfort and deeply disturb. They are a bulwark of faith against unremitting doubt and perturbation. That which can never be fully said in a poem was her subject: an undying love of God and the hollow, often failed, experience of the self. Just as haunting, they bore no lasting reconciliation for her, save the symbolic renewal of the Eucharist to which she returned again and again, as in these stanzas from the title poem of *My Bones Being Wiser*:

My flesh is
the shadow of pride

cast by my bones
at whose core lies cradled a child tender
and terrible, like
the Lamb he prays

to have mercy,
lest the hands held up
fall empty, lest
the light-as-air Host be only air.
Yet the Child within
my bones knows better.

I do not have the good fortune of looking ahead fifty years, but
if the past is any example (Melville, Dickinson), Miller's poetry
will come to be viewed as witness to living in a time that could
not know her. She balanced the ineffable with such immutable
force, that I can only believe readers will return to the vast emotional landscape she has left as in "Embarrassed":

Why am I here if I
must pose such questions to the darkness
whence no heavenly fire consumes my offering.
No propriety of an Amen ends my prayer.
I stumble from
this wrong room while my apologies
freeze my tongue tight.

Miller cherished the morning rituals and repetition of the
Episcopal Church. In many ways it gave her structure, not unlike
her formal poems in the "Christ-haunted landscape of the South,"
to quote Flannery O'Connor. In the afternoons, the liberal Baptist
congregation freed her from tradition. She wrote poems and a
sermon that were not altogether welcomed by the Baptists, but
she could rebel, be the skeptic, and sleep with two faiths twined
at her core. Conflicted to the end by the unanswered question of

her worth in this world—whether flesh or spirit, she held Sundays like bread to her lips.

On religious themes, Miller could parry with anyone in the room. At home, the answers readily delivered in public were slow in coming. Before her caretakers sold her house, she wrestled with the contradictions of flesh. What she wanted more than anything was love. What she found were scraps and pieces of lives and a religious community that would not forsake her—St. Stephen's Episcopal Church and Covenant Baptist Church.

She also found an angel in the presence of Sue Nash. When Miller could no longer live alone, Nash purchased the house. Of her many caretakers, it was Nash who finally negotiated the legal system to bring Miller some parity and dignity at the end of her life. She had never met Miller but was overwhelmed by the deplorable situation in which she was left: a dwindling trust, few friends, and failing health. Not surprisingly, as a consequence of *not* having wheels or love, Miller could be utterly disdainful with the knowledge of her wan existence.

Still, I can't help feeling we have much to learn, and we will learn it without her now. Those words she left us will come like snow, and, to quote Kenneth Patchen, another poet who knew the rancors of flesh with pain, "Snow is the only one of us that leaves no tracks."

Vassar Miller is ephemeral in America. We cannot see her, because she looks like a woman who may not be from this time. And her words read like a woman who may be timeless. Not quite two years before Vassar Miller died in 1998, Governor George W. Bush presided at her induction into the Texas Women's Hall of Fame. Miller looked radiant that evening, and if she could not go to the podium like the other women, she stilled the room with her diminutive frame. The governor was overtaken with emotion and did not know what to do, so he handed me her award. Politics and religion came perilously close that evening. He was effaced and without instruction; she was surrounded by a few friends and waiting for his hands. It was the ultimate moment for Miller: she was a woman finally regarded as a poet in her own time, a small measure for a life spent carving words.

Doubt was her laurel. This is not a contradiction. Over and over she fought with depression and doubt, and even when she saw her books they were like women she once knew, not the artisan skillfully bearing down on a passage from Ecclesiastes.

Bhutanese artists aspire to paint in anonymity. The relative impulse toward perfection in modern poetry is driven largely by conformity. Faced with the choice of denying herself the one thing that provided pleasure, she chose instead to write a poem that would answer the voice within. Vassar Miller lived within the room she created, and it was not unlike Virginia Woolf's room. Certainly it was created for the same reasons: to have a place of meaning, an intellectual life beyond the world outside. If it was a room that could not be understood by the era in which she lived because she chose poetry *and* religion, among those who spend their lives one syllable at a time hers was nonetheless a sacred act.

— 2000 —

14

From the Ash of Human Feeling: Teaching Poetry behind the Fence

THE MORNING STARTS with a collect call; the voice on the other end is tranquil, as if to soothe me. His name is Johnny. How often I have thought of other collect calls, but the man on the phone is pacing a concrete room, one that is barred from the world outside.

He tells me of the book he is reading on poetic forms, the subtle intonations of blank versus free verse, and wonders out loud if we can incorporate such lessons in the workshop. "Why not?" I sing back, knowing that the lessons we learn have so much to do with living the other six and a half days a week, the formidable hours in which there is no *Razor Wire* workshop to dream.

Johnny has been coming for eleven years, has read enough poets for at least one graduate degree, and written a book that sears. When it finds a home, people will regale him with laurels: because of the poems' muscled texture, they are closer to original scores on desire. Like the composer John Cage, who pushed silence to sound, Johnny's poems imprint flesh without flesh. Desire sprung from rueful, sinister feeling that has found expression in poetry.

Johnny has six more years. In Mandarin time—in time without calendars—flowers, families, and countries bloom. But he will not bloom until those years pass. For now, the ebb and flow of poetics and paint must sustain him. I remember a letter of his that started, "Dear Captain, (pretty much my only captain)." In the eternal sprint of human evolution, prison—yet another form of marking time—must finally be regarded as one of our failings.

Lest I give the wrong impression, Johnny is one of many in the workshop, and scores of other men who have been in it. We have notched our chairs with birth, death, marriage, and divorce— nothing the outside world would not recognize as fundamentally human. And we've risen with the tide of prison rules and rulers—from benign to unkind and some that were inspired. The workshop has persisted out of obstinacy more than anything else. With very little instruction, we began to publish a journal, *Razor Wire*, which despite its black cover and ornery title has found a niche in northern Nevada literature. Three years ago, we began getting submissions from the outside. The men voted and decided to open the journal up to the free world. Last year saw our first perfect-bound issue. We almost became respectable but for the outlaws united under one spine.

Perhaps most remarkably, in over a decade, not one man who has participated in the workshop has come back to prison on a yard where the recidivism rate is at least 50 percent.

Later that Sunday I call a former member of the workshop who lives in the centuries-old civilization of Malta. Doc answers the phone and tells me he received our letters the same day. He means Johnny's and mine. Doc was a biochemist for a pharmaceutical firm whose assets were liquidated by an unscrupulous son-in-law. He was released from prison two years later but not before leaving his mark on all of us in the workshop. Of all that I have learned from grown men struggling with W. B. Yeats, kindness takes root in the darkest places.

I share the news from Malta. Ray, a Vietnam veteran in the workshop, smiles. He knew Doc well. Then a small poem on AIDS rises from Ray's lips. It is felt with more than death's cursory needle:

Fatal
Forgiven him for giving me his

skinned venom love sweet forbidden
my tent slowly becomes dust again.

It is felt as the "dry lethal injection of time without parole," as Ray says in another poem, "Calambro." The chaplain's clerk for most of his fourteen years in prison, he has found hope in many things—songwriting, lay clergy, and a cummingsesque poetry that rivets my reading to the page. Ray hasn't found a way out but rather some peace to endure the way. No dime-store Christian, he holds verbs to fire and out of that very personal faith comes an epigrammatic poetry that is uniquely his. Nearest to Dickinson in style and emotion, his lines are buttons on a much larger tapestry of human healing. I often say that to write is to redeem. Ray sheathes his days with poem and prayer.

To the cynic I must sound gratuitous. But the writers have earned their praise. Indeed, of the more than sixty men who have participated, several have published poems, chapbooks, essays, short stories, and nonfiction articles. As with anything, it is the quality that matters. Their voices range from tentative to strong, rough-hewn to high-brow, but however they may be perceived, their words have rippled out.

The first time we read Strunk and White it was like chloroform. I could do nothing to save them from the ruin of independent clauses. Every person in the room taught a chapter until we finished it. From that day on, they began to own the workshop like you own soil or suffering. It became a kind of honor to telegraph syntax or punctuation. To do so without my prodding was like mastering Gaelic. The foreign language had finally come to mean new poetic strength. They were no longer afraid to wrestle with me or disagree when my explanation seemed improbable. But the real learning was yet to come as it might to a silversmith or a farrier—after years of practice and contemplation when the poetic form was freed from its shackles.

Among my happiest moments in the workshop are those times an elder statesman sheds light on the process of revision. "There's something wrong with the music in this line," you can almost hear him say. "The music of your voice is missing." Born of language no one can prescribe, they teach each other as if it were bread they were making. Not to be outdone, they read voraciously and have begun reviewing books for the journal. Although other prison workshops have had more visible success, the men in Carson City have found their measure of self-respect and to be fair, challenge. As any working poet knows, you will die with the best line on your lips. They too suffer the finality of never quite knowing and with even less to lose, they keep writing.

A long time ago, the poet Richard Shelton advised me to "begin. The rest will follow." Were it not for his guiding hand in many things—not least of which were my early fits and starts in poetry—I doubt I would have begun the workshop with virtually no tools save a modicum of practice. But I could not have known how many lives would be at stake and what faces would drown in the sadness. Faces I would not recognize until much later, like the day Tillman abducted the prison doctor and pinned himself to the wall in a hail of gunfire; the day Skip wrote his last poem on the Ruby Mountain Wilderness only to die of a heart attack, younger than I was; the day I was cussed out for being too white to teach a black man poetry; the day that same man wrote to apologize; the day the truly good warden was forced from her job only to later open a restaurant with a former inmate; the day I read "First and Last Things" to Stan in a Washington, D.C., bookstore, a poem I wrote upon his release after eleven and a half years; the day Joey was admitted to graduate school; the day Charles Wright lovingly answered Preston's letter after an earnest attempt to understand Black Zodiac; the day Vernon got married, and the day my boss told me he was a volunteer fireman in the town where Vernon once lived (leaving me to infer the attendant shadows); and the day Barry Lopez wrote to say Cliff's poem on the narwhal was "remarkable." Nine years ago a regent from the University of Nevada, Reno, wrote to tell me how moved she was by their poetry. A spiral-bound chapbook, *Razor Wire*, was barely more than an idea let loose on the yard. Today, while not yet an institution, the workshop is much larger than those first timid poems copied for friends.

It is April in Virginia City, and several people have gathered for an exhibition at Sun Mountain Artworks. The gallery owner, Nolan Preece, has painstakingly matted, framed, and hung the paintings, cross-stitching, leather work, and jewelry. This is the fourth year we have had a prison art show. To commemorate the event, poets Tom Meschery, Bill Cowee, Gailmarie Pahmeier (all of whom have helped with the workshop), and others read from the journal, published annually in conjunction with the opening. Shannon Montana, a photographer, videotapes the reading, asking family and friends to comment on the art. The painter Emily Silver sends her regards—she worked in the prison with many of the artists before leaving Nevada. Soon another painter, Karen Kreyeski, will mentor one of the artists. And there are others: the sculptor Suzanne Kanatsiz singlehandedly arranged for their artwork to be shown at the University of Nevada, Reno's, Sheppard Gallery. Their collective support is a kind of grace holding the workshop up—not one but many hearts that hunger for kindness.

When I play the video the following Wednesday, it is like church. Breath hangs on every word, every subtle glance to and from the artwork. This is the one time of year when the men are without labels. They are synonymous with what they have created. Whether poetry or art, it is stripped of pretense and emotionally compelling. For one hour out of the long day that becomes a year, there is release from what haunts—Aston's watercolors (who is going blind); Tiny's Hobbit-like oils; Randy's perfectly stitched Victorians; leather purses; wallets; and belts from Tom and his younger brother Tim, inconceivably incarcerated together. These names have faces that cannot return to anything more than tomorrow, a not-altogether-sacred pact with creation. All of us live on slippery footing. As Seamus Heaney confides, among "the disregarded ones we turned against / Because we'd failed them by our disregard," slippery footing is commonplace, ergo even the littlest living thing is a gift. A spider under the cell door, the marigolds trimming the warden's lawn, or the momentary touch of a loved one in visiting.

Forget the rhetoric on prison; it destroys. It is an idea and an effect for which we have no tolerance. To survive it is to become an anomaly. I pray that every man in the workshop will live to see its steel gate close behind him. Do I condone what brought them to their knees? It is silly to partake in a discussion the poet Su Tung-p'o was not able to reconcile in 1071. It was Su's job to pass judgment on the "Pitiful convicts in chains."

> Don't ask who is foolish or wise;
> all of us alike scheme for a meal.
> The ancients would have freed them a while at New Year's—
> would I dare do likewise? I am silent with shame.

Nor can I judge 930 later. What I know is that the library in Unit 4 is an oasis on the yard. For a brief ninety minutes every Wednesday, time is displaced and we gather to read and discuss fine writing. Our tastes are eclectic—from Jeffers to James Joyce. This spring we read Irish poets with a healthy mixture of Robert Hass columns, book reviews, journals, and articles sent from friends, bits and pieces from *Harper's*, and the occasional Carruth poem on CD. When they read their work, the others listen and respond as if it were lightning on the tongue. The burly Greg who almost died from a nerve disease, now back in the workshop, anchors the give-and-take: "Cut out some of the emotion and say what you mean. Who you trying to impress anyway?" Ten years for the law clerk to arc the frustration of a beginner with the appetite of a poet.

Early May, and a new man sits across the table. I extend my hand and ask his name: "Nobody." I ask again. "That's what they call me on the yard."

"Do you have a name?" I ask, feeling I may go wrong.

"Lonnie."

"I want to use Lonnie in here—" my last offering before he grabs the reading from the Formica, the poems that frequently confuse and occasionally please. Johnny tells me on the telephone, "The new guys are lost—"

I want to say, "Any more than I?"

"Maybe we can read something about form, about each line—"

Outside, walking the perimeter back to the gatehouse, Adam asks how I knew Frank O'Connor's story was a kind of desperate rendering of 1950s Ireland. Adam, who has struggled more than any man to know a poem, to bend its fine legs and set before him the words that come so hard. Hunger again. "How is it Yeats knew so much, made all those disparate references to an imagined place, Byzantium? How did he do it? I feel so stupid reading him." I wish I could dispatch truth from some far corner of the universe to answer Adam's question. Putting my socks on in the morning, I tell my wife, "What am I doing teaching Yeats? He intimidates the hell out of me." She chortles from the bathroom, "You've never done what's easy."

Adam's almost ready to leave. This is the hardest part of prison: the last waiting, the unknowing months and days when tomorrow really is closer to superstition than reality, when the yard becomes a finite square on which to live. No mistakes, no furtive eyes, no shank from the unseen hand. All of the old ones we talk about in past tenses—"Remember what a cocky SOB he was?"—have stiffened through this maze of patience and muddled endurance. I liken it to the final weeks before birth, when a woman has to find strength she only imagined months before. Adam, who after nine years in and out of the workshop, is writing lines that ring sorrow from the bars.

A young man holds a chill
In afternoon sunshine
Of a prison visiting room
He cannot hear the rotor blades
Twenty hours away, as Careflight waves off,
His body bled white from the shank.
Years later my mother
Would walk by the same vending machine
That ate dead change

Until I almost forget it is prison, not poetry, he is trying to leave.

At a dinner house in nearby Reno I recall the miles Sam ran on the yard, carefully measuring out the distance of fences squared. He is one we talk of in past tenses, having squeezed through time's hourglass. Although Sam is not here, I cannot embrace his fiancée without thinking of him. Nor can my family. A busy manager, she serves us more Italian food and red wine than we can possibly consume. This by way of saying they are happy. Sam is in graduate school and working with people who could not stop drinking or drugging their way down. An old, worn story that has wrinkled Sam's face, but out of this darkness has come some peace. I remember the poem he wrote about taking X-rays of a new prison employee, how the woman thought he was an employee before she squirmed back into her nightgown when he told her otherwise—an embarrassment he shared.

But the new ones still look upon me perplexed: Peter, Angel, and Winston—a Texan marooned in the high desert—and most unlikely is James, who has cataloged all references to learning through his graduate degree and could, I suspect, teach this class but for the saving that must come to his life. This ninety minutes that would otherwise disappear. He hands me the *New York Times Book Review* and I tell him it will only sit in a pile of postponed reading. But it is given to savor, and days later I do, asking who is teaching whom, my qualifications for wrestling with words a scant quarter century of trying.

Tiny opens the door to the library, late from work with draft-
ing students, ponytail curled to shoulder blades. His angular face
is an off-and-on presence in the workshop for years. Tiny, the
painter of J.R.R. Tolkien fantasy who stretches far to read and
write of the closing day:

Embrace

Night wraps me in her arms, filling me, my soul,
darkness.
Lying on this narrow rack, a gaping hole through
the springs where my weight rests, I contemplate
another mundane day, passing uneventful, thankful
for the night, pleasant is
darkness.

At the end of the semester I ask them to pick the books they
would like to read in the fall from the bullet reviews in the poetry
issue of the *Bloomsbury Review*, then thumb the Daedalus catalog
for any poet who looks like he will breathe new life into the room.
Which, I would imagine, makes me guilty of trafficking in books.
But they stretch time to mean something where there is very little
meaning, save survival.

We have called prison many things but rarely by its true name—
slow death. The lives that skin the yard know its name and, I suspect, a few others closer to death than I. What does matter is that
we do what we can, if only the act of putting faces to memory so
that we never forget that *all* life is sacred. Not just life we see, but
life closed to human hands. In this, we are like so many others who
have tried to judge, and failing, sentenced ourselves to live with its
shame and hypocrisy. Prison can only be measured by its losses,
the ignominious consequences of grief and revenge. Until human
dignity returns to this equation, I doubt it will change.

Out of the small hope that a poem would tender a life, the
workshop has grown to be part of many lives and, perhaps, an

island of perpetual wonder where the very act of reading is a political one. Writing, even more so. No good-time credit, no grades, no college units, just a desire to write. That is what draws them to the workshop. What happens after that is a mystery, but some write poems that for an instant—maybe eight or nine calendar years—keep them alive.

—2001—

15

Looking for William Stafford on the Yard

The late Thomas Ferté introduced me to William Stafford. Tom was the founding editor of *Calapooya Collage*, the eclectic journal that emanated from Western Oregon State College every August. Tom was very close to William, Dorothy, and their children—as were so many Oregonians—but it was through Tom's eyes that I got to know William Stafford. Late in Stafford's life, Tom edited and printed two beautiful books by and for William Stafford from Adrienne Lee Press: *The Long Sigh the Wind Makes* and *Stafford's Road*. The latter were poems to his dear friend from many poets, and it is hard not to think of both men as being here still—in fact, I often do. I say hello to them and share their stories freely, especially when I'm teaching the prison poetry workshop where such things are ephemeral and for many of the men, this life, the life you and I partake in, has not existed for some time. Anything I can do to make poetry relevant to what they experience is worth doing. I shared these books, I shared them repeatedly, as I did all of the good journals that Tom produced.

I have been looking for William Stafford with the men in the workshop for more than twenty years. Every year we make a concerted effort to find him. We return to one of his essays, read it aloud, and try to implement what he said about the process of writing. We read his poems to discover what it means to keep writing, especially when we run into difficulty, which on the yard is everywhere. Reading Stafford in the workshop is a paradox. I remind the men that he was a pacifist, a conscientious objector when it was not cool—and still he found his way to poetry. Maybe it is the example of his life that I want them to emulate: write, whatever the consequence. Then I paraphrase his admonition: lower your standards and keep writing, because to write poetry in prison is just as radical a choice as he made to choose peace over war.

Two of the men in this poetry workshop just went up for parole—again, for the fifth or sixth time—and may or may not be granted parole by the time I return. They have been with me for the duration. This requires infinite patience—to practice an art form inside when there is little chance of release. It is almost a Buddhist principle to rid oneself of all things save this kind of deliberate practice. Something in Stafford's poetry and essays defies the logic of the outside world and embraces this patience, this willingness to be vulnerable among people and things, to observe or say what must be said. This quality of being a resilient observer is yet another part of Stafford's character to emulate—an example would be "Dreams to Have," in *Writing the Australian Crawl*:

> I don't think there is any poet writing today, man or
> woman, who is as great as Emily Dickinson.

> For me, writing . . . is a process of relying on immediate
> pervasive feelings, not an escape from them at all . . .

Stafford's ideas are antithetical to being in prison because they require personal risk, something that takes months and years to develop in the workshop, as he writes in "Whose Tradition":

> To curry favor by saying what you do not mean, or what
> you do not feel, is as damaging in poetry as it is in politics
> or business or other parts of life.

How can the men avoid such conversation on the yard and by inference, such falsehoods in their art? These are not easy questions and Stafford admits as much, but we return to his poetry to look deeper into the riddle of his example. Sometimes we pretend to know enough to fathom the distance between the yard and Stafford's inquisitive character. That is when I listen to the two men who have been with me the longest. They lead the others; they show them how to approach this incredibly demanding art of poetry with patience. I listen to them and think they have more knowledge than most who study this subject in college. But I am biased—I have watched them sift through years of practice set in this place where hope, even the hope of finding release, is blunted.

What saves them, just as I imagine what saved Stafford, is the imagination: they see the particles of light beyond the chapel where we meet and try to absorb what he and so many others have written. They lean on these writers for instruction, for exposure to technique, and for a critical perspective on the melancholy journey through much of what passes as poetry. Occasionally we get fresh perspectives. A young Iraq veteran has joined the workshop. His work reminds me of an early Brian Turner. He has every reason to be angry, to be a witness when the thought of war is foreign to most of his generation, and yet he is a witness inside, which it seems is also the perspective of the poet. Last week I shared with the men the late Vietnamese poet Nguyen Chi Thien, who was shackled for most of his adult life before finally being granted asylum in the United States. It was the imagination that kept him alive. He talked often about being in conversation with the French poets and then did the unthinkable: memorized all of his poems because he had no hope of being released. Stafford welcomes imaginary intrusions, even ones we may not choose, as he expresses in "Finding What the World Is Trying to Be": ". . . I would rather be whole-hearted and be welcome about anything I write."

William Stafford came to Nevada in July 1989, for a writer's conference. He worked tirelessly over the two days. My good friend Bill Cowee, the conference organizer, was beaming because Stafford had made the trip from Oregon to the state capital, Carson City. What struck me was Stafford's vision of poetry in the American grain: wrought from particulars, he wove a universe of localities far beyond the Pacific Northwest. When I started the workshop a few months later, I tried to relate the many anecdotes and memories of other Stafford encounters. What finally emerged was a poet of disciplined awareness and joy—the man who woke early to write every day and the poet who articulated the experience of his senses. It was not unusual unless, of course, you tried to do it—as articulated in "Whispered into the Ground,"

> The wind keeps telling us something
> we want to pass on to the world:
> Even far things are real.

Before he left for home, Stafford wrote Bill Cowee a poem on the conference letterhead. It was an evocation of the high desert where we live and more—an unspoken urge to uncover its beauty. When I shared that poem with the men in the workshop, they were awed because they felt like it was their poem, too. It transcended landscape to behold, as a child would, this place.

When Bill Cowee died, the poem was given to a family friend. I had not seen it for years. All I had was the memory of those Stafford lines written in his hand, almost effortlessly. It took seven years to find the poem in Stafford's posthumous collection, *Even in Quiet Places*, but that doesn't surprise me. Stafford didn't write for the literary lights, so a poem—even a really good one, which it was—could be left in Carson City as a gift. When I began to work on this essay, I called Bill Cowee's indefatigable caregiver, Terry Forde, to ask if she knew where the poem might be. It was stored in her garage with Bill Cowee's papers. She gave me the poem, which I cherish because of Stafford's presence in this place, then and now. Here is the last stanza from "Looking Out in the Morning: Carson City":

But the universe turned over once and stayed,
when I looked up and my child across all
that ever happened or would happen was staring
everything that there is into my eyes.

In 1991, the year Tom Ferté published his two-volume set, Michael Markee and Vincent Wixon produced two videos on William Stafford, *The Life of the Poem* and *What the River Says*, with helpful teaching notes inside. When we watched these videos in the workshop, I no longer had to transcribe who William Stafford was. The men could see that he cared deeply for his craft and gave them repeated examples of how to do it. They followed his practice of observation and careful movement beyond simple description. When the proverbial question arose about how Stafford sprang from the deer to all of us when we read "Traveling through the Dark," I deferred because there is something unanswerable about that poem—just as there is in so many of his poems: "I thought hard for us all—my only swerving—, / then pushed her over the edge into the river."

That's how it should remain. I am not here to dissect— Wordsworth said this long before—but I challenged them to pay attention, to listen to the reverberations in his lines, the tension, the apparent ease with which line followed line, and the deceptively uncertain quality of their revelations.

These are poetic qualities to aspire to, but Stafford made them seem *possible*.

That's why I turned to him—on the yard, so little is possible. The workshop is the last station before feeling shuts down. I ask the men to return to the language of feeling, and frequently quote Richard Shelton, himself a veteran of decades of teaching prison workshops. Only at this most vulnerable place can the men begin to say what hell has become for them. Stafford made writing this down possible. He never veered from what was just beyond cognition—that well of unconscious belief and foment. Like him—this gray-haired man who validated their struggle—they had to trust the process of writing to reflect upon their situation, and then proceed. This is a powerful tool when you have so few tools to believe in. The young guys in the workshop don't know that I have shared Stafford for years, but they will hear him soon. They will hear him when we read his work again this January in honor of his birth. They will follow the example of the older men in the workshop who understand him to be a mentor. They will read his poems when I leave the yard.

Tom Ferté did something else for my understanding of William Stafford: he opened up an entire galaxy of writers from the Pacific Northwest, people who made good books in Stafford country. They were drawn to the annual publication of his journal that took place at Powell's Bookstore. It was something to behold: Grey Elliot reciting a Dickinson poem on demand; Dorothy Stafford watching William or Kim read; Tom Ferté heralding most everyone, including the unofficial king of Portland, Bud Clark; Carolyn Kizer shining her light on the next young poet or poetess; and readings by Ingrid Wendt, Ralph Salisbury, John Daniel, Joseph Soldati, Paulann Petersen, Carlos Reyes, Vern Rutsala, Ursula K. Le Guin, Lisa Steinman, Jane Glazer, Madeline DeFrees, and how many more—people for whom poetry was as necessary as rain. I learned that Stafford came from this shared conviction that you could write and belong to a place. And for reasons I will never understand, Tom invited me into this community, so that by the time Stafford finally reached Nevada, I could not help but think of him in this context. There was the man I knew, to be sure, a poet of many minds, never easy to pin down or explain, but a poet who nonetheless was a member of a community of writers and readers. These people were friends and colleagues and had one thing in common: the written word.

Much as Stafford made writing seem possible for the men in the workshop, his community helped me to imagine there could be a similar community of writers here in Nevada. Something must be said for this: this is seed planting, the cultivation of a place in which we can write and coexist as writers. Poetry requires supreme, isolating effort and hence my desire for such a community. Nevada does not have Oregon's poetic legacy and this place surely cannot be the green one that he came from. But Stafford's personal commitment to his family and friends, his involvement in the political landscape, his willingness to be an emissary for poetry—these are what I draw upon to stoke the fires of community here at home.

MORE THAN ONCE I left the workshop with a contradiction. Out of their desire to understand the first steps to write, there was an overwhelming need for order, something that Stafford simply wouldn't give. I tried to assuage their uneasiness with his process, insisted that reading and time would be the greater teachers. One poem, in particular, seemed to be the greatest contradiction. How could a pacifist write this poem? How could Stafford be so certain about this instrument when it stood for the very thing he opposed? I had no answers to their puzzled expressions. We just read the poem, ".38," over and over, until we could find a way into the duality that so often accompanies his art.

> This metal has come to look at
> your eye. Look at its eye—that
> stare that can't lose.

> There's no grin like a gun—
> as if only its calm
> could soothe your hand.

> But metal is cold,
> cold. In the night, in the risk,
> it's a touch of the dead.

> It's a cold world.

This poem from *My Name Is William Tell* required no transcription. I didn't share it because it was a prison trope; I shared it because Stafford opened the revolver to consider just how far it had traveled, how it did not judge its reader, how it chose indiscriminately. These are things a pacifist sees; these are stories a pacifist hears. A pacifist learns to walk alone. A pacifist intuits risk as an advantage: having no things foreshadows poetic vision. That is how Bashō wandered and why Su Tung-p'o was exiled. Without the lens of perfection, they could not be something else. Stripped to its essence, poetry comes into the world like light and leaves even less visibly and its practitioners expect the light to be sufficient.

Why is this necessary to practice? Without concern for its place in the world, poetry has purchase in the intrinsic activity of being present. Stafford did not wait for intention to write. Stafford wrote to affirm the particulars of a pacifist's journey: isolation, resolution, and forbearance, living, as it were, without comfort. Stafford's work was inclusive of others—the viewpoints, aspirations, and divisions—and able to set things apart from what divides as in these lines from "Scenes of Rain in the Mountains":

You hear the lake and you fall and are saved,
again and again, in the kind eye,
deep and gray, millions of times.

Deceptively direct *and* complex, Stafford's poetry was vision for a world beyond a limited range of seeing. Every day he returned to the well of being alone to see things, to record their existence.

To reflect and write like this is almost beyond comprehension in a prison. It has no place where violence begets violence, which is why I share Stafford's poetry. I ask the men to emulate his vulnerable stance, to let down their guard and walk with him. This takes years; trust is not easily found. They distrust my intention, initially fearing what it might mean: I'm weak, I can't cope, or I put on a strong face. Poetry requires none of this, only that you look inside.

One of my closest friends in the workshop was paroled. He had been out five years when he threw a rod in his pickup. He was sitting on the side of the road when a highway patrolman asked him if there was anything wrong. My friend insisted on showing him his identification, said it was a requirement of parole. The patrolman asked how he survived prison? My friend said it was a poetry class: "One of poetry's first requirements is that you examine yourself." Not a small lesson but one Stafford understood and wrote about for sixty years. He is not without his faults, nor are the men in the workshop. They just aspire to learn such lessons. Inside or out, it matters not. The hard work, breaking open a vein to affirm allegiance to a line of poetry, happens everywhere. I've asked them repeatedly whose allegiance they serve, and for what reasons. Stafford answers in the dark. No one chooses prison any more than they choose hunger. Poetry is the medium through which they pass to the outside, even if it is only imagined. Stafford knew this. He passed through to the outside as a conscientious objector and his beliefs became secondary to their presence in his poetry. I hear him every time I read him—"Awaken, awaken, you have much to be startled by" (my paraphrase). In the workshop, that is like announcing the sun has risen. Reading him permits expansion; they rise in small stanzas, give credence to an ally of warmth. That's why it's such a mystery—no one believes it's possible.

Here are some questions, in no particular order, the men posed to Stafford:

Can you bend the rules?
Can you surrender to anonymity?
Can you start over as a child—every day?
Can you believe what's around you?
Can you survive poetry's unintended clues?
Can you live alone with your thoughts?

Can you recommend the art form to the warden?
Can you sit without answers?
Can you suffer the indignity of having no success?

Here are some answers they may have intimated:

And if
Because
I don't know
I cannot
Go away.

— 2018 —

16

The Magnetic Pull in a Poem

Many readers find modern poetry difficult,
and difficult in a special sense.
—CLEANTH BROOKS, 1939

. . . the small, closed world of poetry.
—MARGARET ATWOOD, 1991

THERE IS A THUNDERHEAD moving in, black, gray, and white, blue where it has not yet reached. But soon it will reach into our lives and root out the dry with wet. All of us have touched rain, all of us. We shy from the fear such clouds incite. We gnarl bedposts with grief and wait for the clearing sky. Such is the influence of a cloud.

And a cloud restores.

Into that cloud comes a raven, the birth of an image.

I have hungered for that confluence of great untamed sky and ravenous bird to bear down on poetry, have scoured its arid landscape, indeed have prayed for rain to fall from its inky presence, but found little moisture.

As a twenty-year-old I wished for a poetry that would scald me. As a poet who struggled with the texture of his toil for the next quarter century, this hope belied the reign of private verse. A reluctant Luddite, I have been hushed for asking where is the tedium of our lives? Where are the poems that move us to tears with the taste of such feeling?

This small crown of words is my attempt to find the junction of reader and writer, the interstices of poet and public that hoped-for union about which Walt Whitman spoke.

Not long ago, I returned to the ancients with Red Pine (*Finding Them Gone*) as he retraced the steps of the Chinese poets for whom the act of writing was reason enough to do so—Li Po, Su Tung-p'o, Pai Chu-yi, each headstone a murmur in the wind. Their words gave flesh to the daily grist—loss, tedium, or the search for shelter—with which one could identify, touch, and retreat from. All wrote poems with a force of gravity in them, one that accounted for the poet's most personally held beliefs. They sent angels into every line, every cherished pore of the poem, as in this one Pai wrote in Hangchou, "Saying Goodbye to the Townspeople":

> Elders crowded the road leading out of town
> at the farewell banquet the wine overflowed
> I didn't sit under a pear tree
> I don't understand this torrent of tears
> people here were poor yet my taxes were heavy
> farmers were hungry and their fields were parched
> all I'm leaving is a lake full of water
> to help when the years turn bad

Much like the thunderhead moving in, there is a place for intellectual rigor in a poem, just as there is a place for emotional scrutiny ("Only what is human can be truly foreign," wrote Wislawa Szymborska). Both qualities should be honored as the coil of imagination unwinds around them. But to burden a poem with the ornaments of art—whatever the tastes or the time—is pitiful.

To bring context to this cartography of poetry, I return to the nineteenth century. Leo Tolstoy wrote a scathing review of three "new" French poets, entitled *What Is Art?* He asked "[how am I to read] obscurity elevated into dogma among the new poets?" Tolstoy was wrong about Arthur Rimbaud, Charles Baudelaire, and Paul Verlaine—they haunted generations to come—but the veracity of his question is undeniable. When the intent of an idea is blistered, it cannot hide from the

cells that divide. So too with a poem. It must first be a living or-
ganism. Then we move to define what we value in a poem. After
Anna Karenina, after *War and Peace*, Tolstoy wrote this meager
folio of essays. And to whom was it directed? Not the reader, but
us—the poets who triangulate the ephemeral but neglect the
human. A good many critics have gone down this road but few
have asked so basic a question—how can I understand this inde-
cipherable poem?

One hundred years later, this move to decipher, to decode,
even derail, accrues in the journals of literature. It is commonplace to read of the follies in contemporary poetry, each "new"
school accusing its predecessor of greater degrees of detritus,
with poetry the antihero of the literate class. Indeed, many have
claimed it for their king and marched from its soil triumphantly,
having conquered the region once again.

Poetry belongs to no one. Charles Wright wrote, "The New
Poem . . . will not reveal its name." It exists in the landscape of
a fertile mind, redolent of possibility. When Neruda walked into
the mining halls and the smelters fearing for his life, he did not
taunt the miners' intelligence. He read to his beloved Chileans,
and they chanted until he came back, knowing their poet had spoken a language they lived in those bloody copper mills. It is not
the job of art to ruin a thing; it has nothing to do with ruin. Art is
an act of reclamation, the taking back, bit by stony bit, of oneself
before the all too final moment of dying returns. Poetry is the
viscera that precedes language. If there is a magnetic north in a
poem—and mine is surely different from what I am led to believe
about polarity—it is this quality of feeling, the unmistakable flesh
that sets bone to life. Its presence must never be tampered with
as if it were a toy.

If you think of just one poem you *love* by Elizabeth Bishop, T.
S. Eliot, or Ezra Pound, you know they sing the words with feel-
ing, just as Gerard Manley Hopkins, Thomas Hardy, and Emily
Dickinson did before them. But the choices they made were not

arbitrary. Instead, they focused on the poem's redemptive quality—a sense that our lives have not been wasted—and it is this quality that first speaks to the reader. This is part of the magnetic pull in a poem, what I believe to be true north, something we can point to for direction. There are few words for this transcription. It is the veneration of self on paper, the emptying of one's self to print.

A poem moves over things we cannot see—it precedes voice; it is silence presaging sound. Frost said that all five senses must be in a poem, but the spirit, the thing unseen, must also be present for the poem to finally transcend experience, emotion, intellect ("We all must bow down to *l'homme—ou la femme—d'esprit*," said Hayden Carruth). This transcendent voice cannot be prescribed in a poem. For a poem to be transcendent, it *must* be written. Stanley Kunitz talks about trying *not* to write. This is what he means—he knows this quality is fleeting. Form brings a poem to its proper place, but a poem without spirit is a poem devoid of any emotional depth. What a poet like John Ashbery lacks in clarity has never been accounted for in rudimentary terms. "Hermetic," my friend says when she refers to poetry that is impenetrable. There is nothing to rely on save the empty stations of language. Where is the human frailty that would touch the mother on a bus? Sure Ashbery—but it could be any number of others—has made the connection more than once, but the thrust of the poetry is to a north that cannot account for the lack of people. The spirit languishes; the poem dies on the page.

Poets and their poems are pulled by their influences. If the magnetic pull in such a poem is ideas, the sought-after gravity is unspoken, not known, but calling infinitely to vicarious experience. This kind of poem may be desired, but it stifles many readers. A terrible generalization, I know, except when you stare into the faces at a school, library, or bookstore—the faces of people who want to hear a poem that is remotely spun from the web of their lives.

If, on the other hand, my compass points to feeling, not the mask of words, if it points to the frailty of human expression, if it teeters on posts of recognition, the vulnerable qualities that make us so fallible, if it is directed at any of these, then the reader will seize it as a piece of life that flitters from him, as a hint of unspoken proportions. The poet has functioned as many things through the years, but above all, he has functioned as conscience. To swim in words with no bearing, no reference to even the smallest point of personal, of home, is little more than exercise. Not my north, but a north we recognize to be more than a totem existence.

Tolstoy's point was that we have no business acting so arrogantly. Even though Richard Howard decried the loss of poetry to the public transit systems, art is not made for the blessed few. The reason Alexander Pushkin's bust was surrounded by people and flowers on a cold October Tuesday one hundred fifty years after his death was that Muscovites knew him to speak their innermost desires. That is not a mystery.

The steady outpouring of unreadable, private verse should alarm us. It has lost us an audience. The public is convinced that poetry is difficult, arcane, and desirous of no one. What matters is what's on the page, and there is precious little in these poems to make such a claim. I'm asking that we rethink the norm for what is cogent in a poem.

A poem pulls from the inside. It pulls long to its origins and returns with each reading, evanescent over time. It is not Robert Lowell's simplistic reference to William Carlos Williams of the "cooked versus the raw," not the metered toil of Robert Frost, not Randall Jarrell's advice to Stanley Elkin careening through the cornfields of Iowa—cut that line. A poem is the Patagonia of our individual landscape, the four compass points that we navigate for a lifetime. They are unrelenting in their telling. It is the layering of a life, the shards of experience piled one on another that distill such a thing as poetry. The poems that last are from poets that people have known as salt or wine on their tongues—Dylan Thomas, Boris Pasternak, César Vallejo.

Before Su Tung-p'o was exiled to the island of Hainan, he wrote a poem to his late wife, "Ten Years—Dead and Living Dim and Draw Apart":

> . . . In a dream last night suddenly I was home.
> By the window of the little room
> you were combing your hair and making up.
> You turned and looked, not speaking,
> only lines of tears coursing down—
> year after year will it break my heart?
> The moonlit grave,
> its stubby pines—

No one needs a code to enter this poem. The blue hour of doubt rages in all of us. Su Tung-p'o had the courage to articulate it. His magnetic north was human suffering, what he knew to be true for the laborers and the people who would shudder in the face of words. That is why we read him nearly one thousand years later. We do not read him because of his ability to hide original meaning in text; we do not translate him because of his ability to swallow whole passages of feeling with inference. We read him to know the humility of what he lost. The darkness is not a friend, and we do not read to befriend it. If your words must pull you hither, go with them, but do not tell us of a place that never existed and will us to follow with the ephemeral.

I like to think it is no coincidence that *fear* follows *fealty* in my *American Heritage Dictionary*. *Fealty* is the Latinate derivative of *faithfulness*. Underlying the twin poles of magnetic north and its opposite—the absence of feeling, of meaning—are the emotional correlates: love and fear. To write a poem without faith is to distrust the very elements of one's essence—the core markings we associate with being human. Fear cannot be a place of origin, rather a place of escape. Escape from what one knows to be true. To hollow a poem from its core, to deny its fealty, is to write in the service of fear.

In its plainest, undressed form, the poem is passion. However it should finally be embellished; it is ultimately a roil of human emotion. All other masks, the art mask, the erudite mask, the diffident mask, reduce a poem to words without feeling, without experience. In short, it is little more than a puzzle, not a poem. The poet must not fall prey to its spell: the willful disregard of meaning. This is an old saw in art—from painting to choreography—is it private or public? More often than not, it is both elements, but the harness to which the composition is leashed is fundamentally human, else it fails as an essential arc of experience. It is an ornament with no remote tangent to our lives.

All of this is patently obvious to the banker, the plumber, and the man on the street, and yet we squalor print in the name of what must be left misunderstood. I am not decrying mystery in a poem. I crave mystery in a poem but it is the pull toward unreasonable doubt, the nascent flesh scrubbed out of a poem and in its place the terrible soldiers of disregard. Disregard for the bone and flesh that make up our scudding toward final ends. We have no capacity to doubt veracity. We doubt chicanery and imitation. We doubt the thing made in its own image. We doubt the darkness when fear is entreated like a friend because none of it is true.

We do not seek original thought, but thought originally rendered. For a poem to have any corollary with being, it must first start as a reckoning with experience, an utterance of faith that what is lived is real, and whether translated to mean real in the mind or the body (not René Descartes's dualism), it is being written in service to that other. To not know this when one sits down to write a poem is to render the poem obsolete. Some of our best writing has come from our outsiders—Adrian Louis, Jimmy Santiago Baca, Bruce Weigl, and Yusef Komunyakaa—and more recently Reginald Dwayne Betts, Zeina Hashem Beck, and Ocean Vuong. Mold breakers, they don't hide from the truth in their poems.

This truth is missing from the high-tension lines of much poetry because the words do not have origins in experience. They are like fire tossed from the fictive elements of syllables, not from the coals of one's central beliefs. If the magnetic pull in a poem is nothing more than one's most personally held beliefs about staying alive, then the poet must make that known in a poem. For the reader to be anything but bewildered, it must first be true to one's own experience and not the decadence of a clever mind. We must scribe soul from a rock much as a petroglyph is left to speak without explanation.

Whatever else may be said, a poet will not end this discussion. It will be a reader, steadfast with a book of poems at his or her bedside.

IN THE LATE 1950s the painter Stephen Greene abandoned figurative for abstract art, as if excising a blemish on the pallet. In that small act, he similarly abandoned a threshold of comprehension that we have given over to the visual artists. I have no truck with edge breaking in the visual arts, but the visual image does not require a reader's understanding. Taut with metaphor and impression, sight is but one of the sense organs, and the painting may or may not succeed on those terms. When poets take such chances, they do so at the reader's expense. This litany of impression in poetry—fireworks, as a friend calls it—asks very little of us as readers, save to be sense organs for the immediate, the transparent. What started as an earnest desire to break from poetic tradition has since become a sort of tyranny over language, the power to refuse understanding, as if that were somehow vaunted, more elemental than the connection of writer to reader.

There are people lined up on both sides of this fence, but they seem to miss the point. The point is not the loss of meter in contemporary verse. Even when Vassar Miller was alive, she was looked upon as an anachronism. Nor is it the melancholy searching of Sylvia Plath or Anne Sexton. It is a poetry that has become "so derivative as to become unintelligible." How is it that Marianne Moore could foresee the undoing of what was only then an incipient urge to distill abstraction from the poem? As poets, we simply do not have the luxury to abandon understanding any more than we have permission to abandon ink or paper. Our tools come with certain requirements, one of them being the juxtaposition of thought and emotion—not irrelevant sisters on the page, but formidable adversaries brought together for a leap to freshness, to something not previously beheld. A poet chiefly is the author of wings, flight to that holy and central place of our essence, and he cannot do this with abstraction alone. Whether or not the painter can remains to be seen. Mark Rothko wore thin the horizontal line, but we do not synthesize the painting for abstract understanding of human values. A poem, by definition, must succeed on other terms. It is not simply a flight of fancy; it is "the authority of direct perception" as critic Meyer Schapiro wrote of Claude Monet's painting.

A poem is not a license to obfuscate; it is a tendril of belief held close to the primacy of human experience. The magnetic pull in a poem is nothing less than a sacred force with which it must reckon. To ignore this most urgent requirement is to render the poem a fetal understanding.

I have heard poets discard all notion of common perception as if it were possible to avoid our stake in art. Ask an English teacher why poetry remains an enigma. For all but a few, the transit is not set on the joy of reading Frost, Jeffers, or Whitman; it is culled from the burden of repetition of their prior learning. In a word, the teachers fear poetry, and do so because it refutes what they know to be true—the poem is an abstraction of their lives.

For a poem to live anywhere but in the mind, it must have a thread of recognition else it is little more than stone on the page. Not a stone of my making, but a stone of artifice, one that belies a magnetic north as compass point—the pull to our most vulnerable, exposed selves. In this the poets are complicitous. They have chosen language over meaning and no amount of dialogue will hide this. A poem is not a decoration. It is a central story that we heard as children and that we hear in death, and I am loath to hear it now. "My life was never so precious / To me as now," James Wright wrote in desperation. An apology felt as prayer in a poem.

This is the compelling emotion we must aspire to, the final correlate to north that I struggle to know these many years. It is not an ending but a constant revelation of self in art.

— 2001 —

17

Sing, Before the Long Silence Returns

RIDING A GREYHOUND BUS into San Francisco, a young man was reading *A Coney Island of the Mind* to anyone who would listen. "Poetry, man. This is poetry." It was 1967 and that was my introduction to the words of Lawrence Ferlinghetti and the long roots of New Directions Publishing.

Hundreds of miles and dozens of books later, I read the winter news of 1997: four seminal figures in contemporary poetry had passed from the scene. And while theirs is a legacy that someone much larger than I must name, the void left by Denise Levertov, William Matthews, James Laughlin, and Allen Ginsberg will not soon be filled.

Robert Hass, in a column for the *Washington Post Book World: Poet's Choice*, quoted an early poem by Denise Levertov about the loss of Williams and Pound:

This is the year the old ones,
the old great ones
leave us alone on the road.

He was trying to say goodbye to a poet who wrote these words in 1963—trying, as we must, to make sense of the silence.

Not that their leaving should be any different—we all must pass—but the absence of these four poets will be felt for decades. To reconcile it, I must return to Rapallo, Italy, in the 1930s, where the young James Laughlin found Ezra Pound decoding a Chinese dictionary, trying in vain to read sense into the small characters. Frustrated by Laughlin's early poems, Pound wisely counseled him to become a publisher if he wanted to put his imprint on literature.

And publish Laughlin did—for more than half a century. I count on my shelves fifteen authors published by New Directions, many more copies given away, others lost or hiding in the stacks on my floor. From Dylan Thomas to Gary Snyder, I read them by the season. Not a December goes by without *A Child's Christmas in Wales*. This chapbook, filled with woodcuts, brings some sense of hope to the men in a nearby prison poetry workshop, just as school children light up when they hear Kenneth Patchen, William Everson, or Pablo Neruda. Laughlin had the good sense to reach beyond the ordinary and the literary tendrils are spreading to this day.

There are few contemporary poets who cannot trace some part of their history to Laughlin. It is no coincidence that Denise Levertov's poem was an homage to William Carlos Williams. She was among the scores of poets encouraged by him, and like him she would eventually turn to New Directions to publish her books. As a teacher, she was steadfast in her desire to see poetry perfected on the page. Levertov taught me that a poem is not simply a vessel for expression, but an ark for the precise, delicate transcription of feeling and purpose. Whether good or bad, she never minced words. When it came my turn, she roiled at my obvious mistakes. Without precision, she intimated, the poet cannot express the visceral lens through which we sort our lives. I can almost hear her say to us, "You must bring a critical eye to your work."

It was the voice of a poet who spoke in that apartment at Stanford, a woman who taught herself to read and write poetry through years of hard work—nothing more, nothing less. It was the monotone exasperation of an English nurse who willed her way into the world of modern letters. Years earlier, in one of my first college classes, it was her poems we read. And there were many poets who early on championed her work. Hayden Carruth wrote in the foreword to *The Voice That Is Great Within Us*:

> I remember a day when my mail unexpectedly brought me a little pamphlet of poems so beautifully articulated within their own intentions that I spent the afternoon reading them over and over: my first experience with Denise Levertov.

I once read to my father from Levertov's *To Stay Alive: Poems 1968–1972*. His curt remark: "She has a political viewpoint—and if I don't agree with it?" Meaning, her art was never far from turmoil, which of course is why I shared it with him. Much has been written about the dearth of poetry on subjects other than the self. This was never an issue for Levertov, and it no doubt kept her from mainstream American readers. But her best political poems were poems of craft—"V Report" is just one example:

> O holy innocents! I have
> no virtue but to praise
> you who believe
> life is possible...

During the antinuclear campaign, she contributed "Watching Dark Circle" to the anthology *Writing in a Nuclear Age*. This is a poem about killing pigs to simulate the effects of radiation. So frightening were the images that I see those pigs burning to this day. This is what she meant by precision.

During the 1960s she was the poetry editor for the *Nation* and later *Mother Jones*. It was in this capacity—her critical eye—that she came upon the work of Jimmy Santiago Baca. As a poet frequently in the maelstrom of protest, she must have felt a certain respect for the work of another who was imprisoned. To her credit, she found in Baca's poetry a passionate street wisdom that most can only imitate. Much like her mentor, Williams, she encouraged those early drafts and wrote the introduction to *Martin & Meditations on the South Valley* (New Directions, 1986). She was self-taught, self-reliant, stormy, and strong.

These were words she knew well: the long history of others whose voices were silenced. We owe much to her tenacity, her stubborn refusal to say no. Later in life, her poems and essays returned to her Catholic faith, the woman made stark by her years. I will not forget her playing the piano in that dimly lit apartment on campus, trying always to master something larger than herself, trying to set the sound on fire.

Caught in the hail of stateside Vietnam, William Matthews was twenty-nine when he, Robert Bly, and Allen Ginsberg read before 2,500 people in Portland, Oregon. And not just once, but twice, because there were more than 5,000 people, and the hall held only half that number. He must have been scared to death—so young to be on the podium. I remember him much differently, as a middle-aged father, with less hair and a voice cracked with cigarette smoke. Whether in Berkeley or Reno, when he read his poems, they were like long riffs from a jazz club in "crass" New York. He seemed to possess boundless wit—not one to limber up before going the whole night, then on to the plane that would carry him home. For Matthews, humor was central to his view of the world and his poetry. It kept him from taking all of it too seriously.

In our infrequent correspondence between readings, the question kept recurring—a midwesterner in New York? "I have a seven-room apartment and I love the faces—immigrants from all over the world." City College was the last place he taught. A friend to many students and colleagues, he was also generous with assistance. I remember him happiest when he met Pat, a fellow teacher from upstate. We had lunch in a basement café in his busy city. But then came the letter about her: "Pat is soldiering through chemotherapy."

A poet rarely finds quarter in the world; it may be a prerequisite for the words *I don't know*. But I was heartened to read Mark Strand's review of Matthews's *Foreseeable Futures*. This is "one of the best books of poetry in the last ten years." Although Matthews characteristically shunned such praise—in fact, disliked altogether the notion of poet as sage—his poems were transcending the eastern stairwell, they were moving in ways all their own. His earlier *Selected Poems and Translations, 1969–1991* include some that will last the distance—"Herd of Buffalo Crossing the Missouri on Ice," among them.

On the barn wall at Frost Place in Franconia, New Hampshire, is a poem that begins "So here the great man stood." William Matthews stood on that same porch fifty years later, taking stock of the valley below the White Mountains. Not much has changed since Frost's time save the influx of people during the summer workshop. Walking the trail behind the house dotted with Frost's poems, I wondered what finally led Matthews to call creation home. Matthews walked a different labyrinth to leave poems behind. He should not have gone so young, but it was how he started and I will try to remember that. The final lines from Violeta Parra's poem "Thanks to Life, (Gracias a la vida)" say this best:

> And so distinguish happiness from grief,
> the two ingredients that shape my song,
> and your song which is the same song
> and the song of everyone, that is my own song.
>
> Thanks to life which has given me so much.

Curiously, both William Matthews and Denise Levertov found solace in at least one poet who could not be more unlike them: Vassar Miller. But if the sound of Miller's voice should quiet such disparate souls, it is that singular appreciation of the aftermath of silence that drew them to her, as in "Precision":

> The leaves blow speaking
> green, lithe words
> in no man's language.

Although I would
translate them—better
living in silence

letting the leaves
breathe through me all men's
in no man's language.

William Matthews said of his brief tenure as poetry editor at Grove Press that the relationship between poet and publisher is of necessity adversarial. Perhaps not, but to say anything worthwhile, one must risk. James Laughlin knew this, and he constantly put his small house in jeopardy by publishing many poets no other firms would take a chance on—Nabokov, Miller, and Williams.

Nothing I have read comes closer to defining the doctor from Paterson than James Laughlin's chapbook *Remembering William Carlos Williams*. This long poem, which is part of Laughlin's book-length poem, *Byways*, stands as a crisp reminder that among the finest writers published by New Directions, the word is spoken one day and silenced the next. Williams self-published five books of poems before Laughlin came to him at age twenty-two and asked to be his publisher. It took guts and a good ear to make that leap, a leap he would not soon regret. Though theirs was not an easy relationship, they reconciled their differences and felt, I think, extreme kinship with one another.

Many years after that bus ride to San Francisco, I took my sons into City Lights Books, wanting to show them the literary birthplace of Jack Kerouac, Neal Cassady, and Ginsberg. By sheer coincidence, Ferlinghetti happened to be upstairs working. I told my sons, "This is the man who gave me poetry." He stood up and walked to the door and confided, "No one has ever said that to me." I thanked him, and my sons and I said goodbye—as if words could be enough.

Whatever you remember of *Howl & Other Poems*, the Six Gallery reading, and all of the nights to follow, Allen Ginsberg remains one of twentieth century's true believers. Although loathed by some, he has become the very definition of poetic respectability in the last decade. Stanford Library paid a million dollars for his personal effects. Over a period of nearly twenty years, I saw him give four readings, the best of which was when he was in his late sixties. In the midst of a terrible nationalism, he delivered a long, owlish poem on Desert Storm. For two hours he read some of his and others' most compelling poetry, putting himself on the line with every turn of phrase. Not all of the poems worked, but he mesmerized us with his indefatigable persona, his outright balls in the face of so much poetry that whimpers. Not one person in the standing-room audience of a thousand people left the room untouched. This is a man who sang "the body electric."

Robert Pinsky said, "Great writing makes us want to write." I can think of no greater legacy than that. These four poets—Levertov, Matthews, Laughlin, and Ginsberg—have written dozens of poems that will make others want to take up the pen, and make some keep writing when all else fails them. Each of these poets, in his or her own way, reminds us to sing before the long silence returns.

—1998—

Ismael 2018

III

What Border to Cross?

18

A Poet Returns to Ireland

THE GRAY LIGHT, the green shadow, the misted window. The hickory veil of memory. These things haunted me after a journey to Ireland, these and the discovery of so many poets, playwrights, and musicians. This was a journey to a place that heralded from so far that I could not recognize its name. But I would come to know its name as poetry.

I was hesitant to call myself Irish, much less a poet abroad. A storied place to begin, I touched down in Dublin, weary from some twenty hours of travel from Nevada. But this time it was sunny, midday, and greener than I could paint. I spent the day tracing family names—an American wandering in parish after parish, tickling one file, then the next, hoping to find a match: Griffin, McBride, Brennan, Hickey. The genealogist tells me I am four generations from the marriage that holds the key to our time in the new land. So I must query the vital records office in Buffalo, New York, where they set down and died. This to learn their faces, the mortar that held them all these years since the potato famine sent them fleeing for food. What a melancholy irony: 150 years later, I work with hungry children in a land where we shave potatoes for fast food.

I wanted to stay longer in Dublin. You cannot come here without a kind of prescient visit to all of them: Jonathan Swift on exhibit in the National Library, Bram Stoker's house across the street, and Joyce's ghost muttering in the closet. I live in a town where Mark Twain spent three brief years; much of English-language literature as we know it unfolded in three square blocks in Dublin. But this time I turned north, to the tiny village of Rostrevor, home to folksinger and peace activist Tommy Sands. For over two decades, he has broadcast a show on Saturday night on Belfast's Downtown Radio. When all talk of peace had nearly died in March 1998, he wrote and performed "Carry On" for Gerry Adams and David Trimble, music being the only voice both men could hear. Tommy lives quietly—to the outsider at least—on Carlingford Bay with his wife, Catherine. The phone rings for him to perform in Germany, Boston, Brittany, all hours, and yet he is more than civil with every repeated request.

Rain but deep rest. One more day and we would leave for Belfast en route to the writers' conference on Rathlin Island. The sun shone again. I was beginning to think this was another Ireland, a place devoid of gray. If such a place exists, it was on that road to the city so long under siege. But for the Peace Wall, the barricaded police headquarters, and Falls Road, Belfast is a warm, bricked city, filled with the good voices of children, Protestant and Catholic.

By dusk we arrived at the ferry station in Ballycastle. Gale-force winds were forecast. Tommy needed to return the following day for his radio show in Belfast. The five miles to Rathlin Island seemed so close; Scotland was just beyond. We took our chances with the wind. Before we set foot on the boat, Tommy spotted Dave Duggan, novelist, playwright, and film director, who was also going to the writers' conference. I was unprepared for his savage wit, eloquence, and charm. Although a year had passed since he was nominated for an Academy Award for writing the short film *Dance Lexie Dance*, it has changed his life so much that he is often asked if he has a life beyond *Lexie*.

The Ballycastle Writers' Group hosted writers from Sligo to Derry for the weekend event on Rathlin, an L-shaped island of approximately 3,500 acres that has been home to Irish farming and fishing for centuries. Its appeal lies in the stark coast and the puffins that annually migrate to its western shore. At the center of the conference was Heather Newcombe, poet and mother of six who was quietly orchestrating sleeping quarters for the forty-five writers descending on the island. From the moment we arrived, she and her husband did everything to make the gathering memorable.

Even though Tommy had spent most of the day traveling, had a radio broadcast to prepare, and was still organizing the following day's workshop, that night he sang in the Rathlin Pub as if it were a recording studio. They lifted a bruised sound system from the school and transformed the only place to eat and drink on the island into a music hall. He prefaced one of his songs with notes from his tin whistle and then recited Seamus Heaney's poem "Follower." Not a skip in the rhythm, and it was well after 11:00. In a place where he needs no introduction, he nonetheless treated islanders and writers alike to an almost private concert, and then retreated to sip a Guinness and attend to their many thanks.

Gray light and more wind than the desert of my home, the sea churned with a nautical grief that would keep us on the island for another day. Six-foot seas, force-seven winds, and only one boat would cross the channel that day. The ferryboat, with a flat metal tongue spanning its bow, bobbed in the harbor. Tommy had to find someone to do the broadcast that evening, the first show he would miss in more than twenty years. Restless, I sipped coffee in the Rathlin Guest House among the aspiring writers: Peter, an ambulance driver who later that night recited a poignant short poem that closed with the line "what could I do but reach / my hand to hers under the sheets?" A doctor, her Canadian lover who worked with wolves, and many others—all of us woke to storm.

I tried to paint the gray morning. There was so little color, only shades of light. Instead I walked and waited like the others. Dave Duggan, Joan and Kate Newman (mother and daughter poets who had done so much for these writers), Dublin poet Macdara

Woods, and Donegal short-story writer Marie Hannigan worked the island wind and words. At lunch, lentil soup and bread were all that kept us from cold. It looked less and less like a voyage would take place. The sea paid no attention to our small lives.

Feeling the outsider, I read a few poems to the group. I was never more uncertain as a writer. How would these poems set on Irish ears? Ireland is gray, green, and wet. Words bear down on writers with the weight of their origins. Mine were brown, yellow, and dry. An oxymoron, *Nevada*—Spanish for "snow-capped"—is only that way in postcards, much like Ireland's fabled sun.

Blindly, we stumbled from the Manor House after a fervent reading by all, the wind slowing in the dark for one last gig at McCuaig's Bar. Dave regaled us with tales of the BBC, film parties, and toil by the private light of words, his spectral wit chinked with years of reading. He lamented the tawdry state of literary publishing. Not one word for its epitaph, the nearly dead novel worth reading. But we surmised that it has been this way for years, and the literature that peppered our dinner conversation—Honoré de Balzac, Anton Chekhov, and Ariel Dorfman—was just as vulnerable in its day. Good writing goes on. Stranded on the most northerly outcropping of Ireland, Dave Duggan gave temporal feeling to our small offering: writers winnowing lives to the book.

Tommy coaxed every closet balladeer, accordion player, and grade-school singer from their cabins. The Guinness pitched and tossed like a buoy in the harbor, and he kept his tiny recorder at the ready; all their many voices later spilled over the airwaves on his show. We retired from the pub on separate paths, but the sea wind was not howling. Tommy, Catherine, and I still didn't know when the first crossing would come the next morning. "Half-nine?" she said, wrapping the shawl around her neck.

I awoke to phones and husky voices in the kitchen. The skipper was eating before his day's work. I showered and tried to ready myself for the prospect of leaving. When the diesels burst forth, I had but minutes to run to the metal hull. Gray with sea mist and floating on the waves, our ferry's passage was more like being pulled through an endless canal. Swift must have sailed here, must have known our fright. And I would pull hard at my stomach until the breakwater in Ballycastle.

The drive back to Rostrevor was quiet and wet. This would be the parting. A final lunch of lentil soup, and I set out for a writers' conference in Clifden, six more hours in the rain. I could not bring myself to say goodbye to Tommy and Catherine. They had nearly broken all rules of greeting and let me into their lives as if I were blood. That kind of friendship—unexpected, cherished—is rare among all peoples, not just for a poet returning to Ireland.

At the Alcock & Brown, Deirdre, the hotel's hardworking proprietor, welcomed me with red wine and salmon. With the rain still coming down, I began to relax after the winding drive through sheep and fly fisherman on the rivers that separate County Galway. A longtime friend of the Clifden Community Arts Week, Deirdre knew that the festival meant dollars in the cash register and visitors from all parts of the Continent. For more than twenty years, the Arts Week's founder, Brendan Flynn, has hosted poets, writers, and musicians from Europe and beyond. Every pub, hotel, and restaurant comes to life when the sky goes dark here in late September. The principal of a secondary school, Brendan has a house that is home to art in its finest sense—the shared belief in a world where creation is central to existence. Self-effacing and gentle, he has created an arts festival unlike any other in Ireland. Miraculously, it runs for the duration with his seamless hand moving from event to event. Not bothered by the constant intrusion of phones, late planes, and deadlines, he manages to keep the tethers of joy and performance taut until the end.

Michael Coady, the poet-in-residence at the festival, walked up to the podium. "Are you Shaun?" he asked and proceeded to introduce me to the crowd. I began to read from Vassar Miller,

William Carlos Williams, and a translation from Pablo, a Chilean teenager whose parents had "disappeared" into Pinochet's hands. In Clifden I learned of the general's illness and incarceration, a not-altogether unpleasant end to the dictator's life. Left up to its children to articulate the horror of his seventeen-year rule, we sift from the poems and stories of their Chilean shantytowns to grieve in translation. Not one breath escaped the room without being touched by their words. When Tommy and I had taped the radio broadcast in Rathlin, I recited Pablo's poem to Pinochet: "Words are not enough / to describe / all you have done / friend of hatred." Translation—the process of sifting song from bloodlines.

In heavy rain we made our way to Brendan's for a gourmet meal with poets Michael D. Higgins and Mary O'Malley. Folksinger and expat Thom Moore was also there. Dinner was electric with the voices of poets and places and music, each wishing it would continue forever. By the time we made it to the next reading, it was as if we had been together for days. All the writers insisted that their words travel abroad, and I filled my suitcase with their books.

Come dawn, it would be my last day. Thom and I spoke with the students at Clifden Community School, and Connemara Community Radio did a live remote. I walked into Brendan's office and attempted to find words to thank him for making all this possible, but there were none. I took a photograph of him as I tried to convey the fullness of these few days, the richness I would carry home. As I left, I blew a kiss to Clifden, and then drove through the potholes and rain to Dublin for the flight home. Strangely but completely, the clouds began to lift from the highway as I circled back to Dublin until, finally, the city was replete with sun. When it set that evening, I remembered again that the journey had started just days before—waking to sun on St. Stephen's Green.

In the small constellations of our lives, once in a very great while we are privileged to meet our kin, and whether poetic or personal, they make some part of our experience real and genuine and meaningful. For the week I returned to Ireland, I was at last where I belonged. It is a riddle to me why this is so, save all that the poets have come to define as spirit.

I returned home to a scripted letter from Ireland. The poet Nuala Ní Dhomhnaill had written, but I had missed her letter by a day. Writing in Gaelic, she is one of this generation's few sculptors of the old text. And so my visit ended as it began, with a welcome from a poet. This journey will stay with me for all my days. It was not complete as I stepped from the plane, rather only beginning to unfold. I now believe it will never end.

— 2000 —

19

In the Library of Chile Pickers, Fishermen, and Vicente's Stone

INTO THE STREET before dawn, hardly upright, a whiskered man beneath a straw hat pedals the bicycle to its place. Perhaps it is below the welcome arch to the chile fields, or to the bay with the fishing boats that for a century have kept this culture alive. By the time I wake, the bicycles are all about, the fat tires worn to rusted rims with one, two, or three children riding astern of mother or father en route to work, school, or home. The bicycle is a motorcar in this village of few cars and the dirt roads make no exception to their transport: the bald rubber has washed them for a hundred years. Were this smallest of villages farther south, it could be the hundred-year village of Gabriel García Márquez. Maybe he found his way home after coming to Teacapán. Maybe the shorebirds drew him in, the roseate spoonbills, a collage of ducks and flamingos that coast to the shrimp in this bay. Shrimp so plentiful they kept the entire village fed after just three months' work and now the harvest is thin like the poles that push the boats in this water.

Just over an hour below the bridge to Mazatlán, the Tepaunes Indians and the kingfishers have hunted this place for a thousand years. These rhythms we drive into have been left to sand and dogs in the shadow of Teacapán. A visitor with a guidebook cannot find his destination but he will leave having tasted Omar's churros, the itinerant pastry chef born of the corner who each night finds provisions for the offering to young mouths: his vat of cooking grease, a stiff gun through which comes the batter, and the sugar it falls in after the last fly is scattered for the anointing cinnamon.

Omar watches the dock beneath the mangrove, watches the day-workers build the *malecón*, a walkway for the town to come, and when night returns he blows the dust from the stoop and begins to wait with his son for his first customer. A bag goes for fifty pesos—fifty cents—hardly worth the effort, or an effort we understand, these outsiders who do not belong but come looking for distraction. Omar tells me he is leaving for the border, more business and people. It doesn't make any sense that he would leave for another place, this village being the full portion of place that a traveler would seek out.

Omar looks at the square, a central plaza of green and yellow cement, that for most of the night, is lit with incandescent bulbs on thin wire in the trees, and the lovers below them arc the simple pleasure of public affection. The Catholic Church is always open to the blue walls at Christ's back. During mass, the villagers line up to the square and they listen to the liturgy, let the Latin wash into their lives, and then the bells begin and they move on. A tidal efficiency to this place of water, moon, and fish.

In the long ago, you could not come to Teacapán. There was no bridge to transport the visitor, only a ferry and, before that, a bamboo track laid down at low tide. This kept the weary from the island that my family and friends found at the end of the road from Escuinapa. A road of make-believe: bicyclists, chile pickers, and crowded buses high above the estuary. An egret might have blown down from the cow's back and the palm whiskers flown to the green islands in fields.

In the morning we leave for the school and the road is a border of pelicans, herons, frigate birds, kingfishers, *caracaras*, ospreys, and cranes that make coming to work a miracle of flight. The birds are signposts that lead us to school, a track of wings in the fog. The turkey vultures blow into every backyard and at night, two owls freeze in the palm on our patio, and then screech an unholy catechism that finally lets us sleep. At dawn the grackles and blackbirds beat the same palm leaves until we wake, which comes as punctuation to the fighting cocks that crow from midnight until the stars of last light. I leave the village in a car on the road to Escuela Secundaria No. 36, but I do not remember the journey. The birds help me find the way.

Ricardo and Marta Topete founded this junior high school with five others, including Bonafacio, to serve three small villages: Celaya, Isla del Bosque, and El Palmito del Verde. Bonafacio believed in education because he had none and wanted more for the children than chile fields. An old story in these fields of birds where compulsory education ends in the eighth grade. The fields look like blossoms or mangoes in bloom, the air sweet with their scent. How could you not heed such beauty when to eat, sleep, or swat mosquitoes is a privilege? We visitors understand the scripture of birds, but we do not understand a land of separate beauties: the island people and their labors.

With almost no preparation, Ricardo, my son, and I set out for Rosario to find a hardwood that will hold books in the humid air. A wood that will say no to the termites and rot of salt and wind. Rosario is over five hundred years old, a colonial town founded by the Spanish, but we never get to its center. We stop and ask for help to find the *maderería*, then, after being directed to many such lumberyards, shake off all instruction and walk across the street to negotiate the purchase of four beams of *guanacaste*, a wood from the neighboring state of Nayarit. The sawdust is thick; we cough and speak with signs: the shelves have to be cut to one meter, the braces and sides the length of the beams, all in a width of one-third of a meter. The beams are wet and have to be roughcut, then planed, and then if the sun rises by Tuesday, they will be delivered from the sawmill.

My other son spent hours designing the library, which did not account for the sheer cement walls that need a second coat of a milky primer. In Escuinapa, Ricardo's daughter, Marta, helps us ask for screws and paint poured from five-gallon buckets. We must have seemed the confused lot of Moses: pointing, gesturing, wishing for a miracle in the *ferretería*, where each screw hangs in galvanized order and the TV distracts the serious men who gather over such things, and the horns from the buses begin. A parade of vendors float by in cars with speakers whose words are almost intelligible from the counter. We take 250 of two varieties, knowing they might not fit their purpose. The owner writes out the receipt by hand and punches in the amount on a register old enough to be my father. Somewhere the birds are singing at our misfortune: we have come so far and nearly purchased the right screws.

We drive back to the city with Arim, Ricardo's eldest daughter, calling to the buses and tall trucks on either side. The *libre* highway or the *cota*—free, being the highway of taco stands, mango fields, and unfinished bridges—or the straight line of the toll road. Over the weeks we choose them both, and once make the mistake of choosing the latter to save time. Ricardo narrates in slow, deliberate nouns: the fields, the mountains, and the makeshift pyramids of bricks dug and fired in the red earth. He tells us the history of the place his father arrived in fifty years earlier: no running water, electricity, or doctor. The village without time in which Ricardo's father began to practice medicine. The father whose name, Dr. Luis Alberto Topete, is on the arch above the park, the father whom the customs man knew before we opened our passports, the doctor whom Marien, his granddaughter, wants to emulate when medical school and the work of learning are done, the doctor who cannot remember everything now because a stroke broke the lining of his will at ninety, but who walked and served every day until then. This is the man whose son drives the free road home to Escuinapa.

I will not understand Ricardo's reticence for days; he has too much to say but cannot force the words from their cave. I am the foreigner who for a year had his middle daughter, Marien, in our house, where she studied English and learned to enjoy the high mountains of snow. In all the language he gives to me there is thanks for taking her on the free road into our home. She could not have gone farther away from her mother and father but she came home to them a woman of some resolve, sure in her skin, and Ricardo's wife said, for the first time, without shyness. She began to walk as the doctor or the priest that tells the village which way to lean in the storm. She began to be the person on whom people rely. She began to imagine the books were like mangoes, bloated in the crates by the side of the free road. She dreamt of coming home, saw one or two people that might understand her fresh, undaunted command of English.

Marta is the woman with whom Ricardo started his life in the bare, essential sun of Escuinapa, and the woman who gave her three daughters the wellspring of God's laughter. She taught them to rest beneath a country of monolithic rule, and found in the four blocks of home, her entire extended family into which these daughters became the fountains of green and brown eyes, miracles of confession that came from Marta. Mother of sustenance on Calle Morelos, and a woman unto her sisters of blood and marriage: Cheche from Puebla, whose *pollo poblano* makes me cry, and Marichu who comes to the school dressed for a contest of beauty but it is the beauty of her eyes and wrapped brown hair that make us feel like we have never left the free road. Marta, whose mother and father have a stuffed eagle in the fruit tree in the patio of their home where sister Mónica's pressed aluminum paintings hang on the wall and a fountain welcomes us when we come through the door.

The toll road ends in a labyrinth of left turns and little bumps that slow us to corn and smoked fish by the roadside. The vendors hail from each stack of wood, then the barricade of five soldiers who cannot rest because it is their job to wave us on to what must be the paradise of tacos we are late to eat on the wood benches of Los Monitos but Arim wisely counsels us to stay, visit with *horchata* and tamarind in the midday traffic. There are things on the menu, painted to the wall, that might imply other things: *vam-piros, chorreadas,* and the vestibule of small freedoms swings at the back: *hombres y mujeres.* We wash our hands and return to eat what has been proclaimed the best, and she is right: she becomes the taco doyenne, the woman with whom we entrust our longing to indulge the fits of never-ending hunger.

In the day that becomes tomorrow she stands in a Chinese restaurant, announces the food is bad *and* it is not Mexican, marches out and redirects us to the doors of a restaurant near the family of foursquare blocks and for whom the praise of others is needless. Arim has studied in the country to the north and she has found one or two ways to become the teacher of international beliefs and wisdom: she cannot remember the name of governments who bring people raisins and move on. It is the supreme gift of her melancholy stare that draws us to her table in the back-yard with the sangria and a lemon slice. She calls out to the birds and the buses that surround her patio and then, beneath the aw-ning, she becomes the lawyer who will redistribute the wealth, offer the last bunch of green bananas from her tree and take you down the street to the Ley, the big store with the trail of boys and girls in red uniforms boxing goods for sale, leaning on the cart for a peso after the groceries have been stocked in their shelves.

On the sidewalk is the bicycle warehouse, rows of interlocked tires that wait in the makeshift lot so that the patrons may shop without theft or greed on the tiny island of intersecting streets. The big trucks bound for Tepic keep the horn still, and the parade of loudspeakers champion soap or dry goods or melons at cost. Arim is almost home. She has returned to the land of privilege and inequity and cannot forsake its bounty of fishing villages and art. She believes there is an owl outside her door. She has become the language of dark and light when there is nothing to eat.

Armando holds a bottle of unborn armadillos, and then boas, and then a lizard with the tail crooked off, but it is living. Armando has taught science at the school for many years and he knows what the taxonomy becomes in later life: labor for hire. At the morning break, the loudspeakers boom with Elvis somehow overdubbed in ranchero Spanish and soon Jerry Lee Lewis, Little Richard, and the others join Elvis and we stomp across the pavement. Armando smiles from the classroom, wants to dance for the duration of the snack time, wants to help us build the library. He eyes the *guanacaste* and tells me it is too wet. It will bend to sculpture when it dries and the shelves twist beneath weight of the books. I know he is right. My sons think I am forgetting the basics of woodwork. He turns the shelves over, sees they are not finished and decides they will begin a long gestation, which if we return, may see completion.

The paint, of course, will not stay on the walls. One of our students, Sarita, asks for the roller. Susie joins her. And then Peter, the lithe cat who will perform in the hunting dance of the *indígenas* on the night we leave, moves the heavy metal ladder. Soon we are all painting and the walls will do nothing to acknowledge this.

On the other side of the wall, Vicente sings deep in the baritone of subtraction and addition: *dos y catorce son . . . dieciséis. Quince menos cuatro son* and Moisés parrots the answer: *once.* I am afraid to use the drill because it will disturb his musical subtraction; he might miss the harmonic flutter between question and answer. He spins the numbers over their heads—Jorge, Iris, and María—and has spun them for thirty years. On Friday he will retire from teaching primary school, his afternoon job, and only work here for the pleasure of giving math to his students.

When we get to the other side of the island, Vicente tells me all of the fishermen are his former students. They are making poles to guide the boats, scraping pine logs to make thatch huts for the fish camp, leaving their bicycles behind to gather shrimp. It is hot and muggy when we push the *lancha* from shore. He has organized a tour of the bay for us. We don't know what will happen, but it will not disappoint.

Around the corner of mangoes a fisherman pulls on the line. There is no rod, only a string on a piece of wood. He nods at us.

This is his day, as slow and imperfect as a day can be. He will bring the catch to the table and his wife will ask him if it was a good day. He will nod with the *róbalo*, the sea bass of these waters. Vicente gestures to the trees: *halietos*, fish hawks, he translates, pelicans, herons, egrets, and crabs on the banks, hundreds ducking in and out of the mud. The estuary ends at another village and the driver, Savrando, poles us into its grip. He and Vicente leave for water but we tell him there is no need. Our water bottles are full. He comes back to the boat singing the deep song of his land. He is not capable of any other voice and wants only to please the twelve white faces in the boat. He has pleased them already; they will not be able to give him a tenth of his gratefulness.

Ofelia comes to the door. It is foggy and early. We are sipping coffee. She asks us to her house just as Vicente did the night before. In this place without time, they have been married for a long time. She is the wife who lasted. The wife in Escuinapa wanted five pesos for her trouble of raising his other family. After deliberation, Vicente decided against the added expense and took the bus back to Teacapán, happy to be singing to one less bride. Ofelia wants to know what we will eat in the evening. Anything, I tell her, anything at all. She cannot believe this; we are used to riches on our plates. And so she begins to prepare the meal: our forks will lay down in supplication before we leave. Her food becomes the table of wild things: a soup of exotic fish, *pollo* with prunes, carrots, tacos, and pasta that climbs from the ordinary kitchen to tell each of us: be thankful, I have come to cook for you and it is the gift of my hands that you are eating.

Julie and Dory have returned with *churros*. In the time we are here, they will bankrupt Omar; he will leave for the city to buy batter and grease and sugar, and they will buy more *churros* when he returns. They are the ones in charge of sweet things, and they have become friends with the ants who line the kitchen door like the soldiers on the toll road. There is nothing in the house that will prevent them from entering. The door is metal; there is no air space through which they may crawl, but they do, even when the basket is empty and the *churros* have been eaten and the greasy bag discarded. The ants are part of the kitchen. They move something every night. When we arrived, Marta and Arim cut fresh flowers and put them in every room. The next morning the ants found the carnations. They must have thought them *churros* because each yellow petal was on the back of a thin red ant moving to the window, which was unable to close, and through which they could escape. I had no idea what sweet was in their beauty but watched as the flowers began to shrink until, in desperation, I put them on the patio, the patio beneath the words, *habemus tempus vitalias*—we have more life than time. Ricardo's father painted the Latin on the beam over the door to the patio, the house it took him fifty years to construct. His home by the water, the place he comes to for rest.

I have not asked Ricardo's father but I am sure he has read Pablo Neruda and must have seen the pictures of the home in Isla Negra with the names of poets and writers and friends on the beams of his bar. There is in every man a little bit of Neruda and the distillation of time in the house in Teacapán is the recognition of daily surrender to sand and ants and heat.

There is a belief on the island that no stones exist. The *indígenas* had to make rocks to hunt. They were fired over many days beneath the rain forest. Then they were wrapped with the twine of palm and bark and used to kill the birds that were bigger than owls, and in this way Vicente's ancestors found the flesh of wild things.

Vicente holds a stone in his hands. I do not know what kind of stone. It is gray, and has chips fallen from its nearly round exterior. He says it is perhaps fifteen hundred years old. I do not believe him although I was in the classroom next door to the library, adding numbers that somehow became larger than their chalk figures. Again, he says it: perhaps fifteen hundred years. That wild anomaly of time now suddenly present in his hands: he is there to present the stone to us and we have not finished the library. He comes to proclaim its perfect resolution in our palms. A stone, an artifact of the *indígenas*, pilfered from the island of Vicente and Ofelia.

I have never given a stone to strangers, have never wanted to see the stones of my ancestors recovered or given to strangers. But I see the stone of his people in his hands. And it is mighty. Vicente cups my hands in his. His eyes tear and he turns for the patio.

At dinner he arrives by voice after the work and the dishes are done, and he takes Ofelia home in his green Chevy Nova which he distorts to mean *no va* or won't go—but it still runs on four of the six cylinders. He tells me every night it is the best night he has had in all of his fifty-eight years on this island. Until I believe him because to do otherwise would be to doubt the daily gift of his life to ours.

We close the house of ants, drive the dirt to the *churros* on the corner, and find Carmen in the dust. She has washed almost everything of ours by hand. Her children stand with her in the bougainvillea and we cannot say there is more time than life in this hallway where she hangs every day out to dry. In Escuinapa, the Topetes want to know what the laundry cost and we say not enough. Armando cooks flank steak on the barbeque and Ricardo tries not to send the coals flying to the grass. Arim makes a pitcher of lemonade and we ride down the highway in the shadow of Teacapán to what might be another land of ants, coyotes, and sage.

The next morning that is every morning the children run from the chile fields to the library, but Armando thinks it is a sculpture of *guanacaste*, each shelf adrift with books in the humid air. In time, he will take them down, one by one, plane the wild planks, reassemble them and we will disappear like Vicente's stone, and someone will remember how the village of El Palmito del Verde was once nothing more than the dust of spiders and colonial history.

—2006—

20

Below Swifts in the Albayzín

FIVE DAYS FROM SPAIN and still I wake with my mind in the Albayzín, on the *torreón* under swifts, the wind rocking the canvas at my side. It is late for morning. The sun crests the ridge after eight. I rise, go down three floors to walk Maggie, the aging Labrador, to the courtyard where she noses a fresh stone to pee on. And because there is time, time which we do not understand in the West, the boiling water steeps in the coffee press until I turn up the tile stairwell to sip *café con leche* and read to my wife who is not far away. I see the Alhambra when I close my eyes and have nowhere to turn—the vendors, the café people, and the good, clogged arteries of Granada. The fountain moves like wind in the patio. The murmur of water is in my ears, one of a hundred Arabic gifts left from their cultures.

The bells wail from the churches. Our first night they drove me mad but soon they were a refuge for the day left behind, an indication that what had gone had really departed. They became the doorway to the sun: their crisp ring shook me from sleep to find my clothes, make my way down the curled stairwell where Maggie greeted me with her quiet bark. I fixed her food in the cool kitchen, the orange kitchen with the painting of the poor woman asking, *Soy pobre sin trabajo, tengo hiros* (sic—*hijos*), *ayúdame, gracias*, her exaggerated expression surrounded by wallet cards of Catholic Saints and roses. She watched what we ate, if we left any scraps for the visitors who might come.

Again, I walked Maggie to squat on the stones and relieve herself. One night, I turned the corner to find a young woman squatting on the same stones, grateful for relief in the anonymous dark. The stones became the talisman, the trail markers under my sandals.

I went up to the *torreón*, the balcony on which we slept. There was canvas on three sides but we tried to keep it open, hot as the sun became, and I read Lorca to my wife in that light. Sometimes she reads to me. His face was never far: he stared up from the books to ask what had become of Granada?

We left on the bus to Alfacar, determined to see his place of rest, which was debated in the newspaper: was he really there, should he be dug up? All of this would cause much grief for the families of the thousands who were killed in the Spanish Civil War. At the memorial one of the tiles had the words from his poem, "Sleepwalking Ballad," "*Verde que te quiero verde.*" Green I want you green. I wanted to know everything about him. Why did he want green, how could it give him what the fascists took away on that terrible night? I read the poem again and again but could not answer his question and looked from a distance at his imperfect garden. There was another book in the library off the *torreón* on six Spanish poets. I opened it to read Antonio Machado, Miguel Hernández, and still more Lorca—poets who gave us Spain through the lens of sonnets, and who without a country, could not be kept in the silence of graves. Poets who did not understand the futility of singing in praise of the color green.

Andalusia is brown, almost sepia, in summer. The hills are dilated with olive groves but they are not green. Their silvered leaves are closer to the green of Greece or Turkey, and it is not far from those places. At least a dozen civilizations have settled this region of Spain—from the Phoenicians in eleventh century B.C.— to the Romans, and of course, the Moors. Their influence is pervasive: the Alhambra—on a hill just beyond the Albayzín, is a paragon to Moorish architecture. The Arabic phrase, "The only victory is God's," is repeated throughout this region, a region where the three major religions lived in relative harmony for seven hundred years until roughly 1500. That is unthinkable today—that Jews, Christians, Muslims should live in relative peace, *convivencia*—which is why my friend (in whose house we stayed) moved to Granada. He reads deeply from Arabic and Medieval Spanish history to learn what quixotic blend of religion and humanity permitted this union. He hopes, when he is done with his sonnets, to put the ideas in a novel that may join hands to our time in history, may bring relief to the wounds we cannot heal.

In the middle of the day, when it was hot and the stones were whitening, we hiked up the hill to Plaza Larga where we found almost anything for purchase: fresh fish, meat, flowers, espresso, newspapers, and fat, grumpy old men and happier women talking endlessly. Their lives looked blissful; they did not know how to behave otherwise. Their clock was set for open time, time without borders and we looked on like curious passengers: through them we were leaving our regimen of hours and minutes and seconds. We were alone with the sounds of their voices. Sycamores and trees of heaven lined the plaza. There must have been five hundred years of conversation in that square. And then, almost like shadows, they were gone, the plaza closed and the only feet were children's, slipping their bikes over the stones.

Another afternoon in our friend's house spent in rest. Then the long lunch when the heat was mesmerizing and the choice to do anything was instantly flogged with sweat or the idea of sweat. There was no hiding from the way in which the weather grew to enclose the Albayzín. In August, the tumbleweeds gave up their brown sticks to the last season before rain. But even the heat was not heat which prevented us from wandering beyond the safe and familiar: we hiked in midday to discover the water that ran from the Sierra Nevada or the wall built around that ancient city of stone on the hill.

The paradox of the Albayzín is the green that floats from wall and roof and windowsill: the morning glories, the bougainvillea, the passion flower, the wisteria, and the grapes tangled in arbors of old bent steel and wire, grapes that shield from the midday sun and now were heavy with fruit. In our backyard were old trees: a persimmon, an olive, a lemon, and vegetables our friends planted before leaving. In the middle of this greenery was a wading pool that gave such pleasure I lay down to read on the nearby brick, and when the heat grew like hands on my body, I stepped in and closed my eyes to its cool presence.

There is a reading room below the *torreón*, and the window is crowded with morning glories. When we arrived, the flower was just beginning to bloom. By the time we left there were blossoms on two floors, in two rooms, and over the top of the garden shed. I began to think of their blue and purple eyes as a library of color, a warm place to gaze in. For the first time in months I painted, tried to capture the color in the reading room, in the patio, on the faces of the Arab women in the market, and the Alhambra to the south. A hundred painters better than I had done all of this but it made no difference—the joy was letting the colors run to the page. Watercolor is a quiet escape from what is exact. Like time, watercolor eludes us, finds its own way, and frequently designs an altogether different image, which is part of the process. I cannot order it and so it was the medium for the journey, the way in which the story of each day was relayed. I found a different view by opening my eyes to swifts, to clouds and wind that rose from the green rooftops and shook the canvas to let me know: I was alive; I could not sleep outside without its shuffling. One night, we were away and a storm blew into town. By the time we got home, the air mattress had blown over two houses and was standing perched on a corner down below. The wind I could not paint.

I listened to the last words from Lorca in a play on the anniversary of his death—August 18, 1936—under starlight in the Alhambra, where the wind and flamenco dancers and the man who dressed as his likeness, performed to a crowd of a thousand. This was to celebrate the poet who for decades could not be read in his birthplace, Fuente Vaqueros, just west of Granada. I should not have been chagrined and yet I believe it must be otherwise: poets recount their stories for people to survive the long heat of midday.

One day I went looking for broccoli but could only find vegetables that looked like broccoli: cauliflower, leeks, and lettuce, nothing I might be able to persuade my wife with, and so kept riding farther and farther up the river path to Cenes de la Vega, then Pinos Genil, and finally up the switchbacks to the dam that fed Granada. Still no leafy green bulbs and so I rode on to Güéjar Sierra, another mountain town settled for more than 500 years, with men talking in the square and the bus twisting the labyrinth of streets to the hilltop, and the broccoli was not there. The stores were closed by then. I rode by the large markets and the fruit markets and the street vendors and I saw nothing. Of course, it would take us to our last day to discover the precise place where fruits and vegetables were in abundance, but still it was not to be found.

Exhausted from the fifteen-mile climb, I spotted a mountaintop café in Maitena, with *cocina típica*, *platos rurales*, and I coasted my bike through the grapes, figs, and olives that lined the one-lane road. What was remarkable was the commerce at this altitude: three thousand feet and they plowed every inch of ground for food. In August the streams ran day and night to irrigate with snowmelt from the nearby Sierra Nevada. I tried to imagine working this field a hundred, even fifty years ago with goats or donkeys as my primary tools. I could not, even as the donkey hobbled the stones of the Albayzín to this day.

I was as hungry as I'd been in weeks. It was late afternoon and I had gone through breakfast miles back. I swallowed a mouthful of garlic shrimp that was so hot it made my eyes water. How could I eat this rich food and ride home? And then a cold beer, pork slow cooked with braised vegetables, and bread. An hour later, I rose to ride back up the summit and then down into Granada as the day was ending. I called my wife from the base of the hill and told her: I was looking for broccoli. She laughed, knowing I did not have a thing to show for my journey but a smile.

At night when it cooled, we walked up the hill to Plaza Larga and beyond to a *mirador*, a lookout, where we sipped from something cold and looked again at the Alhambra. Food was an afterthought, there was never any hunger in that heat, only waiting for hunger to return. From the edge of the café, the city below looked surreal—the lights and traffic fading into long fields of darkness. I tried to imagine where the poets lived and wrote as we sat there. Below us was a path up past Sacromonte dedicated to the poets who had come before us. Antonio Carvajal, Rafael Alberti, and strangely, a quote from Thoreau on being alone. Everywhere I turned I was reminded of the Spanish reverence for literature, for art. One night we found an open-air café with huge canvases on display. Inside the building were thousand-year-old columns and these paintings were on display as if they were part of the landscape, part of the idea of Granada.

As the day wound down, we stopped to watch the people walk from square to square and converse on the benches at the edge of fountains. This is a ritual, a way to navigate the return to activity later in the evening. The culture is designed to allow for conversation. I can't imagine anything getting done, but in the absence of work is rest that is necessary and normal. When I went to look for a bicycle for my wife, I walked for hours across much of the city until I found a bike shop that would rent bikes. I asked him when I could come back to show my passport and pick up the bike—of course it was after the long lunch, which I did not hear. And so I walked again, to the cobblestone road where nearly every store was closed—furniture, clothing, and toys—to find an art college as steady as the oldest church in Granada.

At the corner of the street was a mural of the bombing in Madrid painted by a tagger. It looked like a painting. It was on a piece of cement scaffolding—it would come down shortly and disappear in lime dust. The red and yellow words were in English: scream peace. What made these outward expressions so dramatic was the contrast of the people working regular jobs: the street sweeper in our little corner of the Albayzín, the bartender in Pinos Genil who in that still, afternoon sun, washed every plastic chair for the evening crowd who ate tapas and drank *cañas*, and who despite the heat, smiled all the time. We had just peddled five miles and he brought us a beer, and soon small sausages, olives, bread, and cheese. This man was like the server in the bus station, crowded and not nearly as peaceful, but there was no complaint. And he was like the waiter in the café near Lorca's grave who was pleased to be serving two others and us. I'm sure they were not making lots of money, but they were visibly happy. This is so foreign to the idea of work in the West, that labor can be its own reward: fresh, new, and visceral.

One night we went to the theater and watched *Fahrenheit 9/11*. I spent most of the evening translating every fifth sentence to my wife. Almost no one was inside: it was early evening and an American film. I felt alone in that audience: Spain was the lone member of the "coalition of the willing" in Europe, and it had cost their president the election. The socialists were back on top, but there was acrimony. I heard the echoes of 1933. I heard the voices of derision that made Franco's rise to power possible. It is an anomaly we cannot understand. American politics are ruled by other forces, no less sanguine, but others nonetheless. Still, with our election weeks away, our rhetoric was beginning to sound a lot like theirs. I worry because this is not how tolerance finds its way; this is the way of might. We may well be in for changes that none of us can imagine; we may be cutting down the last flag to raise the icon of the next ruler.

I think of Diana who came to the house every Thursday to clean. An Ecuadorian, she studied business in Granada and cleaned homes to pay for her studies. Her perception of her situation was far different than ours: she was seen as the underclass, an emigrant, and a person of little faith or imagination who was there to take their jobs. This sounded too familiar, this strain of xenophobia. It was the same strain that was eating at America and pushing the globe closer and closer to hostility. Curiously, because a Guatemalan woman was traveling with us, Diana became very close to her, in fact Elena was her first real female friend since arriving in Granada more than a year ago.

I tried to paint the room where Elena slept. The window was filled with morning glories, hundreds of heart-shaped leaves with the blue and purple flowers calling to anyone who entered the room: be still, listen to the fountain below, lie here and read.

I read from a history of Spain, an eloquent and loving portrayal of the centuries of writers and poets who had given the Western world its greatest novelist, Miguel de Cervantes, and a long, complex history of poetic roots from Luis de Góngora and others. Then one morning while reading from the jacket notes of an Arabic CD, I found still another form of poetry—the *moaxajas*, a spoken, rhythmic poem, a story, which reminded me of the Japanese haibun. In the den below the reading room was a chest stacked high with coffee table books, Lorca's drawings, Antoni Gaudí's architecture, and the history of Granada. I could not fathom so much literature set in a place. My place is in the West; I did not know what it was to live with three major religions and cultures save what I was told in these books. I remembered the Arabic letters tiled in the reading room: in the name of Allah, the compassionate and merciful.

In Plaza Larga was an old, whiskered man with gray slacks crumpled at the waist. He stood at the cash register of his market like a sailor at the helm of his ship, picking out eggs by hand for our purchase. He knew intuitively where every item was. One day I needed shaving cream and after looking for twenty minutes I gave up. He pointed me to the precise location of the last two canisters. When I brought a bottle of red wine to the counter he held it to his lips, so delicious was its contents. Each day when I walked to the plaza I looked in to see him, to register his presence in the Albayzín. There were other markets, larger and smaller, but none with his ebullient face. He brightened always, wanted to know if we found everything or needed anything, took care of us like we were family. And I learned to buy what I needed: we walked with our groceries to the house. You could never buy too much because it could not be carried. It was a precious rule: don't take more than you need. It meant we shopped for fresh food: meat, fish, vegetables, all sold for the first half of the day that felt like the first half of ten days. They were languorous, they lasted until the last breath before siesta.

Sometimes we sat in the plaza and sipped coffee until the flea market or the flower market filled the square. I bought a succulent and potted it in the window, which was really an excuse to listen to the classical piano being played across the street. The faces, the doors, the sounds became a collage of color and hopefulness. Hope that I could paint and write and read again, these small things we took for granted.

Across from the market was a coffee bar that sold chocolate *churros*. It was air conditioned and invariably there was a man, Quixote's ghost, squabbling with the owner, but that good squabble, that "I know you know I'm talking because I like to talk" kind of conversation. The street sweeper, who hours before was brushing the stones at our door, was inside, with his *café con leche* and *churros*. The smoke was thick and the young mother with her stroller, waiting for the *café* to cool, swallow, and walk on, and the English tourists trying to hide their clumsy Spanish, and the ice cream melting, even in the cold, and then it was over and we were the last to be in the coffee bar with the beads, icons, and the hundred Catholic saints.

I returned to the orange kitchen of home, to the *pobre señora* who stared at us all hours of the night and day, and whose sorrow comforted with what could not be said, and I put Miles Davis on the phonograph. Miles had never been to Spain but did the quintessential album with Gil Evans—"Sketches of Spain." There were times when I wore that disc out, played it night and day, and played another from a Spanish flamenco guitarist, Tomatito. Again the muted answer of music. The kitchen table grew to be a giant easel—there were paints, brushes, canvases, and poems stacked in their quadrants—and it made the two of us feel like we were building something greater than ourselves. We were making an art that was of Spain, and although it was not art without limitations, it was art born of the hundred faces we had come to know in our short time there. More than this, it made our marriage a marriage of art. Toward the end of our stay, we found a leather worker who made a large book cover with a design from the Alhambra on the front and we put those paintings and poems and calligraphies inside that leather. We left it for our friends who raised this house from crumbled stone. It had been a home for squatters, an abandoned structure in the Albayzín, circled with razor wire. Now it was a house, filled with the toys of a young girl, and a mother who built consensus to manage the environment, and a father who was a writer and a reader, and who wrote sonnets in the *torreón*, and a young woman who sheltered the child from the world when her parents were at work. This was the house we came into; this was the home of art. We left that place, left the smell of brick and tile and stone and leaf behind. We closed the door, the hundred-year-old door of wood behind us, and scurried the pathways to Plaza Nueva where José picked us up in the 4:00 a.m. dark. The people were coming home from dancing. It was Saturday and we were leaving for Málaga, then Madrid, then New Jersey, and then home in the high mountains of the West where I woke for days at 2:00 a.m. to the bells of Granada. And could not rest until I wrote their ringing down.

—2006—

21

Fourteen Days in South Africa: Healing and Contradiction at Land's End

IT HAS BEEN SEVEN DAYS and still I do not have words for the country at land's end. In the eyes of this Westerner, South Africa will remain an enigma, a place understood only by those who call it home. There is contradiction in everything and into that contradiction we flew. Some twenty-four hours of travel from home left my wife and me delirious but thankful to once again be on solid ground. At the airport in Johannesburg, Darcy and Beth met us. They were Irish sisters whose parents had immigrated to South Africa in the 1930s. We loaded our bags into the trunk of their Toyota and drove the ten minutes to home.

The elder sister lives in a middle-class suburb—middle except for the barbed fences running the perimeter of most houses on Darcy's block. What we take for granted in the West, a modicum of safety, is not taken for granted on Topaz Street. It was summer when we arrived, thirty degrees Celsius, and her yard was florid with color: lobelia, pansy, geranium, all of them carefully bordering lush grass and river stones—a beauty I was not prepared for coming from winter in the Intermountain West.

We set our bags in the hall and dropped to the couch. Darcy made tea and we tried to find a name for this temporary home: Africa, a continent not widely known to Westerners save the torrent of news telling of its demise. As the days slipped from our hands my ignorance of place and history would unravel. I would find no solace in this undoing but a reason to return.

We woke from deep sleep to nightfall. Winding our way through the capital, we arrived at a colonial building heavy with trees and the scent of age. Inside we met more family for a Malay dinner of bobotie. The four traded barbs as only siblings can. My wife and I watched through the blur of jet lag and candlelight. The meal was exquisite—part chef, part connoisseur of all things reverent, our hostess baked this dish for her youngest sister, Beth. Somewhere between curry and chutney, the flavors were wild with banana, rice, and turmeric, spices I would have thought home to Thailand, not South Africa.

Like so many who immigrated to South Africa for work— whether freely or forced, the Malaysians brought with them indigenous foods, language, and culture. The movement of tribes to a common land. There are faces that belie a journey but those I remember moved beyond my imagination: they were the faces through which their legacy of love and grief was told.

At dawn—much earlier than our own—we packed the car for the journey to Kruger National Park. Six hours to the northwest across cornfields and villages on a soil so red I thought it blood by the roadside. Mangoes hung from market windows like swollen apricots. Tin roofs slipped to hillsides. Improbably, a mother in green, yellow, and black walked the shoulder, her dress so perfectly printed against the clouds it was closer to paint than cloth. Always the spectrum of fear lurked overhead, until I had no bearing for its origins. For months we had heard of its unlucky victims and would be warned in all places: your life is a small thing. The buckling of peoples below one post-apartheid roof. What was once tolerated was now only violent, once forgiven, now expected. We tried to be nothing more than roadside witnesses to the Combis (local taxi vans) zipping workers down the long South African highways.

What most startles is the country's infrastructure: it is a place of raw beauty and for many, extreme efficiency. A place built for ease and utility that until very recently probably functioned as orderly as the tides which border this land. But for the occasional pothole on the road to Phalaborwa, it could have been Mediterranean Europe. This would exacerbate the parallel experience of place: the hidden and the visible, what we could only imagine as flesh and less than flesh.

Almost to the park entrance, we found a cold stout under a thatched roof that doubled for a bar in the humid sun. There was a family playing in the pool, singing Afrikaans over the water. Faintly German in tone, it is a derivative of the Dutch and Malaysian languages brought to the Cape centuries before. Two men at the bar gave us instructions on finding the most animals but I could not listen. Work and worry had taken me down. Coming here was like being released to the endless green of Africa known to us through books: elephants, giraffes, and gazelles. Released to the not knowing, to living without orientation to every day, a dress rehearsal for being—and not just alive. That which anchors expectation to the unruly tedium of travel rendered us passive strangers, unprepared for all that lived below the surface.

Driving through the wooden gates of Kruger I felt an immense gratitude for something much larger than self or country—the spectrum of animal life without human interference. As if to portend our three days in the park, Beth warned us, "Look carefully. They are hidden from view." Not twenty minutes from the entrance I saw a phantom bird: the carmine bee-eater. Just days before leaving, I had turned the calendar to December and read the caption below the fluorescent blue-and-red bird to find it was from Namibia. I thought, never in my life would I see its plumage. And here, not just one, but many flew over us in the car. The male is one of the most colorful species I have laid eyes on. We tried to capture it on film. But even before I see those pictures I know they will pale. This bird lives where Jorge Luis Borges lives—in the world of imaginary beings.

By the time we reached Olifants Camp, our eyes were heavy with storybook texture—zebra, nyala, guinea fowl, African fish eagle—some of these almost legend in the dry land I call home. The elephant tore at the baobab tree, chewing the bark for digestion. Olifants River flowed below and tucked in the islands of sand and wood; hippopotami and crocodiles moved with prehistoric grace. As far as I could see, green and brown flowed together.

At dawn we sat over the same gorge. Baboons swung from tree limb to tree limb, the littlest ones playing like cats on the cliffs above the river. Made so small by all before me, I wondered how far Homo sapiens had come, and remembered it was of little consequence to the wailing of water on stone. Thousands of tribal feet had passed this ground and still it was untouched, as wide a river canyon as the Colorado before dams did their work.

Without speech, my wife and I sat motionless for the hour of sunrise. Fog lifted from the tropical canopy. Every limb came to life. The temperate gave way to the sensate. The yellow-billed kite floated the gorge, the sky seethed with mist, the barbarian hunting for food at first sun. This I tried to paint sitting on the porch of our thatched room but found only failure. There is a momentary redemption that follows all rendering of such beauty, but this day would not be held by word or brush. We would look but release all longing to capture the wild.

We never saw the mythic lion or leopard. Perhaps they are better left to the fiction of green lands. My senses shook with elephants bathing in wide rivers, African fish eagles soaring over us for minutes as if we were prey, and the Lariam reeling in my stomach for the lone, infected mosquito.

At the gift store I held out my hand to the cashier. Short by nine rand for a bag of ice and postcards, she asked me to bring her the money later. When I returned, I wanted to know the Swazi word for trust but simply handed her the rand and felt welcomed on her terms, not mine.

Unwitting volunteers, we came to a country of many names—Swazi, Xhosa, Zulu, Sotho, Indian, Asian, Malaysian, Dutch, and English until the vocabulary was not one but several, the aural landscape of nation layered upon nation.

Kruger left me empty of ideas, of ambition. The healing had begun. I knew also, what was to come would unsettle. Driving back to "Jo'burg," as Beth affectionately referred to it, the questions percolated to the surface: What place is this nation South Africa, what place for all these faces living in the distance? How did their rueful stares come between three centuries of sorrow?

High on a mountain ridge, we stopped to buy wooden spoons from the vendors. The tallest woman, nearly naked in her darkness, moved with the grace of a heron. The rand became straw we traded for spoons. The sun was a yellow stone pushing the women to knees, to the cardboard under the miniature sculptures oiled with shoe polish. There were six or seven shiny cars, visitors with cameras and accents. At once the two skins crossed, theirs, and ours. It was as silent a border as I have touched.

Driving this silence to Dullstroom, I began to *feel* the South Africa not known to me before setting foot in this land. Or if known, only through public faces—Mandela, Tutu, and others who spoke without a mask.

At the gas station a rainstorm kept us in our car. I was told not to pump fuel. It takes away jobs. My notion of Western helping was of no use: he will come when the rain stops. Admonished by my lack of understanding, I waited my turn to refuel.

Rain followed us to land's end. Outside the Cape Town airport, we drove by Langa, the first township we would later visit. The tin and plywood squares against the roadside. In the distance stood the relentless skyline of seaside commerce. It could have been Monterey or La Jolla two oceans away, not South Africa outside my window. The shoreline drive to Simon's Town, a sleepy naval port almost immune to Langa, was skirted with surf shops, restaurants, boutiques, and sunburned shoppers. But for the few blacks in the streets, it was Southern California, and I was no less chagrined for having noticed.

Grateful to be still, to read and paint on a hillside above False Bay, at least some part of the Cape was what I hoped for in long-ago Nevada. But each moment brought its private reckoning: Evan, who comes weekly by train to polish the car and water the garden; Evan, whose farthest reaches into post-colonial patios would not buy my gas back to Cape Town; Evan who teases his Rastafarian co-worker about being less a man because he is not circumcised; Evan who cobbles wood and glass and stone for the shelter he built in Langa; Evan who owns the plot on which he now lives; Evan who almost has enough rand to visit his dying brother in the Transvaal.

When an East Indian professor took us into the townships—a euphemism for residential poverty—I said to Beth, "This is the day the feel-good part of the journey ends." He worked with student teachers in their skeletal schools, and knew many people who called Langa or Khayelitsha home. This did not assuage my guilt at driving into the eyes of so many with so little, and I could not escape its human consequences: we have failed one another as people. When I travel over eight thousand miles to a place where boys strip power lines like they were cigarettes, children bathe on sidewalks and scab the street with flesh, where women whisk flies from entrails drying in the sun, stitch shoes in an eight-by-ten storage shed, send laundry to the salt air with no hope of returning, where dogs bloat in the fields of refuse, where cricket is played with rocks and rocks are the last natural thing, when I come to such a place, no words unchain me.

High above Cape Town in a bar on Table Mountain, we tried to find excuses. Even the rudimentary explanations were nothing more than wasted breath. What country has *not* conquered another? If I was sickened by what I saw, so be it. But let's not pretend we have changed. The fact remains a Sotho name, a Zulu name, a Xhosa name lives in what I can only describe as terror.

Blood sense tells me Mandela did not leave jail for this. Nor did the thousands of others whose skin dictates their demise. I wished for a minute to be free of skin, but knew also the terms of human suffering would not permit me such indulgence. As long as flesh enslaved flesh, I would understand how close we were to death.

It had been a decade since the death of postcolonial rule. The orderly transition of power in South Africa was no less a miracle than the fall of the Berlin Wall. Under the indelible weight of hatred, it is a wonder the country did not simply collapse.

Very few of us are privileged enough to understand how fear names its soldiers, and terror, in turn, its victims. What may never be understood is the caprice with which such violence lights upon a life. When the professor drove us into Manenberg, his words came as subtle reminder: your life is paper, not worth more or less than the paper blowing in the street. I thought of Tu Fu returning home to find his son dead of starvation, how guilt had begun its masterwork once again, to eat the poet from within. The professor pointed to the street corner, "That is a gang. Nothing more than thugs. They would kill for your watch."

The laundry hung overhead like failed flags. From tenement to tenement, the wires were stretched with clothes, the closest thing to wings over the street. His colleague at the university lives a mile from this corner. They go to sleep to the echo of bullets. I kept wondering what a child does amidst such disparate worlds. And who will unchain him when he grows old?

Paradoxically, I would later read that a student at the university where the professor worked was selected for the lead in the opera "Carmen." A student living in Khayelitsha, a Xhosa word meaning "new home." To think that a woman who barely has potable water to bathe in will be singing before all Cape Town by night, is not just a contradiction. It is an adumbration of feeling, a numbing of human context that I cannot appreciate. The audience will not know she studies her lines in darkness. They will imagine her coming by limousine to the theater having been the understudy of a prestigious soprano at Julliard. They will not know it is the ratchet of gunfire she has studied under. They will not know thirty-nine people were murdered in Khayelitsha in December.

I AM TOLD by many *there is nothing you can do.* If it was death we wished for, I would agree. But whether Dutch, English, or my own bloodied Irish kin, we do not wish for death. Nor do those who were conquered. But that is probably all we have in common. Which, of course, leaves me with the disquieting futility of revenge. And hope that such revenge has outlived its usefulness.

Much as the landscape in Olifants Gorge, I would never capture all that scoured my senses that day. Waking to red-winged blackbirds in the top of a yucca flower, there was precious little to reconcile the two Capes. When I mentioned this atop False Bay, there were quiet disclaimers: it is better now. Things are much improved. The lens shifted over and over until our experience was refracted through so many eyes I felt like a fly. All that I touched had multiple meanings—not one or two, but scores that made the touching implausible.

That morning a friend took us over the mountain to Red Hill, a small township in the pines. Because of the flora, the abundance of firewood, and a preschool, this place seemed almost tolerable. Many of the residents traveled by foot to Simon's Town, a distance of several miles along the charred road. The lessons were not lost on our host: "Before relocation we lived together in relative peace. When they were forced to leave and live with no shelter, campfires nearly burned Simon's Town to the ground." Further still, we drove by Ocean View, yet another settlement with no ocean view, then to a smaller township with a modicum of roads, power, and roofs. When our friend's son left home, the young man was chagrined to learn he had no squatter's rights in the township. He would have to pay one thousand rand—about one hundred thirty-five dollars at the time—for a plot of land. This was not fair he intoned. Fairness? There is none. There is only black and white and the loss of country between them.

When the Portuguese explorer Bartolomeu Dias christened the tip of Southern Africa "Cabo da Boa Esperança" in 1487, he could not have known what so innocent a name would herald in the coming half millennium. I stood at the Cape of Good Hope. There was no truth but the meager offering of two oceans. By then all my resistance was gone and I held out my hands to sea wind. A few men were chasing abalone; further still, lobster nets bobbed from skiffs. Over coffee and toast, two East Indian women made us feel like we were a part of something larger than land, an unchosen human history that binds us to place, to context without explanation—even in so lowly a thing as a café they could now freely run.

We returned to Johannesburg, our Western curiosity reduced to the genesis of what we had seen and heard and felt over the intervening weeks. Foolishly, I was reading a book set in the American West, a book that seemed empty of solace so far from that landscape. I would have no home here, not even in fiction. Not until many days later would I come to find some respite in the South African poets. There was only Yeats to console in Jo'burg.

At dinner Darcy invited many friends who had spent their lives entwined in the two South Africas—detainees (I would never learn the definition of political torture save its referential identity), AIDS activists, legal strategists, physicians, teachers, thinkers, and all the faces from whom we would nevertheless return without answers. If there were other stories, I would not assimilate them. The longer I remained, the more dissonance defined this brief period of travel.

A Sotho woman came to the house. Regal in black dress, she warmed to the strangers in the kitchen and by lunch she was eating crepes with us. I wanted to know all that she thought, all that brought her to this place of work and trust and hopefulness. On the piano was a notebook with her name on it, a place to trade ideas and family information, how one culture learns the ways of another. She played with Darcy's children like they were her own. It wasn't long before the black and white codes became diffuse; there were no rules for acting. When she hugged me goodbye, I had only her sacred whisper to remind: not one but many in the hands of home.

Distracted by her leaving, I had not noticed a young couple had arrived to adopt the last cat of the litter. Darcy's youngest cried at losing so good a friend. His crayon pictures adorned the kitchen walls. The dogs slept the heat away. In the bathroom, a horizontal poster of Yosemite. What country had I flown into? I tried to write a postcard but felt helpless at transcribing what could only be true for those who lived here. I was a foreigner and knew nothing. How naive to think one visit would change that.

In the supermarket we fished for the right ingredients but found few for the dinner my wife would make. When we drove out of the parking lot, Darcy gestured, did you see the rent-a-cop looking for keys in the ignition? The chill of theft was ebbing to the regimen of daily tasks.

Over pasta Darcy's friends wanted to know all that we did and thought in America. The conversation drifted to the botched election and then miraculously back to a recovering South Africa. A dozen years of healing and contradiction flew about the room. My lungs filled with trepidation at being called upon to answer for any person or country that late January evening.

When I returned to the white silence of northern Nevada, I told a co-worker the journey changed what I believed about truth. Not knowing how to fully articulate the death of an idea, I now believe there are very few absolutes. Having no other choice but to dismantle hatred or die, I hope we choose healing over death. It is the only choice I can abide, but then I have never been enslaved. And so these words are nearly weightless. It will take all of us to rein in terror, not just the political or the powerful, but all of us. Gandhi would have said kindness before blood. A hundred prophets have said hatred kills. As a species, we can do better than this. We must, or we will surely perish.

— 2000 —

22

Letter from Zimbabwe

LYING ON THE ZAMBEZI RIVER, no hope for recollection of what really happened in all these fourteen days and nights of constant movement from one post to the next in the florid interior of the former British outpost, Zimbabwe, I begin to lift from its truculent sway, begin to release its unabashed vendors who line the streets in Harare, its swarming currency which has fallen to new lows, its unrepentant outlaw dollars which double their value in the queues at teller machines and Western Union outlets, its almost Biblical regard for Robert Mugabe, now ninety-two, and yet absolved of so much that is necessary.

With a group of Westerners, I went in search of something redolent of southern Africa. I was not a stranger to its rivers and mountains—my family had been to the region, had seen the unbelievable flora and stood among thousands of migrating flamingoes—but still, I was not prepared for the kingdom heralded by Stanley Livingston, and later colonized by Cecil Rhodes. It's hard to say in any concrete way what Zimbabwe is to a Westerner. By turns it can mean a country of thirteen million people, a sprawling, open land, a tribal place of multiple origins—Ndebele, Tonga, Shona, and more, names like recluses in the corner of history, yet they are very much alive. We had the pleasure of visiting one chief, Mr. Nelukoba, and listened while he explained what was happening to his Mabale village: the young were leaving. Their cell phones were taking over; there was little time for family and tradition.

"How," he asked, "would the next generation know what to do?"
We could not answer him. Chickens and cows were close by, his
only protection against his tribe's economic well-being.

It is the constant rub of first- and other-world ideals that
make this region of southern Africa so hard to explain. In the
many parks and preserves, they are doing serious conservation
work. In Antelope Park in Gweru, its director was leading a team
of over a hundred researchers and volunteers who were trying to
bring lions back from their threatened status. Outside our hut
I woke to two women fishing the reservoir with long sticks and
empty plastic bottles floating above the silent water. An egret
poked in the mud. Their children walked back and forth while
they waited. This was their morning ritual—fishing meant eating,
even as they baited the hooks with small pieces of bread. It seems
paradoxical—the world traveling at warp speed and these women,
on the shore of a shrinking lake because the rainy season had not
yet started. There was contentment, a peace unknown to my wife
and me as we walked across the wooden planks to the main lodge
for breakfast. Again, how could I name what was left unsaid: we
were about to sit down to a breakfast of every possible food, and
feet from here the women splashed the water with handmade
poles and hooks.

We learned to eat with eyes open because there was never a
time when hunger was absent from the journey. This is one view
from the West: there are two Africas, what we are able to absorb,
and what we are able to intuit. I longed for more depth and definition. I remembered our time in Fish Hoek, outside of Cape Town,
when we became close to many and were involved in their lives
without some degree of effort and worry. I wanted to sit by the
water with the women and ask what they were doing, how they
lived by such filaments of prayer and longing? I wanted to know
how their husbands worked, what they believed about Mugabe,
if they believed, and what they did to flatten the horizon of an
unknown future? But you see, these are my questions, locked in

my furious understanding and over and over, I was shown how little they mattered. In Hwange National Park, Kennedy drove the Land Cruiser and pointed to bird after bird—the gray-crowned crane, so beautiful it must have been painted, the gray go-away-bird, given its name for the call it emitted to warn the animals of an approaching lion or cheetah, the African spoonbill, almost overwhelmed by its beak, the Marabou stork, whose bald head looked like it had been in the sun for days, and so many more—these birds Kennedy knew like family. He shared endlessly, the impalas, springboks, waterbucks, hippos, a lion cub we followed for a quarter mile until it snorted at our proximity, its mother high on a hill with another cub, the zebras, almost surreal in the green landscape, the elephants that lived beyond my notion of time, the three types of termites whose mounds were over six feet tall, and more that my words will not convey.

Kennedy knew we wanted this knowledge, and in his sharing we found a friendship of depth. He and his wife had lived at the park for five years, made a decent wage and had housing. His children were grown, trying to make a living in the city. He seemed happy—the blessed curse of the Westerner—because he did not try to trap it like a fly. We were grateful for the two days spent in his esteemed understanding of that place. One night, we were near one of he last water holes when elephants came to its shore. Dozens of the leviathans and their young, some who were so small they walked beneath their mothers. The dominant male snorted an ungodly cry to let the others know who was in charge. They were feet from us, sucking magnesium from the earth after bathing and drinking. They needed this mineral for digestion. Somehow they inhaled it without the dirt and dust choking their mouths closed. Another anomaly: they live longer than humans. They have wandered this land for millennia. We must look so small, so referential, and still Kennedy and his colleagues throughout the country work to save them. A tusk, a thin white tusk protruding from their mouths, fells the beauty of this mammal, but poaching is on the decline because the penalties are far more severe. The game wardens can shoot if someone is caught in the act.

Rodney was our guide on the old Mercedes bus with the trailer behind. He, Hillary, and Edward kept us from flying off the road into the green mist. Rodney had the countenance of a priest and his wife, Bo, taught French. The language of learned people—one I still cannot master. They had two children, lived in Bulawayo, a bucolic city in the southwest of the country. He ran a travel agency and laconically said that tourism was the country's number one source of revenue. Bo would soon start to work with him. He had optimism that the business would thrive. We would tell others about our experience and they would want to come. He hoped to bring people to this country for similar exchanges and could sense, that if Mugabe's transition was peaceful, there was a future for Zimbabwe.

We ate lunch in a café on a long porch as the rain started to fall. A young couple ran it whose family had been in the former Rhodesia for generations. This was home; how else to define it? They were trying to prepare the best local, organic food in the region and it was—we felt as if we were in Palo Alto—and felt also, we were not. It brought commerce to the city and their black employees were grateful for the work. This is the conundrum—the whirligig of who is in charge and who is not. For Rodney and Bo, they were trying to share their homeland, wanting to give us some part of its essential beauty. Without apology, without reference to what it could have been. A story still in its making.

Over the course of the two weeks we became part of that story. Not shaping it; rather, absorbing it. In the embassy the cultural attaché said this was the one place she and her family had been posted that she loved. I could see why—Rodney and Bo were like ambassadors. They gave us what diplomats frequently miss—the personal, the most profound form of address. Later in Bulawayo, we met one of the Mandela Fellows who had visited the states in 2015. Andrew and his wife, Vivian, welcomed us as if Bulawayo was our home. They hired chefs to make a barbeque in their backyard and let this unwieldy group meander through their house of many rooms. He confided that he might have to fly to South Africa to get the parts and the cash to keep his recycling business going. But he would come home one week a month. It was the way things were. Vivian said the water was stored for the days when it did not flow; the drought had come like thieves. They hoped this rainy season brought relief, brought some prosperity to the land and its many inhabitants.

Water is a commodity except at the orphanage: they had drilled four wells, only one produced. Andrew was on their board. He shepherded their many projects through a web of like-minded leaders and miraculously, they managed to shelter twelve young people from harm's way. It was hard to be in their house; it felt like usury but the children were grateful we had come. We were part of a string to a larger universe that meant food, clothing, books, and shelter. The charity model does not work. Andrew and its director understood this; they were building a small chicken farm to sustain the orphanage. It was hard selling fresh, organic eggs, but it was a living for the young people. In this corner of Bulawayo they found some dignity, which is not unlike water— you can hope for its existence and sometimes touch it.

The light rain in the baobab thorns kept us alert as we walked back from the coop. There were three thousand chickens inside and atop the perches the pecking order began. This, the director told us, was the origin of the phrase. I wished for another order— less dramatic and more resilient. Maybe the order of the eyes in those young people—maybe that would suffice—but my question would be left unanswered. The Western lens must codify, but there are few codes here save the obvious and so we drove on. There was a large hut on the side of the road. We took the meandering path to its door: a sanctuary for the painted dog. This animal that looks like a collie with yellow blotches on its flanks is also under threat. Trappers use thin wire to snare the dogs, but invariably they are injured or killed. The guides live at this facility, too, and they take pride in teaching the young people in nearby schools about the painted dog. There was a creation story on the walls of the overlarge hut—it gave meaning to the dogs' lives but it also gave the children an intuitive understanding of what was at stake. Equally important, the trap wires had been recycled as art: small faces of the dogs and their habitat. We brought one home; it hangs on our porch, looking east, looking to find solace in the open space. I cannot imagine a painted dog in the high desert but it runs here, runs all the way to Bulawayo.

At Victoria Falls, one of the seven natural wonders of world, there were tourists from every corner of the earth. And more gracious people, hosts who had seen us walk into their land for decades. This journey to southern Africa represented a migration, a way to define what was missing, and for us, a way to define what was needed. If, in the abstract of the present, with our businessman having taken the helm of the states, we cannot find some semblance of common good in one another, I fear for all of us. It is not for the usual chatter of nations, but for the eyes in the orphanage, the ones left most vulnerable by our incessant exploration. I was heartened by so many loving gestures and people; heartened by what could not be said because I was not of their tribe. But they did; they said it over and over: you are welcome here. I worried my white skin would be a cloud overhead. It was not, which again, made me all too aware of the magnanimity of our leaders on the old Mercedes bus.

So, this is what we came to: an unraveling, a story within a story that will need decades to be told. These are images that float over us like wind. They let us into another place for a brief time, and then they leave us. What we do with them is our concern. I choose kindness; it is the only affirmation left to me on this long return to the West.

In customs, they took an orange but left an apple and a plum, the twin gifts of fruit from the hotel staff in Harare. I declared nothing; I wanted to declare everything. The form would not have it. I had to be brief. I cried in the darkness the next morning, trying to light a fire in the sixteen-degree cold. Cried because the words I hold up have no meaning in the winter where I live. But still I try to say them, pretending, as I must, that spring will thaw more than ice and we will listen to the echo of others when it comes. I wish Rodney and Andrew and Kennedy a peace of nations, if only on the next old Mercedes bus of tourists, and if it stays on the road to Bulawayo, a time in which to laugh.

—2017—

23

Fadhil in the New World:
How Humor Saved an Iraqi Poet

The role of poetry is to confront lies and fraud.
It pulls the masks off the faces of those who peddle delusions,
by uncovering the truth from under a stack
of commercial, repetitive slogans.
—FADHIL AL-AZZAWI

I HAD NEVER met a man so lean. His every breath was a concentration, a ritual for leaning into words, for making the music of Arabic come to life—and that was in a bar in Armagh, Northern Ireland, at a writers' conference where such things are tolerated or even expected. In the wild empty of Nevada, the sound of his voice was like being in church. He was reading from the poems of his village, "Elegy for the Living (Iraq: January 17, 1991)," his Baghdad that had become dust and rubble and now was the bane of some new government—but not the place of his childhood:

8

This is your night, Iraq:
Mothers stand at the crossings of battle-bound roads,
waiting for their sons who will never return,
young soldiers who never grew up,
whose life is only the time of their death,
left in the desert
for the wolves to mangle.

When Fadhil Al-Azzawi left Iraq in the first days of 1977 to attend graduate school, his country was leaning to the edge of intolerance and its poets were being jailed. He fled to Leipzig, East Germany, on a student visa and never returned. Squatters have occupied his house since then, and his immediate family is in clandestine communication with him. Fear, it seems, has become the hoe in their lives. It has turned many a night into the warm Baghdad air of supplication, where, he tells me, they wish for a homeland without fear and where he may live as the poet he is esteemed to be, as lines from "Mr. Edouard Luqa's Dilemma" exemplify:

> So that poetry tears out the masks of convention,
> so that the word encompasses the world,
> I am crucified in this exile
> outside the guidelines of the profession
> flogging the faces of the poets.

Fadhil came to the Great Basin to read from his poems and talk, however briefly, about building a global community in the post-9/11 era—if such can be said of this time. What he did was sing the poems from the podium, in Arabic, and on the last night in Las Vegas, in English, so that the readings became a mosaic for living in this time. He wanted, he said, to put a face on the Iraqi people. He gathered us for a night of incantation, of spinning in and out of the dialogue that Western Civilization has had with the Middle East for two millennia. We were left without words to proceed. Instead, he winnowed from his thoughts a recipe for his survival, which, to almost everyone, seemed unbelievable: humor, as in "Newton's Apple,"

> . . .He remembered
> that what tied him to earth
> was not the law of gravity
> he'd just accidentally discovered,

but the hope
that the apple would fall
upwards.

When we drove around Lake Tahoe, snow still on the ground, a live radio signal faded in the distant Baghdad with an Iraqi doctor practicing in the Green Zone. The interviewer asked with trepidation, "Your wife is pregnant with your sixth child. Why are you having another child *now*?" Fadhil, who doesn't do anything loudly, let out a frantic yelp—"What a stupid question!" In three weeks he was never so strident.

"What do you mean?" I asked.

"We have lived with oppressors and dictators for a thousand years. This is not new. When a man and woman go to bed at night, they do not stop loving because a war is on. They do not stop eating, they do not pretend to love their children less when the sun comes up again. We are not fatalists but we keep going. We have for centuries."

I was silent with the fallacy of my Western thought, my nearly perfect plans for child rearing. This must be the beginning of what translators understand: that to bridge the world of thought and culture is to step into the void of both and recreate an image that might satisfy a piece of the twin linguistic landscapes. Fadhil was always translating for the riddle of post-modern Iraq, and I could never take enough notes. In his childhood, he played with Sunnis and Shiites alike; he played with Christians and Jews; he played with atheists; he played with children who did not know king from country. These were his blood relatives, his kin, his relations, and they were not disturbed by the differences. To which tribe did he belong, I wondered? "To none. We are Iraqis; we are one people. It is only the extremists who are tearing us apart." Again, the contradiction of the Western press and the poet of few words. "We are Muslims, we want the same things—safety, schools, jobs, and peace. We want our country back. Now it is in the hands of dust and darkness." Almost reflexively, he asks in "The Prodigal Son Returns," "What have you gained, O poet, from your wandering?"

Fadhil married an Iraqi woman, the journalist and novelist Salima Salih, and she, too, has never returned. He worries for the safety of his relatives, fears they will be threatened for having proximity to him. That his family is a meal ticket for kidnappers is the paradox of his critical success. And so he returns to his room where he smokes and works on the novel, the current novel of Baghdad, the one he hopes will tell some of this story, will share a piece of the light in his desert. In some ways, Fadhil has never left. He is the sculptor of the Iraq that might be, the Iraq that has become memory, the Iraq of his poems. His "Elegy for the Living (Iraq: January 17, 1991)" is a look at what was the temple of Baghdad, and it murmurs over and over to us, the reader, for solace despite the death of birds and things that would sing:

> In the distance I see airplanes coming, flown by Bedouin
> dictators, their shoulders studded with stars, piercing the
> clouds, frightening birds in their skies.

When Adrienne Rich reviewed a recent collection of Iraqi poets, she quoted from his poem "Every Morning the War Gets Up from Sleep," as if to underscore what might be said if we listened to its poets. Harbingers have come and gone for centuries, they have looked for people and places to ignite controversy, and some, like Fadhil, have wanted only to strain the full volume of humanity with a poem:

> Ah! Every morning the war gets up from sleep.
> So I place it in a poem, make the poem into a boat, which
>   I throw into the Tigris.
> This is war, then.

THERE IS A FAMILY of piñon jays in the birdbath outside. They are playing in the water. They do not imagine one being different

from the other. They are like the characters in Fadhil's poems—
they dance and light on the rim of what we understand to be sorrow. They help us to see when only darkness prepares our way.
Much as he finds humor in the world, his quixotic blend of humor
and futility finds its way into the poems. They never really arrive
where they set out to go, but he delights in the journey. They tilt
the world a bit and draw a new picture of what might be beheld.
They are frank, funny, and deceptively unburdened, except of
course when they must be as in "From an Open Window Unto a
Dark Street":

> The torturer comes to wash his bloody hands
> under my faucet. . . .
>
> Many will knock on my door
> before morning arrives.

His poems make no pretense to have answers. They are like
wind in the feral empire—they rise up and disappear only to return from the inside of a book. He is the joker, the one who would
not laugh in the car by the river of snow. He does not want to be
in a land of poets who are forced to choose between eating and
writing the king's verses. His friends, he tells me, still must make
those choices, to become the scribe of the oligarch or move to the
border and learn to dissect sand. An old choice for poets, older
still for people.

He parodies almost everything—God, Satan, even war (from "No
Matter How Far"): "All these wars, how can I lose them?"—to affect
the larger reality, the one we live in without recourse or, he might
say, without recourse for all. And then he ducks, jabs, jumps from
the ring to the outer ring where, in a line, he becomes Abdullah, the
cherubic Arab who wanders the desert to teach or trade epiphanies,
if there is a voice to share when the warring is over.

When he first read in Reno, he barely rose above the podium,
his diminutive frame haloed against the curtain. His poems came

from a place of other origins, and they asked that we in the audience join him on this quest to set the words free. When he read in Arabic, it was rendered as song, a language made musical by his insistence on rhythm. His small hand rose and fell as he filled the room with the idea of Iraq, an idea unlike the desert we visited nightly on the news. Later, at the university, he read from an essay on poetry that follows *In Every Well a Joseph Is Weeping*. He talked about his childhood in Kirkuk, how the dervishes came home reciting quatrains, *khoryats* to the sun or moon or a lover, each quatrain improved upon by the others traveling with them. A poetic process like the *renga*, the Japanese linked poem that informed his "sense of play between poetry and life." He grew up in a howl of dervishes and the sounds of Turkish, Kurdish, Assyrian, Arabic, and English; this is what kept him alive for the three years he was imprisoned as "Prisoner No. 907":

> In my cell the clock of my days
> stops. I enter its darkness like the banished king
> who stays up at night's gate.
>
> . . . In my cell
> I seek a moment of love
> on the face of the world.

The wonder of Fadhil is multilingual and multidimensional: he refuses the ordinary step of diction, of words for words' sake, and replaces them with countries, whole globes of feeling and masterwork that might be conducted under the universe of Fadhil, a universe he does not proclaim to understand or even depend upon. Rather, it is a place of contemplation and laughter, a place of animals and birds and trees that could live in the desert of his childhood. When he spoke of the prison, it too was like the wind. There was no forgetting the monster that swallowed the spirits of the intellectuals, the writers, and the teachers who would not be shamed by Saddam and the Baathists but who, on occasion, read in the wind the sound of another desert without such disregard for human life.

The morning after he read in Las Vegas, we walked by the pool. He was startled to find bathers sitting in the chairs in the March sun. He talked and smoked and took a picture because it was something he could not believe—palm trees and neon without the deafening blaze of tanks. He talked of his new projects; the translation of his early novel, *The Last of the Angels*, by William Hutchins; and how, with very little sleep, he could write in his Berlin study for two weeks at a time. Every phrase was punctuated with the two poles: Berlin and Baghdad, the former home to his grown son and wife, the latter a memory at the dawn of history. The fertile valley, the river that spawned what we know to be the first written word, cuneiform on stone. He asked if I had read the new *Gilgamesh* translation by Stephen Mitchell. I had not and he insisted on giving it to me, a symbol of the time when language was a metaphor for understanding.

Walking beneath the palms at poolside, it seemed as if I was in the desert with Li Po, no compass point but the conversation pulled to the circle of poets and friends and the unwritten words. I did not have the gift of my own small planet to impart; I never would. I could not know the cell he described. It was made from the bones of dictators. When the British-controlled monarchy was overthrown July 14, 1958, the populist leaders were more oppressive than their British predecessors. And so on, until he left when the Baathists seized power. A poem is not a stick or an occasion to say "look at me," but it might be the words people say to survive such cells. In this, he is of a long tradition—Russian, Spanish, Nigerian, Polish, Burmese, to name a few in this century—and that requires a certain deference, a belief in the hope that words might one day be freed of their torturers. The Indonesian novelist Pramoedya Ananta Toer, who wrote a quartet of novels chronicling his country's struggle for independence from the Dutch, asked, "Is it possible to take from a man his right to speak for himself?"—this after composing those novels in prison and committing them to memory because he had no pen or paper.

Perhaps I was walking by the pool with some distant cousin of the Chinese poet, an apparition who was smoking, thinking, and asking me to take his picture for his wife and son in Berlin. He brought a satchel of books and papers, but all of it, even with his clothes, was light as rain. He had no visible exterior except his suit jackets which he wore in all times. It was cold like Berlin, the spring of Nevada. Colder than it had been in ninety-two years. A record snowfall, a record low, a record of searching for reasons that might bring such precipitation. I gave him a heavy overcoat and he looked like an elf poking out from its fur collar. All Fadhil could say was "Thank you," at the podium, at the pool, at the airport. Wherever we went, people were left without words. They had no way to return to the world outside. It was as if he had come like a dervish and spoken in so many tongues that they understood language to be a gift. He never read for more than thirty minutes in four cities, and still the rooms were filled with his generous presence.

He signed his selected poems, *Miracle Maker*, and left in the long column of passengers for home: "For my friend who gave the sense that the world is still full of beauty." But I think it was he who gave that sense. He returned to read in Cairo, Paris, Amman, and still more cities I cannot recall, his name a wafer on the tongues of those who cannot return home. And we, who call this place home, take hold as Fadhil marries the consequence of being alive with its supreme expression—poetry.

— 2007 —

24

Trying to Cross the Island between Us

IT IS HARD TO TELL what side of the fence you're on when you straddle the border. The signs are bilingual and the money runs through pockets like knives. You can walk across or try to cross in a vehicle. You may get delayed. You may find it is not a structure, only an idea through which you pass to the other side. You may arrive like a bird not knowing if any prototype has been erected. On the ground you may not squeeze through. Fear is trying to cross into the lives of those it watches. It hovers above the mannequins of desire on the billboards, on late night radio, and the percussive throb of street vendors.

When my wife and I left for Mexico, we hoped to live for a time in the hands of the Loreteños, rub the dust of this border crossing from our bodies. We were wrong. We could not outrun its corrugated promise of protection, could not escape the ideal of freedom in the country to the south of our high desert home. Even though there are rampant similarities, we were confused. Out the window stood hundreds of *codrón,* the cousin of the saguaro cactus. It was fall and the rains had turned Baja California into a wild green paradise. I saw two bicyclists whom we met later in Loreto. They had ridden from the northern tip of Alaska and now they were in this country, almost free from their British accents, desperately trying to cross from their island to this one.

Long before the politics of extinction grew like weeds in the statehouses, my wife and I came to this country out of love. The

Mexican people were humane, decent people who, while living through three-quarters of a century of near-monolithic rulers, had become so much more—artists, farmers, mothers, and laborers—names for things you do out of honor, fealty, and compassion. You labor in a field when the crops need you. You labor in a house when the children need you. You labor in the city when the vacuum of pretense slips from your grasp and you must eat.

I have come here since I was a boy, seen the murals in Chapultepec, sweated in the hill towns of Sonora, dug fence post holes at a school in Cíbuta, but like a character in a Frida Kahlo film, have not understood how the thieves of language transpose what I believe: How is it this place of such beauty and possibility can be reduced to something like a wall? Something in its very disguise tries to belittle, to steal from what is right and good in the parallel universe of this country.

Most people who live on the border will tell you it is ludicrous to assume any such separation can occur. They are married to spouses who don't live in the same country; they work on the other side of the fence; they cross for commerce; they buy groceries and presents and cars and pay taxes in two places. A wall divides; that is its central purpose. We cannot laugh about such a defining characteristic. When we left for our brief sojourn, the eight prototypes of division were released to the press. I wondered how long we would drive before their presence stole its way into our sleepy path. I wondered who would admit to such sorrow. I wondered if would we would find in our hotel, restaurant, or Pemex station, someone that might understand—it was not us who did this. It was not the five thousand ex-pats who come down this highway every winter. It was not the government of fishermen, dune buggy drivers, mothers on break from the routine of habitual service, students trying to find some respite in the cantinas, and last of all, it was not the solemn voters in the margins of this discussion that hangs overhead like the cinnamon vapor trails of dusk.

I would not ask the waiters how they felt; I would not begin to describe how small it made us feel on the journey, we who were the diplomatic Cheech and Chongs in our aging Subaru. I would not wait for the pause to come in the awkward conversation about things in the states, much less the state of my home, that place in the West that is so often the butt of jokes because here, in their country, this is not a joke. A life is torn on the radius of steel. It is like the razor wire of prison. It is designed to separate, to cloak fear on its transgressors. It is not a new or even bold idea; it is salvaged from the past of excuses for not trying to cross the border of differences. You can see it almost anywhere in the world: think Middle East, Myanmar, or Zimbabwe. We have nothing left to flee; we are ephemeral. This planet is borderless; it is one planet, not two, not 196 countries with borders. It is one planet. We move like wind over its surface—we, being the animals that stand, mostly, when we move. Someone got out their paintbrush before we came and marked the colorful spots for our inclusion, our exclusion. Now we try to remember which one we belong to: orange or red, blue or green? I think I'll choose the space of least color, least identification. Then when I travel there will be no hideous stares. There will be no rationale for misbehavior. When you pull the static line, the Mexicans are the first to intimate we are not perfect. We live in peaceful disarray, but we did not negotiate to be erased from this meandering wall. In fact, we were given a choice—live with it or live with the consequences of ridicule beyond the wall.

Until spring or sometime when those still trying to cross are needed. This fall the growers in the wine country were chagrined—there was no one to pick the grapes. Is it even an irony that César Chávez organized the annual crop migration of families? The black-and-white stills of him and Dolores Huerta in the fields with no money and no idea of whose wall ran between the rows of grapes bracket the last five decades like two orphans in church: What have we done? But the labor goes on, the mothers stoop to feed their young, the boys stoop to feed themselves. The labor goes on into the next story of hands so that when we arrive in Loreto our friends tell us they no longer return. The border has become a threat; its talons creep up and down California, and they who live in radio silence find ways to hide from its crucible. My friends speak passable English; they would migrate from Mexico but it does not seem worth it anymore. The pain of losing oneself for a passport has lost its luster.

I keep returning to the poets for instruction. Perhaps they will know what to do. Surely they will not keep government records. Surely they will lie below the fence; they will mark time with metaphors, with singular images of beauty like the snowy egret that would not leave us on our journey. And the great gray heron that flew to the top of the codrón while I rode by on my bicycle. And the turkey vultures that watched from above with indifference. I was little more than a distraction. I was not of their kind—menacing gatekeepers of the open road. They always arrived before us, trying to cross before the magpie or the crow ate from the killed rodent. It seemed so basic—eat or be eaten—a way to live below the border. I remembered the lines of Homero Aridjis, one of Mexico's finest poets, in "*Juego de silla, 4*" from *Imágenes para el fin del milenio*:

The rock does not know the shadow
in which it rests,
nor the sun that illuminates it,
or the blow that pulverizes it.
Inert in the hand that fans it,
passes air for a moment
to fall again in its repose.

Rock, wind, sun—these three illuminated our journey into the lives of the Baja peninsula—but is there anything to shield them from the threat of this wall? A line from Octavio Paz requires no visa: *Todos los días el mundo muere. Todos los días nace.*

El mundo—the world, the globe, the place on which we reside. It is born every day and every day it dies. But what of us, what of its two-legged gatekeepers, we who confine and rebel against that very thing? What of us whose dialogue with a wall cannot be ordained? It's commonplace to reject any such idea of separation—think of the Berlin Wall coming down—but yet we persist. We define the order of our differences with little patches of earth. I wonder what would happen if we—North American and Mexican—stood on the border and the two countries became empty? All of us. Who would immigrate then? The birds in their silent abandon of things on earth? Who would colonize the refuge of beautiful places? Who would come to claim its king? Of course this sounds like a fairy tale. Wouldn't it be a divine loss of belief to forgo such realities? And yet, when the Spanish came to the desert Southwest, when missions slowly rose like burnished moons in this place, didn't someone ask why? Didn't they want to know if it was more than stone, sun, or wind they were conquering? Didn't they have a chance to sit down and reason with one another? Of course this also sounds like a fairy tale but out of its long reach grows the latter-day medusa of a wall. And so when our friend Chuy, a rural school director, gave sixteen years to the kids who lived on the ranches so they could get an education, he understood why: without some piece of paper to talk to this medusa the kids would be left in the fields where their parents were left, and the grandparents before them whose great-grandparents were there when the Jesuits came.

Love has no honor in these fields. You are conscripted by your family to belong. If you choose to leave, you sour the roots of this foreboding history and choose a kind of immaculate freedom until there is no more border to cross. You may wake in the inspector's office asking what it is you need to stay. You may find yourself in a dishwasher machine searching for lost plates. You may recall the first words in English when the lights came on. You may understand that little belongs on earth, little you can touch or hold or call your own. This is how you make up the room in another country—folding sheets and towels for the family who took you in. This is how you listen to the echo of what you left behind. In the corner of your room is an altar. Their faces are lit with candles. The wax has run down the thin neck of the chalice like a bead of shame. Sometimes the room is all you have, and, in the night, you return there for respite from the day that began in the rock, wind, and sun.

—2017—

25

Without a Way Home

LYING BELOW THE Sheridan, Wyoming, radio signal, I could not hear anything above the wailing on the airwaves: how could this happen in our state? For more than four hours I listened. The station suspended all programming and people called in unable to find words for what had happened. It was October 1998—twenty years ago—and I was dizzy and sickened by the outpouring of grief. What small onus of hate landed in this hotel room I had rented for an art's conference? What visitor had come from another planet? I had no answers, nor did the listeners, who called, one after another, to voice disbelief at Matthew Shepard's murder.

There were about sixty of us gathered in the meeting room downstairs. I left to get something from the room and turned on the radio but instead of music, I heard the thrum of nightmare, something with no antecedent save darkness. That Matthew Shepard was left tied to a fence line, cruciform, relieves us of nothing. The mountain biker who discovered him thought he was a scarecrow until he noticed the tear-streaked blood on his face.

Art has no place in this room. I have not been able to watch *Brokeback Mountain* because being there on that day when his life was taken was movie enough. It seemed the great fallacy to be talking about any art after hearing so much that made us bleed. We struggled to find things to talk about, wondered what skin had been removed to reveal this sorrow, and drank a beer, but none of it helped. I have even lost the name of the person who was with me because the weekend became ghostly, a living outside of living.

When I arrived I walked the streets of Sheridan. There were many things I loved: the prospect of fly fishing the Bighorns, the café with one coffee urn, the run-down department store, and mountains as far as I could see. I was determined to return. What must belong to those flanks pouring down from the west? I wanted to know the stream-fed morning, the sky that clouded with each day. As I am wont to do when I travel alone, I looked for the innkeepers of the town, those few who could describe what I was seeing, who could name the slow, urgent telegrams of the migrating geese. I did not have a map but I had direction—I wanted to be in this place. It was like the place from which I came—broad, expansive, and in need of explanation but understood by its residents. This is the paradox of the small town West, the ordinary prescription of ritual set against the elements: farming, ranching, and limited opportunity except of course, if you what you wanted was here. I imagined that was true enough and that for this brief time, I could fit in, could belong to the cold promise of these mountains. In a few years I would ride Beartooth Pass, about two and a half hours to the west. I would strain for oxygen at nearly 11,000 feet and stand by the sign proclaiming its summit on my bicycle. Nothing out of the ordinary. A motorcyclist stopped and asked if I needed water. I said I was fine, but thanks. And started my descent into Red Lodge, a mountain town you wish could lie at every town center—good people, food, and pubs. There wasn't any anguish on the radio that night. We slept well, my wife and I, in a log home just outside its city limits. When I started up the mountain that morning, I had forgotten about Matthew. I only saw switchbacks that scissored back and forth across the ridge. I didn't know if I could summit but I had stashed water at 9,000 feet the day before. When we drove in from Cooke City, it looked foreboding and I wondered, do I have enough *cojones* to pull this climb off? I told my wife I might come back; I might not if I kept climbing. I tried to flag some tourists and asked them to call her but I doubted if the message got through. Somehow I just kept riding. After the rest stop, I found my water and kept on above the tree line. It was almost seventy degrees and calm. The snow plows were staged on the mountain throughout the year—anything could happen. I was just grateful for a windless afternoon.

Wyoming has so many naturally beautiful hills. If I had more time I would ride them, but now it occurs to me that the beauty was code for loss, what had happened and I could not revoke it. I have been drawn to this landscape for years; even before the night in the hotel it was stunning to visit. I read once in Rock Springs and the college elders told me about the night Allen Ginsberg read to the oil drillers and roughnecks, screaming and drinking and hollering at his disheveled grace. I couldn't imagine a more dissonant crowd gathered in front of an American poet who had been happily gay for most of his life. I did not say unanguished; I said happy for most of his life. He died before the night I was in the hotel in Sheridan. I wondered if he would come into the lobby now. I wanted to hear him wail against this moonlit corner of north central Wyoming. I wanted him to break all of the constructs of our beloved poetry once again to find some way through this night. I wanted to see him chanting in the bar like he did on the stage in so many cities, chanting because it conveyed the depth of his story. His story that even the roughnecks applauded that night.

I almost read in Cody, but my good friend said not many people come to the readings. I wasn't surprised; it's not like poetry is chocolate, at least for most. But I still wanted to go because its beauty doesn't translate to road maps. There's an elemental part of Wyoming that must be felt, be languished in to stretch out its definition. My friend was good enough to put a few poems in an anthology he edited, and he still writes, reads, and teaches students; he does what he can to instill values. Values I imagine were lost that night in the bar in Laramie. It's easy to point fingers, but that afternoon, there was no compass, no prevailing wind, only absence. I was left with emptiness. We had gone back to some other time. We had receded. I did not know why.

I have taught poetry to many men in prison. If Henderson and McKinney, the men who attacked Shepard, walked into my poetry workshop I would try not to judge but at some point, heinous is heinous. I'm fallible. I've worked with many men who have killed. I try to find my way back to forgiveness. It is the only way I can go on. It does not excuse them or me. I sit with the pain in my hotel room, stare out the window—how did this happen, here, to a young man in college? It is an elegy he wrote with his life, a poem to the pastoral field somehow defiled that afternoon. He was Neruda signaling to another god for whom such things cannot be believed. He was the ecstaticist tied to the fence beneath the radio signal. He was waiting for us to come. He was the man that, had he a moment to recover, might have spoken about his ordeal with innocence. It was innocence that led him into that bar, and it was ignorance that led him out. But still. I want him to remain alongside the flowers at the road edge, on the steep hills that lead to the tree line, on the curb in the small town by the Bighorns.

I want you to know we keep trying, Mr. Shepard, to uncover our weakness and repair that emptiness inside. I want you to know that if Allen Ginsberg could come back to read in Rock Springs, he would be welcomed. I want you to know that if Thom Gunn could come back, he would be welcomed—and I don't think Thom Gunn ever read in Wyoming. I want you to know someone has learned how it is to be alive with remorse. I want you to know that the English teacher who asked me to come to her college in Rock Springs met me that weekend in the hotel. She was listening, too. She was trying to hear your voice over the airwaves. She was not afraid to ask how you came into our lives without supposition, how you moved over those mountains that afternoon and touched us. It left little room for art, for anything really, but she knew that something would come from this, some infinitely small act that would return a person to break open a poem with her students. And that's what I tried to do. When I left I gave her those poems her students wrote. They were like the land where you lived, not Rock Springs, but Laramie, and they landed all over your home. They lay in the street for days. No one touched them. No one dreamed they could. They knew they were cables from what it was you saw and they welcomed them. Some part of me drove away that afternoon and foolishly I have returned over and over to recover it. But you know it is not possible. I live without that afternoon. That is where you live. On the radio. Towering over us. Like a border, like a place we cannot visit. This is what Allen Ginsberg could not say, or maybe it was Thom Gunn, or maybe it was you. Thank you for coming into the room, Mr. Shepard. I wished for art but you gave us more than any life can contain—witness to love and its undoing.

— 2017 —

Postscript:
Donald Hall's Reflection in the Sand

WHEN DONALD HALL was selected to be the U.S. Poet Laureate in 2006, it was an affirmation of a catalog of work, thought, and belief that could not be held by one man—and yet, he was at his desk, alone, on the farm in Wilmot, New Hampshire, trying to answer the repeated requests for readings, articles, and poems. He would share that he confided with his good friend, Ted Kooser, on just what to do. As would any acolyte looking to fill a role—except Hall was rounding the arc of his seventh decade and like his closest peers from the generation of 1920–1930, putting an exclamation point on what was a long, illustrious career. Indeed it was an obsession with beauty that kept Hall at it for his many days and a completely unwarranted generous sense of the poetic landscape—what to do, how to do it, and who to mentor. I was one of the lucky ones. When I wrote to inquire about Vassar Miller, a magnanimous note came back within days. I did not know him then; I was just trying to learn about Miller's poetry. I imagined Hall knew these things and more than that; his hands were the unseen guides that led Wesleyan to publish her.

That postmark was almost thirty years ago. In three decades you learn about a poet's work ethic, intellect, and ardor. You learn the inscape of a mind, and you learn that what sustains is not always permanent. Hall intersected with almost every major modern American poet. His classmates at Harvard were John Ashbery, Adrienne Rich (Radcliffe), Robert Creeley, Kenneth Koch, Robert

Bly, Maxine Kumin (Radcliffe) and Frank O'Hara. Seven years after the *Paris Review* was founded by George Plimpton, Peter Matthiessen, and others, he was one of its early contributors. It's difficult to know such a geography of literature, one that we view now from a distance. When Donald Hall left this world on June 23, I was nearly done with this book of essays but it was his influence that let me proceed. I cannot go many days without looking at his picture or rereading an article, or finding him, unexpectedly hidden in a book or letter on my desk. He never wanted much when he wrote. The letters were crystalline messages from the farmhouse, the one he and Jane Kenyon restored and wrote in. And throughout the chronicle of their love and her early death, he was an omnivorous correspondent and friend to the literary public. That is why we ached with him when she left too soon. It is easy to horde privacy when you no longer need the trappings of being well known but he did not. No matter how busy or preoccupied with the daily tasks of his editing, writing, and reading, he wrote back faster than I could send off a response.

In this, he was a mirror also of the other serious correspondents of his era. These volumes of collected letters will soon disappear. The collected emails will be addressed but they will not have the depth of something like Donald Hall's letters. I'm thinking of *The Letters of Robert Duncan and Denise Levertov*. In over thirty years it spans almost nine hundred pages. That is a record, an intimidating one, and Hall's correspondence was equally intimidating. Writing him, particularly in the last decade, I felt as if it was stolen time because I knew it would end soon. What I never understood was why he continued. The light flickered; his many rooms were closing in but he soldiered on. He once told me he never wrote on a computer and his picture at his desk looks as if it's from the 1940s—pens and paper but no modern technology. If I think of my close writer friends, most of them have a letter they cherish from Donald Hall. And if I think of Hayden Carruth's yearlong letters to Hall's late wife, Jane Kenyon, I see the image of a glass of water whose tension holds despite it being filled to the brim. This is how you know a person. Hall intimated to Carruth how much the letters helped her and Carruth understood: you love them as much as you can in a letter.

When I turn to the series on American poets and poetry he started at the University of Michigan—the preeminent series in this country—it is like a vault of poetic knowledge. Without it, we would not have a public record of the lifework of scores of modern poets, those journeys into the wellspring of thought, craft, and practice in this unruly world where poetry has so little import. *Claims for Poetry*, which he edited in 1981 from his Wilmot farm, and which I purchased four years later, gathers more than forty American poets to lead a conversation on the art form as it was emerging from the mid-twentieth-century. Once again, he was trying to navigate a sea of differences: "I found friends opposing each other and enemies in agreement." But what he gave us was a road map for understanding the topography of the art form. An intellectual backboard to push against, to pressure the next wave of writing.

Hall did not suffer fools. When I made a mistake he let me know it, but never to criticize, only to sharpen my ability, my attention. This small postscript, this chronicle of one artist to another will not suffice. Baseball writer, Caldecott winner, deeply felt man of letters, it is a small letter I send to you now. An incomplete draft of what you left behind in my life. A place no amount of writing will fill. It is like the wind in this desert: once it goes through you, you are marked. I will keep looking for your presence but it will have gone. Marked though I am, I trust what you left us not as legacy, but solace for the work to come.

FOUR YEARS AGO I drove down Canyon Trail outside Boise, Idaho, to find Limberlost Press. Inside, Rick and Rosemary Ardinger were collating the pages of their next chapbook by Kim Stafford. The press is historic in that fleeting way letterpresses are: it has published fine volumes for more than thirty years and despite the attendant aggravations, it is still alive, which in the Intermountain West, is like discovering water beneath the trunk of a sagebrush. I went there to listen to Rick talk about the presses, watch Rosemary sew the binding of each copy, and hold the other beautiful chapbooks they had made. We had lunch and a beer. He told me about the bull elk that slept below his porch most of the summer to get out of the smoke from the fire. Then he wandered the shelves and pulled Donald Hall's *Remembering Poets* and gave it to me. He said the essay on Pound was the best. Hall was a young poet on assignment for the *Paris Review* in 1960 and had gone to meet Pound.

I took the book home and started reading. Hall had been in the presence of so many literary giants—Frost, Eliot, Thomas, and Pound in this volume—it seemed as if he was there when the die was cast for twentieth-century American poetry. Looking at that vast canvas where he started, it seemed like our generation had shrunk from its predecessors. Whatever side of the poetic fence you found yourself on, the generation of 1920-1930 made modern poetry what it is. I was also haunted by the absence to come: How could anyone name what had been done when the art form had fractured into a thousand pieces? Still, given Hall's strong editorial attachment to the University of Michigan Poetry Series, there was a template from which to try and name some piece of the shadow left by those who came before us.

Donald Hall helped me on many projects—always generous and specific to the task. He broke molds too: when most poets chose academia to stay alive, he did not, and moved instead to his family farm in Wilmot. He worked quietly, authoritatively, to carve his New England niche. An inveterate correspondent, like so many from his generation, he made letters a kind of reflecting pool for being (his archives at the University of New Hampshire include 350,000 letters). But it was his example that gave me the courage to try and make a book of essays. I considered the structure he used in *Remembering Poets*, his willingness to be vulnerable to the influences of those minds he encountered. I listened intently for the nuanced perceptions, the insight that filtered through the prose.

When I finished Hall's book, I wrote Rick and told him he was right: the Pound essay was the best. Then I wrote Donald Hall and told him his book, which later became *Their Ancient Glittering Eyes*, was the seed I would use for my own timid effort. At first I thought it would be a book about poets and poetry, and thought about the Michigan Series again, but that wasn't its exclusive focus. It was about the desert and poetry and places beyond this country. At each juncture I wrote him, asking more questions. Would it hold up and would an editor like it? He was kind—cheered me on as if it were a milestone but it was only a snippet of the book he presaged. It soon became a very different book. Indeed, one of the central poets in this volume is Hayden Carruth, Hall's lifelong friend. I know of no other correspondent except Hall who could keep up with Carruth, and when Carruth died I thought of Hall as the next in his generation who wrote, almost compulsively, to the end.

As each year passed friends sent me essays from Hall. His piece in *The New Yorker* on aging at the farm was a long poem of anguish ("Between Solitude and Loneliness"). By then he had lost most everything—his luminous Jane Kenyon, his desire to write poetry, his ability to move easily from room to room. Again he wrote to say yet another essay collection was coming out (*A Carnival of Losses, Notes Nearing Ninety*, which was released posthumously). I wrote back to tell him I was plodding through mine.

This is how the vatic tale is passed to the next generation. We believe we are strong when we are young, but our bones fool us and we soon become the reason death no longer overwhelms. When the last letter came from Kendel, his assistant, telling me he could no longer write, I knew his health had failed. I look at his picture on the dresser, among those of so many writers I love.

He is wearing purple pants and slumped in his chair. He printed it along with the cover of his final book of essays and folded them to send to me. He let me live with him for the sweet journey to affirm what can never be mastered—this unlikely art form that so many profess to own.

We live in a time when books generally and books like this one can seem superfluous. Donald Hall challenged that perception and I am sure, sitting with Pound in Rome, in post-fascist Italy, his book seemed no less superfluous. But what we learn, and what he taught us, is that words have no borders. They stream on from generation to generation, taking us further down-current until finally we have made all its discordant letters a refuge for this and all time.

Eagle Pond Farm

—for Donald Hall, in memoriam

A terrible ache wore at me—
I knew this was borrowed time.
Your letters came like thread
parsed with the breath of eight decades.
I opened them like rain in this
high desert. What poet would not?

The reasoned weather of words streamed from your pen.
What I reach for in the June light:
not that Frostian shadow, but yours Donald—
in the chamber now—and have no
recourse but to read without you.
A burden not yet known.

—July, 2018 —

Acknowledgments

The author owes a particular debt of gratitude to the late Tom Ferté, who one night called to ask if I would be the editor-at-large for *Calapooya Collage*. It started me writing essays and it gave me the courage to wade into prose after a long absence. Similarly, Sherwin Howard, the late editor of *Weber Studies*, nudged me to write about the prison, for which I will be forever grateful. His successors, Brad Roghaar and Michael Wutz, were heartfelt champions when it mattered. Without the careful prodding and support of the late Tom Auer, then editor of *Bloomsbury Review*, and his sister, Marilyn, many of the essays in this book would never have been written. To Richard Logsdon, Todd Moffett, Tina Eliopulos, and Erica Vital-Lazare of *Red Rock Review*, I owe many thanks for the opportunity to set the words free. No writer works alone.

To the many poets who have stood close for so long: Gary Short, Gailmarie Pahmeier, William Wilborn, John Garmon, Steven Nightingale, Tom Meschery, Richard Shelton, William O'Daly, June Sylvester Saraceno, Krista Lukas, Suzanne Roberts; the late Stephen Shu-Ning Liu, Bill Cowee, Joe Crowley, and Hayden Carruth; and the essayists Michael Branch and Robert Leonard Reid, you are like a rib cage beneath these words.

To Tommy Sands, Mary O'Malley, Michael Coady, and Brendan Flynn, you shed more light than I can say.

To Margaret Dalrymple and Katja Lektorich, impeccable editors, readers, and confidants, and Betty Glass, special collections librarian emeritus, this book is so much more because of your steady hands.

To Nolan Preece and Bob Blesse whose early belief in this and so many other artists, *mil gracias* for your abiding support.

To Doug Unger, and David Winkler, you make writing and living a sacred influence.

To Joe-Anne McLaughlin Carruth, Howard Levy, Bo and the late Rose Marie Carruth, I hear you every day.

To Marilyn Hacker, Wendell Berry, and the late Donald Hall and Carolyn Kizer, you were there when it counted.

To Monique and the late Robert and Joyce Laxalt, bless you for the ride.

To Lynn Nardella and Sophie Sheppard, Jeff Nicholson, and Jean LeGassick, *un fuerte abrazo.*

There are so many more who were there for the duration—especially Izzy, Cornell, Billy, Michael, Jimmy, and the late Bobby, Greg, and Chip—maybe someday the words will be enough.

To my wife, Deborah, sons Nevada and Cody, spouses Brenna and Suzette, I would not be able to do this without you.

The author wishes to thank the following publications where these essays first appeared, some in slightly different form.

The Limberlost Review, "Postscript: Donald Hall's Reflection in the Sand," Boise, Idaho, Winter 2019.

Red Rock Review, "Letter from Zimbabwe," Community College of Southern Nevada, Las Vegas, Winter 2018.

Anthem for a Burnished Land: A Desert Memoir, "Dressing for Fire," Southern Utah University Press, Cedar City, Utah, 2016.

Vermont Literary Review, "My Journey to Hayden Carruth: Falling Down to Understand," Castleton University, Castleton, Vermont, Summer 2016.

Friends of William Stafford Newsletter, "Looking for William Stafford on the Yard," Fall 2012.

Isotope, "Snowalking," Fall/Winter 2009.

Bloomsbury Review, "Fadhil Al-Azzawi in the New World: How Humor Saved an Iraqi Poet," March/April 2007.

Weber Studies, "Letter from the Blackstone River: Under Fog with the Porcupine Caribou," Weber State University, Ogden, Utah, Winter 2005.

Bloomsbury Review, "From Sorrow's Well: On Hayden Carruth's Resolute Poetics," Denver, Colorado, November/December 2004.

Weber Studies, "From the Ash of Human Feeling: Teaching Poetry behind the Fence," Weber State University, Ogden, Utah, Winter 2001.

Rattle, "The Magnetic Pull in a Poem," Studio City, California, Winter 2001.

Sojourners, "A Genius Obscured," Washington, D.C., May/June 2000.

Bloomsbury Review, "A Poet Returns to Ireland," Denver, Colorado, November/December 2000.

Bloomsbury Review, "Sing, Before the Long Silence Returns," March/April 1998.

Bloomsbury Review, "On 'Earth Bone Connected to the Spirit Bone:' An Appreciation of Adrian C. Louis," Denver, Colorado, July/August 1996.

Halcyon, "Joanne de Longchamps: Nevada Poet," a journal of the Nevada Humanities Committee, 1994.

Calapooya Collage 17, If I Had Wheels or Love, (on the life and poetry of Vassar Miller), Western Oregon State College, Monmouth, 1993.

About the Author

Shaun T. Griffin has been described as someone who has often wondered how to wake America from its slumber. Why are poverty, hunger, and homelessness tolerated? Griffin has dedicated his life to creating a caring community. In 1991, he and his wife, Deborah, founded Community Chest, a nonprofit organization that directs more than thirty programs for northern Nevada including hunger relief, service learning, emergency shelter, drug and alcohol counseling, early childhood education, and art and social justice projects. Throughout this time he has taught a poetry workshop at Northern Nevada Correctional Center, and published a journal of their work, *Razor Wire*. Southern Utah University Press released *Anthem for a Burnished Land*, a memoir, in 2016. He edited *From Sorrow's Well—The Poetry of Hayden Carruth*, published by the University of Michigan Press in 2013. *This Is What the Desert Surrenders, New and Selected Poems*, came out from Black Rock Press in 2012. In 2014 he was inducted into the Nevada Writers Hall of Fame, and in 2006, he received the Rosemary MacMillan Award for Lifetime Achievement in the Arts. For over three decades, he and his wife have lived in Virginia City in the shadow of novelist, Walter Van Tilburg Clark's former house.

About the Illustrator

Ismael García Santillanes published *Indelicate Angels*, poetry, in 2014 from Black Rock Press. He has painted and exhibited for more than twenty years. He lives in the Southern California desert near friends and family.